The Pakistan Army
1998 Edition

With A New Foreword and Epilogue

The Pakistan Army
1998 Edition

With A New Foreword and Epilogue

Stephen P. Cohen

Karachi
Oxford University Press
Oxford   New York   Delhi

Oxford University Press, Walton Street, Oxford OX2 6DP

Oxford   New York
Athens   Auckland   Bangkok   Bombay
Calcutta   Cape Town   Dar es Salaam   Delhi
Florence   Hong Kong   Istanbul   Karachi
Kuala Lumpur   Madras   Madrid   Melbourne
Mexico City   Nairobi   Paris   Singapore
Taipei   Tokyo   Toronto
and associated companies in
Berlin   Ibadan

Oxford is a trade mark of Oxford University Press

Second Impression 1999

ISBN 0 19 577948 7

First published in 1984 by the University of California Press.
First produced in Pakistan in Oxford Pakistan Paperbacks, 1992.
With new Foreword and Epilogue, 1998.

Printed in Pakistan at
Challenger Paper Products, Karachi.
Published by
Ameena Saiyid, Oxford University Press
5-Bangalore Town, Sharae Faisal
PO Box 13033, Karachi-75350, Pakistan.

For Edward, Jeffrey, Peter,
Benjamin, Tamara, and Susan

Contents

Acknowledgments

Several individuals and institutions provided vital assistance during the evolution of this book. My original interest in South Asian military systems was encouraged by Henry C. Hart, Morris Janowitz, and the late Richard L. Park. Financial support for research in Britain, India, and Pakistan was provided by the American Institute of Indian Studies, the Ford Foundation, the Inter-University Seminar on Armed Forces and Society, and the University of Illinois. The last mentioned has provided me with a congenial intellectual home for over eighteen years and has been generous in its investment of time and resources. At Urbana, I received research assistance from Sumit Ganguly and Rashid Naim and superb secretarial support from Mary Anderson and Susan Radzinski. I also thank Dr. Shivaji Ganguly and Professors William Richter of Kansas State University and Marvin Weinbaum of Illinois for their comments and suggestions and Grant Barnes, Phyllis Killen, and Richard Adloff of the University of California Press for their encouragement and sound professional advice.

Above all, my deepest gratitude is to the officers and jawans of the Pakistan armed forces for their hospitality and responsiveness. I hope this book will represent their reality fairly and accurately, and that they will—where they find me critical—remember the British military aphorism that remains prominently displayed at the Frontier Forces Regimental Training Center in Abbotabad:

> Sweat saves blood,
> Blood saves life,
> Brain saves both.

Or, if they prefer, the words of the Prophet:

> The ink of the scholar is more holy than
> the blood of the martyr.

Foreword to the 1998 Edition

This is an interim reprint edition. I hope to write a fully-revised version in a few years. In the meantime, this does provide the opportunity for a few comments on events since the original American edition of this book (1984), and subsequent reprint editions, in India (1985), Pakistan (1992), and China (1993). Although a few errors in dates and places have been corrected, the text remains substantially unchanged. I leave it to a new generation of military and civilian reviewers to determine whether the arguments of the book still hold and whether my concerns about the risks of regional proliferation, the need to develop a strategy for the army's withdrawal from politics, and the connection between the army and Pakistani society remain valid. An Epilogue to this edition develops some of these arguments in the light of events that have taken place since 1984, but the reader is cautioned that a complete revision will require more than the brief but valuable trips I have made to Pakistan almost every year from 1985 to 1997.

The history of this book is of some interest. Permission for a Pakistani edition was denied by Ziaul Haq's martial law regime in 1985. Zia had read the book carefully, praised it, recommended it to several visitors, and had a summary made for the officer corps. However, he told me in 1987 that "Pakistanis were too emotional" about some issues to permit its publication "just then." He later told me not to worry, that a banned book had greater credibility. At our last meeting in June 1988 (a few months before his death), he told Brig.

Sidiq Salik, in my presence, to "let the professor's book be published."
He also stated that the book had more credibility for having been
banned. Zia had many faults and committed some horrific deeds (and
many courageous ones) but he did not lack a sense of humor.

The first Pakistan edition was published in 1992, by Oxford
University Press, after censorship was abolished in Pakistan. This
edition was welcomed in India, where the book has been a text at a
number of Indian army training centers. (Conversely, I find Indian
editions of *The Indian Army* in Pakistan army libraries.) The Chinese
translation was published without my permission or knowledge by the
Peoples' Liberation Army Press in 1993. The Chinese editors caution
their readers about the "capitalist bias" of the author, but the
translation, according to one of my graduate students, aside from a
few hilarious errors, is accurate. Its publication came as a surprise to
me, but also to the Pakistan army, which was unaware of its existence
until I showed them a copy.

While appreciative of the Oxford University Press's desire to reprint
a book that is almost fourteen years old, I am particularly grateful to
the many army officers, scholars, officials, and journalists who have
commented on the book over the years, and offered me advice for its
revision. These include a number of Ziaul Haq's successors who made
it possible for me to revisit various facilities and meet with serving and
retired officers. Their commitment to excellence and professionalism
is exemplary. I hope this interim edition is of some value to their
successors and their civilian counterparts. In this post-Cold War
period "which might better be termed the era of precarious peace"
Pakistanis must grapple with a transformed international environment,
regional instability to their north, west, and even the east, domestic
unrest, and a failed economy. While the odds against success in all of
these areas would seem to be very high, there remains, in Pakistan, a
solid core committed to the peaceful and democratic transformation
to what could yet be an Asian success story.

I would like to thank the Ford Foundation, the Alton-Jones
Foundation, and the Rockefeller Foundation for general support to
the Program in Arms Control, Disarmament and International Security
at the University of Illinois, and the Research Board of the University
of Illinois for support to travel to Pakistan to prepare this edition. I
would also like to thank the many serving and retired officers of the
Pakistan army, and a number of Pakistani civilians for their suggestions
for this revision.

I would like to acknowledge the assistance of three fine scholars of the military of the "new" generation, Sunil Dasgupta, Ejaz Haider, and Robert Mclain, for their help in preparing the postscript to this edition. They saved me from numerous errors, those that remain are entirely my own. Also, two old friends, and real experts on Pakistan and its army, must be mentioned: Prof. Hasan Askari Rizvi, and Brig. (Retd.) A.R. Siddiqui, whose own manuscript on the military's public relations operations was cited extensively (but anonymously) in the first edition.

I also owe a debt of gratitude to Mary Anderson and Merrily Shaw of the Program in Arms Control, Disarmament, and International Security for lightening my administrative load. Finally, the Research Board of the University of Illinois provided timely assistance which made it possible for me to visit Pakistan to work on this revision.

Introduction

In the nineteenth century, a physiological metaphor was often invoked to describe the components of the Indian Army. The transportation corps functioned as the legs, the service corps as a stomach, and the fighting branches (infantry, artillery, and cavalry) as the arms. But the officer corps was special: not only did it serve as the brain of this metaphorical body, but as the Indian, Pakistani, and Bangladeshi successors to the British later demonstrated, it held the power to create or recreate the various parts of an army—given time, money, and equipment.

One hundred years later the preeminent contemporary scholar of the military extended the metaphor in time. "The sociological analysis of a profession," Morris Janowitz wrote in the early pages of his classic study of the American officer, "is the systematic analysis of a biography—not simply the biography of a great leader, but group biography in an organizational setting."[1]

Like the British, we regard the officer corps as central to an understanding of the "mind" (and perhaps the soul) of the Pakistan Army, but like Janowitz we shall endeavor to present a biography of that officer corps. We shall examine the military in its organizational and national setting, the generations of officers that compose it, their collective ambitions, motives, and accomplishments, their critical political role in Pakistan, and finally, the regional and global implications of the decisions on war and peace that they must reach.

Although there is an abundance of public data concerning the Pakistan

1. Morris Janowitz, *The Professional Soldier* (New York: The Free Press, 1960), p. 7.

Army, and many officers of that army have, over the years, provided me with considerable assistance, this can only be a partial biography. It lacks data that are either uncollected or unavailable, and it is necessarily based on interviews with a small sample of what is today an army of over four hundred thousand men.

However, exhaustive detail is not necessarily a virtue in an undertaking such as this. We are more concerned with the substructure of basic ideas than with short-range trends. The former cannot be hidden from outside view; indeed, the Pakistan Army (like all professional armies) engages in lively debate over such issues as the social responsibility of the officer, the identity and intentions of potential enemies, and the military's political role.

Three objectives have shaped the writing of this book. Our primary goal is simply to describe the military of Pakistan, particularly the army, and within the army the officer corps. The Pakistan Army officer corps not only plays a central role in defense policy but has also been central to the politics of Pakistan. It is one of the major arguments of this book that the latter cannot be understood without knowing something of the former. The attitudes held by the Pakistan Army will be examined in detail in chapters 3 and 4. Chapter 1 will place Pakistan's military and defense structure in comparative perspective, and chapter 2 will examine the broader relationship between army and society in Pakistan and the ways in which the present system contains elements of British and even pre-British cultural patterns as well as post-Independence adaptations and innovations. These two chapters must necessarily describe basics, which are not well known even among some in the West who claim expertise about the Pakistan military.[2] Chapter 5 will focus on the question of civil-military relations.

Our second goal is to analyze the strategic choices open to Pakistan. This task will be reserved largely for chapter 6, although there are some structural and organizational issues with strategic implications, such as the balance between infantry and armor, the degree of weapons self-reliance, independence, or even the application of Islamic ideology to military doctrine. Whereas our objective in describing some critical features

2. For example, both the U.S. Army *Area Handbook for Pakistan* and the major defense-industry source incorrectly locate the headquarters of the three Pakistani armed services, placing them all in Islamabad. In fact, as of 1983 the Army Headquarters was still in Rawalpindi, twelve miles away, and Air Headquarters in Peshawar. The latter may, however, move. See Defense Marketing Service, *Market Intelligence Report*, 1977 (Pakistan), p. 1, and Richard F. Nyrop et al., *Area Handbook for Pakistan*, 4th ed. (Washington: Government Printing Office, 1975), p. 387.

of the Pakistan military is to lay out the problems of survival and security largely as Pakistanis see them, we shall also suggest ways in which Pakistanis might yet come to see such problems.

Our final goal is to suggest policy choices open to all of the major participants in an emerging conflictual relationship of enormous and terrible potential. The 1980s have seen the near-nuclearization of India and Pakistan and the forcible entry of a superpower into the region. None of the problems traditionally associated with South Asia (poverty, population growth, political instability) can be independently examined without considering this new substructure of strategic insecurity. The academic community has virtually ignored the military-related dimensions of economic, political, and social problems in the region; the decision-makers of India and Pakistan do not, or have done so to their regret.

A brief word is in order as to how this book came to be written. I have studied Pakistani security policy and the role of its military for a number of years and have written frequently on these subjects.[3] My request to visit Pakistan for field research (in 1965) was turned down. After 1972 the Pakistani attitude towards the objective study of such problems changed, and a number of important studies by Pakistanis appeared. I made two trips to Pakistan in 1978 and discussed the prospect of a major study of the Pakistan Army with senior Pakistani officials. They were encouraging, and I returned to Pakistan in 1980 as a guest of the military—coincidentally, just as Soviet troops were pouring into Afghanistan. Although it was intended as a preliminary survey, this trip proved to be of special value, and I was shown a number of military training facilities and defense-production installations, visited several field formations, and had extensive conversations with active and retired Pakistan armed forces personnel. A number of these interviews were tape-recorded and have been transcribed. These interviews and my other field notes (which date back to interviews in 1961–62 with the first two British commanders-in-chief of the Pakistan army and Sir Claude Auchinleck) come to nearly four hundred pages of double-spaced typewritten text and are used extensively in this book.[4] Given the sensitivity of the issues I raised with them, it is not surprising that a few of my respondents were sometimes reticent to speak "on the record," although

---

3. Especially "Arms and Politics in Pakistan: A Review Article," *India Quarterly* (October 1964): 403–20, and *Arms and Politics in Bangladesh, India, and Pakistan* (Buffalo: Council on International Affairs, 1973).

4. Permission to cite respondents by name was given in most cases, but I have followed my usual practice of concealing identities (especially of serving officers), indicating their level of responsibility where this is relevant.

most were quite forthcoming. My 1980 trip was in part regulated by the Director of Military Intelligence, Army Headquarters, although several changes were made in my itinerary at my suggestion (and a number of site visits were included that I had not even dared to request). Besides the exigencies of military security, another inherent problem in writing a book of this nature was that—like all scholars—I want to return to my research area, and in dealing with sensitive subjects there are self-imposed restraints that may be applied unconsciously.

However, I did have several advantages in my field work. First, I have been writing about the military in Pakistan for a number of years and it was in the interest of Pakistani authorities that my work be as truthful as possible, or at least not misrepresent them to their disadvantage. The Pakistan Army is not a monolith, and some of its officers felt that a reasonably objective outsider should be encouraged, just as there were some generals and civilians who had doubts about my presence. Second, my work in Pakistan was built upon sixteen years of direct contact with the Indian Army. I did not go to Pakistan without knowledge of the regimental system and the British-Indian patterns of recruitment, training, and indoctrination or without an understanding of the relationship between a modernizing bureaucracy and a technologically less developed but otherwise rich and complex society.

Because my 1980 visit coincided with the Soviet invasion of Afghanistan and renewed American interest in Pakistan, I was asked by the U.S. Department of State to prepare a summary of my impressions. This began as a short paper, but because of the wealth of material in hand, ultimately became a much longer monograph, which forms the core of this book.[5] Those readers who have seen that unclassified study will note several changes in interpretation as well as coverage; I am particularly grateful to the several Pakistani, American, and other officers who read and commented on that earlier study, and who allowed me to incorporate their suggestions and some new material that they provided.

5. It appeared as *Security Decision-Making in Pakistan,* a report for the Office of External Research, September 1980, under Contract No. 1722-020167, unclassified, 215 pp.

CHAPTER ONE

Pakistan and Its Army: Historical and Comparative Perspectives

States strong enough to do good are but few.
Their number would seem limited to three.
Good is a thing that they, the great, can do.
But puny little states can only be.

Robert Frost, "No Holy Wars For Them," 1946

THE HISTORICAL CONTEXT

The British plan for partitioning the Indian subcontinent into Pakistan and the Union of India was announced on June 3, 1947, signaling the end of a three-way struggle between the British, Indian nationalists, and the advocates of a separate homeland for the Muslims of South Asia. A number of partition schemes had been proposed over the years since the idea of Pakistan was first raised in 1930.[1] Some envisaged a loose confederation of various Indian provinces, providing some autonomy for those with a Muslim majority; others foresaw the creation of separate and autonomous Muslim states; the final plan created a single Muslim state, although its two wings were separated by fifteen hundred miles of Indian territory.

Very little thought had been given to the military system appropriate to a partitioned India or to the strategic implications of partition. Almost all of the British generals associated with South Asian security matters were unhappy with the idea, and they assumed until the very end that some form of military confederation (in which they would play a major role for several years) would align the two successor states. They reasoned that the

1. A standard history of the origin of Pakistan is Chaudhuri Muhammad Ali, *The Emergence of Pakistan* (New York: Columbia University Press, 1967). An excellent series of maps depicting the various proposals for "Pakistan" is in Joseph E. Schwartzberg, ed., *A Historical Atlas of South Asia* (Chicago: University of Chicago Press, 1978), plate VIII.C.4.

old Indian Army, which had existed for almost two hundred years, had proven itself in two world wars and many minor struggles; it was also vital to the maintenance of internal order within India.

Whereas the debate over the creation of Pakistan largely focused on domestic political and ideological issues, a few politicians did discuss the strategic implications of partitioning India. Mohammad Ali Jinnah, the leader of the Pakistan movement, had once been something of an expert on defense matters. By the 1940s, he said little about the issue except to argue that India would be protected by an independent Muslim state to its northwest, shielding it from both Islamic and Soviet pressures. A few non-Muslims supported the idea of Pakistan for their own reasons, but perhaps the most prescient contribution to the debate was made by a leading Congress Muslim, Dr. Shaukatullah Ansari. He correctly predicted that Pakistan would have insufficient resources to maintain its defense forces at the level necessary to defend the Northwest, that it would have *two* two-front zones of potential conflict (Russia-India and Japan/China-India) and that a united India would emerge as a great power whereas a divided India would probably resemble "Egypt, Burma, or Siam."[2]

The Indian Army that the generals tried to keep intact and that the politicians ultimately succeeded in dividing was a mixed force, with officers and men drawn from all religious communities and most regions of the subcontinent. The Indian component of the officer corps (which by 1946–47 constituted almost 80 percent) was primarily Hindu, but Hindus, Sikhs, Christians, and Muslim officers worked, trained, and fought together with little difficulty. However, there were no all-Muslim units (as there were pure Hindu and Sikh units)—a legacy of British distrust of Muslim loyalty dating back to the mutiny of 1857.

When a timetable for partition was finally announced, it was clear that the Indian Army would itself have to be divided. On July 1, 1947, it was announced that Pakistan and India would have operational control of their own armed forces by the date of partition (August 15, 1947), and a committee was established to carry out the task.[3]

As if there were not enough bitterness between those who were to lead the two states, the partition of the army did not go well. The old Indian Army, the Royal Indian Navy, and the Royal Indian Air Force were organic

2. Shaukatullah Ansari, *Pakistan: The Problem of India* (Lahore: Minerva Book Shop, 1944).

3. This was the Armed Forces Reconstruction Committee, chaired by Field Marshal Sir Claude Auchinleck. Auchinleck was in anguish over the partition of the army, and fought for a permanent joint headquarters to coordinate activities of the two successor armies; although his worst fears—that the two armies would turn against each other—were amply realized, he retained considerable affection for both establishments until his death. Author's

entities with training establishments and combat units scattered through-out the subcontinent. Many army units with large numbers of Muslims were in areas that were to remain in India; most of the defense-production facilities were situated in India, as were the bulk of military stores. The human problem of choice was also there: some Muslim officers and jawans retained their position in the Indian armed services, but virtually no Hindu or Sikh officers opted for the Pakistan Army. Navy and Air Force units and facilities that went to Pakistan were immediately undermanned.

Because of the disparity in size between India and Pakistan, the latter naturally received fewer stores, supplies, and facilities. The two domin-ions shared assets in the proportion of 64:36, which roughly paralleled the communal balance. Pakistan received six armored regiments (to In-dia's fourteen), eight artillery regiments (to India's forty), and eight in-fantry regiments (to India's twenty-one). Of the fixed installations, it received the Staff College, situated at Quetta; the Royal Indian Army Ser-vice Corps School (at Kakul); and a few other miscellaneous facilities, as well as several regimental training centers, important naval facilities at Karachi and Chittagong, and the obsolete defensive infrastructure of the Northwest Frontier. One long-range problem was clear to all of the mili-tary professionals who had studied the issue: Pakistan alone did not have the strategic depth or resources to withstand serious pressures from the northwest, although the immediacy of a Soviet threat had evaporated by 1948.

The immediate requirement for the planned army of one hundred fifty thousand men was approximately four thousand officers, of whom only twenty-five hundred were available. The difference was made up by tem-porary commissions, short-service officers, and the employment of al-most five hundred British officers. The last-mentioned were of critical im-portance in technical branches and as senior commanders, for there were only one Pakistani major-general, two brigadiers, and fifty-three colonels. Only one hundred Pakistani engineer officers, "most of them un-qualified," were available for six hundred appointments. The difference was made up by the British, some of whom stayed on until the early 1950s (the first two commanders-in-chief were British). Thus, what was at first only a paper army gradually took shape.

---

interview with Auchinleck, 1963. See also Maj.-Gen. Fazal Muqeem Khan, *The Story of the Pakistan Army* (Karachi: Oxford University Press, 1963), for the authoritative Pakistani version of these events and Stephen P. Cohen, *The Indian Army* (Berkeley: University of California Press, 1971) for a discussion of officers' and politicians' attitudes towards military matters.

Although this is an army young in years, those responsible for training and doctrine in the Pakistan Army insist that their real traditions long antedate the British Indian Army. The official history of the Pakistan Army begins with references to succeeding invaders of the Indian subcontinent—the Aryans, Scythians, Semites, and Turks. The ancestors of the Pakistan Army's officers and jawans "were the men who fought Alexander the Great; who . . . established the first Muslim stronghold in India" and who campaigned in the days of the great Mughal emperors, helping to "conquer and stabilize nearly the whole of the subcontinent."[4] Even allowing for rhetorical excess and certain liberties with history, such passages do reflect the search for a separate identity in the Pakistan Army, a search that continues to be important to the present establishment. Although the army has grown to over four hundred thousand men and has survived successive military stalemates, moral corrosion stemming from repeated intervention in politics, and the trauma of defeat in 1971, it is still visibly and substantively more British than Mughal, and will continue to be so as long as it remains a professional army. Although it may be true that "the Pakistani officer overnight became in 1947 a 'free officer of a national army,'" he has yet to explicate the meaning of such a phrase in a way that fully meets his own professional standards, let alone the opinion of many of his countrymen.

THE STRATEGIC AND COMPARATIVE CONTEXT

We naturally identify objects, people, and states by comparison. All people and all countries have more or less the same number and order of parts: legs and eyes; parliaments, parties, and armies. It is the proportion of each in relation to the other that creates a separate and distinct identity, and proportion can be gauged only by comparative reference. Pakistan may be unique among contemporary states in that its own reference points have shifted dramatically and frequently during the thirty-three years of its existence, so that its identity appears to have changed during that period. These reference points are both ideological and strategic.

PERCEPTIONS OF PAKISTAN

For many, in both Pakistan and the West, Pakistan has stood as one of the natural bastions of anticommunism. Islam has long been thought to

4. Khan, *The Pakistan Army*, p. 3.

confer a natural immunity to communism, and Pakistan was at once both explicitly Muslim and wedged between the world's two great communist powers. Yet Pakistan has proven to be a disappointment to many of its conservative Western friends. It was one of the first states to open diplomatic relations with the People's Republic of China, and in the late 1970s it was the largest single recipient of Chinese military assistance; Pakistan has accepted Soviet economic assistance and, despite the strong anticommunism of many officers, some military assistance as well. The events of 1970–71, followed by the advent of Zulfiqar Ali Bhutto's government, the discovery of a Pakistan nuclear program, the burning of the American Embassy, and the pursuit of an explicitly nonaligned policy, further diluted Pakistan's image as one of the staunch anticommunist "free world" small states (some other members of the "club" being South Africa, Taiwan, Israel, and Thailand).

However, despite having moved to the left, Pakistan acquired few friends among the world's radical and left groups. Even under civilian rule, Pakistan's few Marxists concluded that the state was fundamentally feudal and the military hopelessly bourgeois. The struggle to retain East Pakistan split Pakistani leftists, and the ties with China were of diminishing ideological importance.

The world's liberals were earlier alienated by the behavior of the Pakistan Army in East Bengal, and Pakistan's generals will carry the stigma of that episode for many years regardless of their personal or professional role at the time. Even the scholarly community has largely lost interest in Pakistan, forsaking it for India, where access and cooperation has been considerably greater. This is in sharp contrast to the early 1960s, when Pakistan was the object of intense study as a model of economic development.

A look at Pakistan from a comparative perspective provides several clues to its shifting image. Pakistan happens to share a large number of characteristics with many other states; this makes it an interesting and important country but also encourages the casual observer to stereotype it. For example, Pakistan, like Iran, Nigeria, and India, is ethnically diverse, and one of its regions tends to dominate the others (as in Iran and Nigeria). It has a substantial population, as do Bangladesh, Nigeria, and Brazil; like Israel, it was originally brought into existence to provide a religious-national home and was born in violence and partition; Pakistan has also been a relatively moderate Islamic state, much like Egypt and Indonesia; it has a high level of defense spending but a relatively low per capita GNP; and like Vietnam, Israel, Cuba and Taiwan, it tries to cultivate an image of being a small but tough state. Pakistan is also acquiring nuclear technology and may be one of the near-nuclear military states, like Brazil, India, Israel, and South Africa. Furthermore, Pakistan is regarded both as a South Asian state (and hence is constantly being compared with India) and as the eastern fringe of the Middle East. Pakistan shares its colonial history with India, yet it does have a precolonial Islamic identity. The territory that is now Pakistan has been part of much larger imperial systems, the most recent being the British-Indian, but it has also been a part of imperial political structures that had their center of gravity in the west rather than in the east.[5]

Thus, depending on the issue of the day, Pakistan can be accused of being on the verge of civil war because of regional diversity or intraregional domination; or overpopulated, with a high birth rate; or in the natural sphere of influence of one or more of its neighbors; or a fanatical Islamic state; or a nuclear proliferator; or a pale imitation of either India or the Islamic world. We hardly need mention a final point of comparison: Pakistan has been ruled by the military for much of its thirty-three years, and its leadership has been subject to epithets ranging from "Tweedle Khan" to the "Butchers of Bengal." Pakistan is of course not the only state where the military have repeatedly assumed power, but—in large part because of its alleged "British tradition"—such an assumption of power has never sat easily among Pakistanis themselves, not to speak of persons in the liberal West.

Underlying these shifts in ideological identity were several basic changes in Pakistan's strategic position. In the 1950s, Pakistan was usually characterized as a large, strategically pivotal, and tough nation, which could more than hold its own with its neighbors. It had achieved this status largely through its alliance with the United States and membership in SEATO and CENTO. These had led to a flow of weapons and to high levels of military training and proficiency. But by 1972, Pakistan was in ruins. Its army had been defeated in a war against both its own rebellious population and the Indian armed forces. Not as humiliating, but of great strategic significance, was the way in which Pakistan and Iran changed positions in the eyes of the world. Pakistan had once been Iran's tutor and military superior, but thanks to massive Iranian purchases of American arms and the development of an expansive geopolitical vision, the Shah's Iran assumed the role of superior partner, much to the chagrin of many Pakistani Army officers. Most recently, Pakistan has been revived—at least by some in the West—as a regional power that deserves

5. This point is made with stunning effectiveness in the series of maps of "Major Powers of South Asia" in Schwartzberg, *Historical Atlas*, pp. 145–149.

military support so that it can withstand and even roll back Soviet pressures in Afghanistan.[6] Yet there are those who make the comparison between Pakistan, India, and the Soviet Union: if Pakistan had trouble in coping with the Indians in 1971, how could it stand up to even a limited Soviet thrust?

All of these different perceptions of what is Pakistan were present in 1980–81 when successive American administrations debated the type and extent of assistance to this new "front line" state. Conflicting perceptions of Pakistan had been laid down, one upon another, even in the minds of those quite familiar with the state, and support for the 1981 aid and arms-sale package was tepid at best.[7]

Later chapters will explore the question in greater depth, but it is important to note here that Pakistanis themselves have been uncertain over the identity of the state, particularly since the traumatic events of 1971. Although Zulfiqar Ali Bhutto provided a new direction for Pakistan's domestic and foreign policies, his eventual downfall in 1977 plunged Pakistan into a renewed period of searching for an identity and a role. Even the senior military leadership was uncertain about the future of the army and the nation before the Soviet invasion of Afghanistan offered new opportunities as well as new risks.

It was small consolation for them to be told by a visitor that if Pakistan were to be transported whole to Latin America or Africa, it would be regarded as a regional great power, and that in absolute terms it is still a populous, militarily powerful state with a large pool of educated and trained manpower. Although such an observation was flattering, it ignored the geopolitical facts of life and Pakistan's precarious location. The Pakistan Army's own late-1970s analysis of national identity emphasized

6. In an influential analysis, Francis Fukuyama claimed in 1980 that the Pakistan Army could serve as a "proxy fighting force" in the Persian Gulf, that equipment for an American Rapid Deployment Force could be stored in Pakistan, and that American naval and air units could have access to Pakistani facilities. In a statement anticipating American policy under the Reagan Administration (which Fukuyama was to join), he concluded that "it is by no means a foregone conclusion that Islamabad could not be induced to cooperate in an American scheme for defense of the Persian Gulf, provided once again that the United States undertakes to protect Pakistan from the consequences of such a decision." "The Security of Pakistan: A Trip Report," *Rand Note N-1584-RC* (September 1980), p. 4. Yet, as aid to Pakistan was being debated in the United States, Pakistan's Foreign Minister, Agha Shahi, was telling a domestic audience that Pakistan was not a Gulf state, would not assume a military or policeman's role there, and indeed, wanted to transform the whole of the Persian Gulf region into a "nonaligned area free of the military presence of the Super-Powers." Speech before the Council of Pakistani Newspaper Editors, June 30, 1981.

7. See the testimony of various witnesses before the House Foreign Affairs Committee, U.S. Congress, between Sept. 16 and 23, 1981. The Committee ultimately refused to ban the sale of F-16 aircraft to Pakistan (as did the Senate), partly because Congress had just lost a struggle with the Executive branch over approval of the AWACS sale to Saudi Arabia.

the ambivalent economic and geographical status of Pakistan, and faced up to some difficult issues with considerable realism. The two hundred or so students at the Staff College have been taught each year that Pakistan stands on "the *lower* rungs of the third world—only a *little* above the fourth," and is just barely a "developing" as opposed to an "underdeveloped" state.[8] The Staff College teaches that Pakistan is so weak that it is primarily a regional power, still trying to consolidate itself within its existing frontiers. Yet one of Pakistan's leading military intellectuals hinted at the broader role that was to be assumed after 1980 by Pakistan, when he added, "I think we are also strong enough to go beyond to the regional setting, not merely as an aid to maximizing national power but also as a genuine contributor to regional stability, progress and development."[9]

PAKISTAN AS A MIDDLE POWER

In the nineteenth century, Helmut von Treitschke argued that the real test of a state's power status was its ability to decide on its own whether it would engage in warfare.[10] In contemporary terms, such a state would have both a capacity to initiate war against weaker states and the ability to deter equals or larger states from attacking it. We have, it may be hoped, moved beyond Treitschke's cynicism in our attempts to measure power and influence, but there are some aspects of his definition that are not inappropriate for contemporary Pakistan, and we shall return to them shortly. However, a fuller definition of a "great" power in contemporary Asia is necessary.

At the minimum, great-power status implies regional influence, if not dominance. It may further include continental or global influence in an adjacent region. Such influence can come about, however, only if a number of conditions are fulfilled. Most, but not all, pertain to the enhancement of national capacities: (1) the capacity to manage the domestic processes of economic development and national integration; (2) the capacity to resist outside penetration; (3) the capacity to dominate regional

8. Professor Abdul Qayyum, "Modes of Approach to Geopolitics," transcription of a lecture, Command and Staff College, Quetta, Pakistan, 1978, p. 5. Abdul Qayyum is one of Pakistan's most distinguished retired officers, and taught at the Staff College for several years. A Bengali, he elected to remain in Pakistan after 1971, and is the author of a major study of Islam and the military. We shall examine his ideas and influence in chapters 3 and 4.

9. Ibid. By "regional," Qayyum meant both West Asia and South Asia, Pakistan being part of both.

10. For an elaboration of this discussion see Stephen P. Cohen, "Toward a Great State in Asia?" in O. Marwah and J. Pollack, eds., *Military Power and Policy in Asian States: China, India, Japan* (Boulder: Westview Press, 1980), pp. 9–41.

competitors; (4) the capacity to deter outside states (especially the super-powers) from lending support to regional competitors; (5) the capacity to achieve autonomy in critical weapons systems, or at least to be able to bargain successfully for them when they are needed most—during war-time; and (6) an awareness that the above-mentioned capacities exist (or are within reach) and a strategic vision of what influence their exercise will produce.

Great-power status thus implies the existence of local military prepon-derance over neighbors through the spectrum of force and the means and the will to maintain that dominance. It may also imply the ability to ma-nipulate the domestic political weaknesses of rival states, and certainly a diplomacy that places power and status ahead of other objectives. Finally, if necessary, a great power is willing and able to make external political commitments and has the resources to fulfill such commitments. These are not the commitments of the weak to the strong, but of the strong to an equal or weaker state.

In Asia, between the superpowers and the smaller (or fragile) states, there are perhaps about ten "middle" powers. These states are substantial in terms of size, population, or economic capacity, and some maintain armies of considerable size. They would include China, Japan, India, In-donesia, Iran, Vietnam, both Koreas, Taiwan, and Pakistan. Three of them approach "great-power" status: China, Japan, and India (and some would add Vietnam to this list). They fulfill most of the criteria listed above, although there are striking differences among them.

There is no international certification of great-power status, and asser-tions as to which states are more powerful than others are based on esti-mates of military capability, political will, and a host of other factors.[11] From time to time this murky landscape is illuminated by a war that pro-vides one crude but vital test of relative military power, and hence greatly influences our perceptions of strategic status.

The 1971 Indo-Pakistan war was particularly crucial in shaping our perceptions of Pakistan. It showed that Pakistan was unable to control the onset of war between it and India, let alone the pace of the struggle within East Bengal; nor could it deter India from attacking, and its own attack (in the West) achieved no significant political or military objective. Even apart from the incompetence of the senior military leadership, Pakistan emerged as a state which, though powerful in absolute terms, lacks mili-tary capacity relative to its chief antagonist.

11. One attempt to quantify such variables is Ray S. Cline, *World Power Trends and U.S. Foreign Policy for the 1980s* (Boulder: Westview Press, 1980).

It is Pakistan's fate that its status as even a "middle" power is indeterminate, although before 1971 it clearly fell into this category. Returning to Treitschke, it is evident that what has changed for Pakistan is its ability to shape its own fate. Pakistan has declined in status and importance for many reasons, but above all because it is perceived to have slipped permanently behind India in a regional struggle for power. One American official who dealt with the region declared several years ago that "there is no 'arms race' between India and Pakistan: India won it in 1971." His judgment may have been premature. Ten years later a new debate over a South Asian arms race—this time including the race to a nuclear capacity—has begun. The debate was triggered by the discovery of a secret Pakistani nuclear program and by Henry Kissinger's offer of A-7 attack aircraft in exchange for the termination of that program; it was revived by Ronald Reagan and his advisors, who argued that Pakistan was pursuing nuclear-weapons capacity because it had been abandoned by the United States and was therefore unable to match Indian arms levels. Even as late as 1981, in analyzing the Administration's aid and arms-sales package, House members and other officials sought hard information as to the "race" or relative military balance between India and Pakistan, and tried to peg United States arms sales to a level that would defend the latter country without threatening the former. The whole question of military capacity thus remains an unsettled but important component of American policy in the region; it is of equal importance to the military of Pakistan for professional reasons, and it may be a factor in their broader political role in the state.

We shall turn to these questions in later chapters, but it is important first to examine the question of how one measures relative and absolute military capacity in the case of a state such as Pakistan. If the data were available, a time-series or trend analysis of both absolute and relative capabilities would be ideal, for these are the measures that most military planning staffs like to use when calculating their power vis-à-vis a neighbor. Let us first look at a series of static comparative measures that point to Pakistan's status as an intermediate power.

STATIC MEASURES OF POWER

Tables 1, 2, and 3 together indicate the force levels and defense effort that a number of Asian states are capable of achieving. They also indicate some structural differences, even where outputs (in terms of levels of weapons) are similar. India and China stand alone as two giant states

TABLE 1   DEFENSE SPENDING, POPULATION, AND ECONOMY

Country	Population (millions)	Armed forces (manpower)	Gross national product (billion U.S.$)	Military expenditure (billion U.S.$)	MILEX[a] per person (U.S.$)	MILEX[a] per soldier (U.S.$)	MILEX[a] as % of GNP	MILEX[a] as % of government spending
Pakistan	88.9	478.6	27.3	1.89	212	3,949	6.9	28.1
India	688.6	1,104	157.8	5.26	8	4,764	3.3	17.3
China	1,024.9	4,000	568[b]	11.8[b]	10	NA[c]	NA[c]	20.7
Iran	39.1	235	112.1	4.4	113	18,723	3.6	10.6
Indonesia	156.0	269	67.66	2.69	17	10,000	3.3	12.3
Japan	118.5	245	1,153	10.45	89	42,653	0.9	4.8
Vietnam	56.0	1,029	9–16[b]	NA[c]	NA[c]	NA[c]	NA[c]	NA[c]

[a]MILEX—military expenditure.
[b]Available figures for China are rough estimates, some data for Vietnam are not available.
[c]Not available.

Source: Data are for 1981 and are derived from the International Institute for Strategic Studies, *The Military Balance, 1982–83* (London: IISS, 1982).

TABLE 2

RELATIVE NATIONAL RANKS: SELECTED ASIAN STATES

	Public expenditure per capita	Public expenditure per soldier[a]	Literacy	Life expectancy	Individual Income per capita
Pakistan	87	118	114	87	78
India	114	112	97	92	115
China	73	81	65	56	67
Iran	18	26	81	87	30
Indonesia	91	76	71	98	82
Japan	40	15	1	2	39
Vietnam	79	127	56	61	130

[a]"Soldier" refers to any member of the armed forces.
Source: Ruth L. Sivard, ed., *World Military and Social Expenditures 1981* (Leesburg, Va.: World Priorities, 1981). Based on 1978 data from 141 countries around the world.

TABLE 3

FORCE LEVELS

Country	Infantry divisions— equivalent (number)	Armored divisions— equivalent (number)	Medium tanks (number)	Combat aircraft (number)	Regular submarines (number)	Major surface vessels (number)
Pakistan	18+	3⅓	1,285	264[a]	6	9
India	31⅔	3⅔	2,128	670[b]	8	24
China	119	12	10,500	6,100	105	34
Iran	3	3	1,110	92	nil	10
Indonesia	5	⅓	nil	45	4	10
Japan	9	1	910	424	14	49
Vietnam	44	1½	1,900	470[c]	nil	3

[a]Includes 45 light aircraft under Army control.
[b]Includes 35 aircraft under Navy control.
[c]Many of these are in storage.
Source: Derived from individual country entries in the International Institute for Strategic Studies, *The Military Balance, 1982–83.* Light tanks and armored personnel carriers are excluded, as are patrol vessels. There is great variation in modernity and readiness of equipment.

based on impoverished peasant societies with relatively small—but in absolute terms, substantial—industrial sectors. Their enormous populations can be organized into huge infantry forces at relatively low cost; their industrial sector can turn out sufficient weapons for such forces. They can also produce limited quantities of heavy and advanced weapons—ships, tanks, aircraft—but often only in cooperation with a more advanced industrial state. Pakistan resembles China and India in that it is largely a peasant society, but its proportionately smaller industrial sector is below a level that would allow it to manufacture any sophisticated weapons; it is dependent (as are Vietnam, Iran, Indonesia, and to some degree, the two Koreas) upon outside sources for critical high-technology equipment. Nor has it—like China and Vietnam—organized its population in a large militia, which would be one way of substituting manpower for weapons (this, or course, could not be done in such underpopulated regions as Baluchistan, for political as well as demographic reasons).

Is the economic defense burden of these large, peasant-based, poor societies harmful to their economic growth, and thus to some extent self-defeating? India and China have come to the conclusion that an indigenous defense-production capability is supportive of their industrial goals, and the Indians in particular defend their massive defense industry in economic as well as political and strategic terms. As will be discussed in chapter 6, many Pakistanis have come to the same conclusion and would like to build up an arms-manufacturing capability. A case has long been made for the positive economic contribution of having men under arms. In India and Pakistan the prosperity of the Punjab can be traced in part to the enormous remittances and pensions paid to servicemen and veterans. (That prosperity can also be traced in part to the Punjabi work-ethic and government investment in irrigation canals.)

Surprisingly, very little serious work has been done on this critical relationship between defense and economic development. One study, by Emile Benoit, concludes that in India during the 1960s there was a positive relationship between defense spending and economic growth.[12] This was possible because in a "loose" society any efficient organization of the system makes a positive contribution because it will draw upon resources that would otherwise be unproductively used, or not developed to begin with. In his recent study of the Indian economy, Lawrence Veit takes exception to Benoit's conclusions, and states his belief that even at low rates

12. Emile Benoit, *Defense and Economic Growth in Developing Countries* (Lexington: Lexington Books, 1973).

of return, India's growth would have been greater had defense spending been diverted to the civilian economy.[13]

This debate over the utility of defense spending is particularly important to Pakistan because, as shown in table 4, it has one of the world's highest relative burdens of military expenditure. Does this mean that more spending, especially on infrastructure and defense production, will stimulate the Pakistani economy (as some have argued) or that it will cause it to stagnate? Some Pakistani generals think that the former is true, and point to their experience in the 1950s, when defense spending, foreign assistance, and the Pakistani economy all experienced strong positive growth. But is this true today, even if it was true in the 1950s?[14] Pakistan's present nuclear program, its attempt to build a defense-production sector, and the maintenance of a twenty-division army may be justifiable in strategic terms, but the leadership of Pakistan has no idea whether such an effort may not destroy the state—or at least the present leadership—without a shot being fired.

TOWARD A BALANCED IMBALANCE?

The comparative measurements given in table 4 indicate Pakistan's intermediate status. They are not the subject of controversy, although they do contradict some stereotypes. Of greater immediate importance are measures of the dynamic balance of military power between Pakistan and its neighbors, particularly India. This is soggy ground: we can at best describe the parameters of contention, for there is no accepted method of measuring such balances.[15] What is beyond question is the political and military significance of such comparisons; they have powerfully influenced the decision of outside states (especially the United States) to sell

13. Lawrence Veit, *India's Second Revolution: The Dimensions of Development* (New York: McGraw-Hill, 1976), pp. 110–15.

14. My search of the literature indicates no serious work on the subject by academics and no mention of defense planning, budgeting, and economic development in the official Government of Pakistan publications.

15. One important attempt to do so, assigning numerical values for a number of military, leadership, and organizational variables is in Col. T. N. Dupuy, *Numbers, Predictions and War* (Indianapolis: Bobbs-Merrill, 1979). Dupuy demonstrates that the classical 3:1 ratio for success in attack cannot be of useful value unless certain other important variables are known. We shall return to this issue later in the context of instructional policies at the Staff College, Quetta. Surprisingly, although the concept of relative ratio permeates the strategic literature of Western and non-Western civilizations (e.g., in Mao, Sun Tzu, Kautilya, Clausewitz, and Liddell-Hart) there is little scholarly consideration of the problem in the context of India-Pakistan conflict; and, of course, the military of these two states think of little else.

TABLE 4

RELATIVE BURDEN OF MILITARY EXPENDITURES BY SELECTED STATES

Military expenditures as % of GNP	GNP per capita				
	Less than $200	$200–499	$500–999	$1,000–3,000	More than $3,000
More than 10%		Egypt	Jordan	Syria	Israel Saudi Arabia Soviet Union
5–9.99%	Ethiopia	China Pakistan	Korea, North	Iraq Korea, South	United States
2–4.99%	India	Indonesia	Philippines Nigeria	Turkey	United Kingdom France
1–1.99%	Bangladesh				
Less than 1%	Sri Lanka Nepal			Brazil	Japan

Source: U.S. Arms Control and Disarmament Agency, *World Military Expenditures and Arms Transfers, 1970–79* (Washington: Arms Control and Disarmament Agency, 1982), p. 6.

FIGURE 1.
AIRCRAFT TOTALS, INDIA AND PAKISTAN

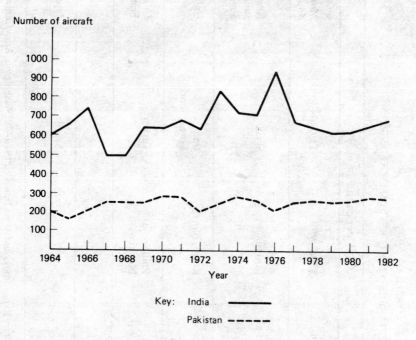

Source: International Institute for Strategic Studies, *The Military Balance*, various years.
        Only combat aircraft are included.

military equipment to Pakistan, and on at least one occasion they have been the determining factor in triggering war in the subcontinent.[16]

Figures 1, 2, and 3 present the data that are least subject to controversy. Drawn largely from the annual *Military Balance* of the International Institute of Strategic Studies (IISS), they show absolute aircraft and tank levels for India and Pakistan.[17] Figure 3 summarizes (in constant dollars) overall defense expenditure.

16. Any war may have complex origins, but it is fairly certain that the argument that was persuasive in 1965 was that Pakistan was going to fall farther and farther behind India, and that it had to make a last-ditch effort to bring the Kashmir issue to international attention. The result was the estrangement of Pakistan's most important ally, the embitterment of its Bengali intellectuals and politicians, and an increase in India's rate of rearmament.

17. Although not as erratic as data provided by the Stockholm International Peace Research Institute (SIPRI), International Institute of Strategic Studies (IISS) figures for India and Pakistan have come under some criticism. Nevertheless, they are regarded as substantially accurate and are used intact in some lightly classified Pakistani military material, such as study papers at the Staff College in Quetta.

FIGURE 2.
TANK TOTALS, INDIA AND PAKISTAN

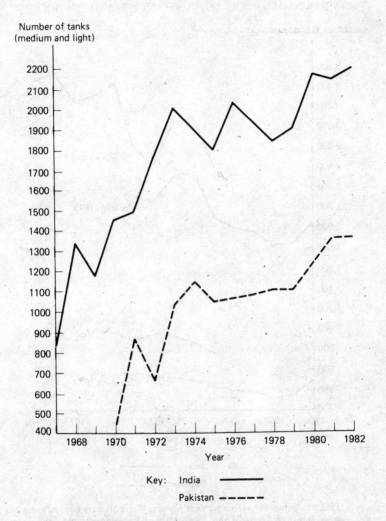

Source: International Institute for Strategic Studies, *The Military Balance*, various years.

. These data are summarized in ratio form in figure 4. They indicate a fluctuation around the ratio of 2:1 for tanks, 2.5:1 for aircraft, and over 3:1 for defense expenditure, all in India's favor. Given the fact that Pakistan has about 12 percent of India's population and 17 percent of its GNP, and spends only 6.8 percent more of its central-government expenditures

FIGURE 3.
DEFENSE EXPENDITURES, INDIA AND PAKISTAN
(IN MILLIONS OF U.S. DOLLARS, CONSTANT 1973 AND 1978 PRICES)

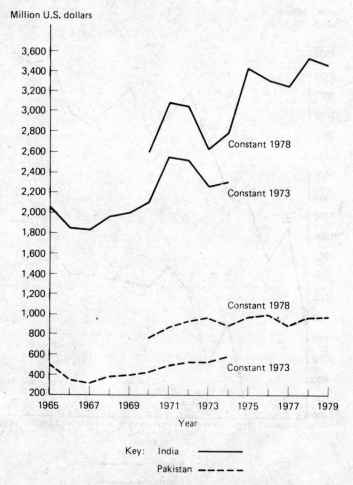

Source: U.S. Arms Control and Disarmament Agency, *World Military Expenditures and Arms Transfers, 1965–74* and *World Military Expenditures and Arms Transfers, 1970–79.*

on defense, it has done quite well in maintaining a military establishment that is not greatly inferior in total numbers. However, these numbers and their ratios do not take into account important overall qualitative differences between the two military establishments or between particular weapons. Looking first at aircraft and then at armor, the difficulty of measuring relative power becomes apparent.

FIGURE 4.
RATIO OF MAJOR WEAPONS SYSTEMS, INDIA/PAKISTAN

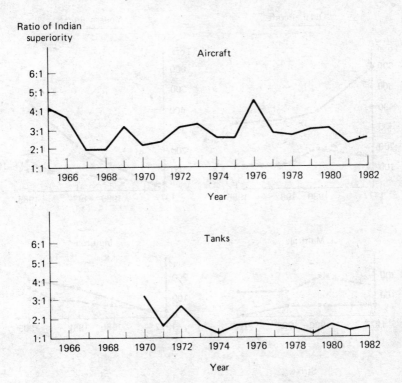

Source: International Institute for Strategic Studies, *The Military Balance*, various years.

The special quality of modern airpower is its flexibility. The same air-craft may be used in an air-defense role, a deep-penetration role, or a close-support role, and "each of these missions should hold a different set of performance characteristics at a premium."[18]

Aircraft differ greatly, however, in their degree of specialization, as well as their combat performance. The Congressional Research Service (CRS) has analyzed the air balance between India and Pakistan by type, and their results—including a projection into the near-term future—are presented in figure 5. These graphs show that if one air force has a larger number of multirole aircraft, certain strategic and tactical options are

18. Richard P. Cronin and Douglas D. Mitchell, *Issues Concerning Pakistan's Possible Acquisition of the U.S. F-16 Fighter Bomber Aircraft* (Washington: Library of Congress, Congressional Research Service, 1981), p. 35. This study represents state-of-the-art analysis in the unclassified literature.

FIGURE 5.
INDIA-PAKISTAN TACTICAL AIR BALANCE, 1977–85 (ESTIMATED)

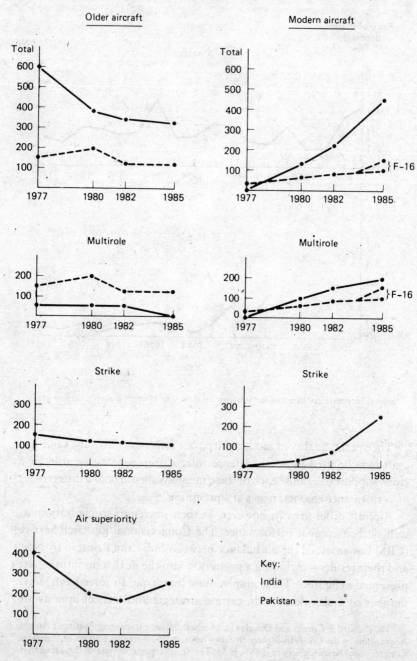

Source: Library of Congress, Congressional Research Service.

available to it that otherwise would not be; for example, the F-16s sold to Pakistan in 1981 have an excellent air-defense capability, although they are even more distinguished for their deep-strike role. Further, some aircraft simply have greater range and staying power than others, or better rough-field capability, or night-fighting and bad-weather capability, or air-to-air combat capability (with radar-guided missiles), and are thus worth more, plane for plane, than other aircraft. This is strikingly shown in map 1—a comparison of combat radii of the F-16 and a proposed new Northrop fighter, the F-5G (later re-designated F-20). In preparing this map, Northrop was trying to demonstrate that its aircraft has a smaller combat radius than the General Dynamics F-16; its aim was to persuade the Administration and Congress that the F-5G would be less provocative to India. Of course, this very characteristic made it less attractive to Pakistan, which ultimately chose the F-16 despite the prospect of coproduction of a much larger number of F-5Gs.[19]

Finally, other technical characteristics of an aircraft affect its overall plane-for-plane value. Some aircraft have a better radar profile than others, some have two engines rather than one, and some have better evasive characteristics. All of these factors influence combat survivability and hence the availability of the aircraft for future missions. Then, too, certain aircraft are easier to fuel, arm, and repair than others; these factors also influence the overall value of an aircraft.

Given the number, complexity, and sometimes the classified nature of these characteristics, it is not surprising that even the most authoritative attempts to quantify and measure performance comparisons admit the difficulty of the task. The CRS study itself points to the inconsistency of performance data available in the industry's standard reference book.

The IISS data are acknowledged as "reliable," but observers have seen armed and fueled aircraft in South Asian airports that have been reported as scrapped (it may be that obsolete aircraft have been mothballed as insurance for the day when even a non-airworthy plane serves some purpose). Even the U.S. Department of Defense's own classified *Performance Characteristics Handbook* notes that despite the many efforts made to compare missions performance for various aircraft, "it is very difficult, if

19. Coproduction, or eventual complete production of a weapon, is an important element in the choice of a weapon, especially if it leads to the development of an indigenous design and production team and the eventual export of finished models or components. This probably would not have been the case for Pakistan, which still lacks an aeronautical industry. One other important consideration in choosing the F-16 over the F5-G was that the latter was a "paper airplane," i.e., was still in the design and engineering stages, and no prototype had flown.

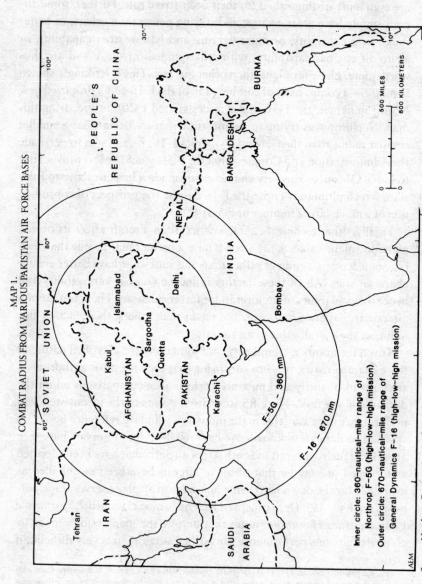

MAP 1.

COMBAT RADIUS FROM VARIOUS PAKISTAN AIR FORCE BASES

Inner circle: 360-nautical-mile range of
Northrop F-5G (high-low-high mission)

Outer circle: 670-nautical-mile range of
General Dynamics F-16 (high-low-high mission)

F-5G – 360 nm

F-16 – 670 nm

Source: Northrop Corporation, Inglewood, Calif., 1981. The state of Jammu and Kashmir is shown by Northrop as part of Pakistan; it is in fact claimed (and in large part held) by India.

not impossible, to make direct comparisons between the various fighter and fighter-bomber type aircraft."[20]

Despite these obvious difficulties, industry sources as well as several governments have not been reluctant to support specific aircraft ratios in the subcontinent. The Defense Marketing Service stated in 1977 that Pakistan "should be able to put up an equal number of ground-attack sorties as the Indian Air Force, have superiority in tactical and deep interdiction, and for an Air Force that is about half the size of its adversary, be almost equally as potent."[21]

These conclusions were strongly rejected by Pakistan Air Force officials in 1980, and they insisted that Pakistan was in danger of falling dangerously behind India in relative air combat capability. This came to be the view of the Reagan administration, which argued that India possessed a very large, well-equipped, well-trained military establishment that provided it with a "decisive superiority over Pakistan in the air as well as on the ground."[22] Looking ahead, the then Under Secretary of State for Security Assistance stated that the Indians would emerge in six years with a still greater edge over Pakistan, even if the latter did receive the forty F-16s then under discussion. "In fact," he concluded, "India should then have an advantage over Pakistan, in terms of modern fighter aircraft, of about six to one."[23] These figures do not correspond with those of the CRS, which admittedly represented a great deal of guesswork, and they were strongly criticized by the Government of India, which took the unusual step of having its Washington embassy issue a rebuttal. Denying that India had any plans to acquire a weapon as sophisticated as the F-16, the Indian position was that India's overall combat-squadron strength would remain at thirty-five; inasmuch as the Pakistanis already had seventeen combat squadrons, with more on the way, "assertions that (India) will possess a 6-to-1 superiority are manifestly incorrect," and the ultrahigh technology of the F-16 represented the initiation of a new round in the regional arms race.[24]

What emerges from these charges and countercharges is the politicization of numbers. It may be that the overall context is such that no numbers

20. Quoted in CRS, p. 34.
21. DMS, *Market Intelligence Report, 1977* (Pakistan), p. 10.
22. Statement of James L. Buckley before the Subcommittee on International Security and Scientific Affairs, International Economic Policy and Trade, and Asia and Pacific Affairs of the House Foreign Affairs Committee, Sept. 16. 1981.
23. Ibid.
24. "Fact Sheet," mimeographed, Embassy of India, Washington, D.C., September 1981, p. 4.

are ultimately reliable, but this debate is clearly based on politics, not analysis. The Reagan administration was determined to show its symbolic support for Pakistan, and marshaled the facts accordingly; the Indians have been equally determined to prevent modern American weapons from reaching that state.

Exactly the same problem arises when divisional ground balances are considered. India has for many years justified its million-man army on the grounds that it must keep at least ten "mountain" divisions in the Himalayas to meet a potential Chinese threat. These special mountain divisions were merely regular divisions stripped of their heavy equipment and given lighter and more mobile artillery. Even today, the Indian Government insists that these divisions should not be included in India-Pakistan comparisons.[25] Recent evidence indicates, nevertheless, that because of the virtual completion of India's road-building program in the Himalayas, these divisions could be quickly brought down to the plains. Furthermore, they are being progressively equipped as regular infantry divisions, and their separate designation may ultimately be removed. If added to India's other seventeen infantry divisions, they may indeed alter the overall strategic balance of ground forces between the two countries. No less important to the actual military balance (although unreported) is the mechanization of regular Indian and Pakistani infantry divisions, which improves—at great cost—their punch and mobility on the plains.

Again, the simple addition of IISS data may not reveal important qualitative differences between armies, or their relative strategic mobility, not to mention the strategic context in which they operate. If India were to establish normal relations with China in the next few years, or even if it were assured that China would not enter a future India-Pakistan war, Pakistan's already shaky strategic position might translate into a position of true inferiority.

This discussion of dynamic military balance has so far dealt only with the India-Pakistan dyad. However, just as India has always claimed the need for force levels that would enable it to deal with both a Chinese and a Pakistani threat, Pakistan itself can now legitimately make such a claim.

Although no Pakistani military official expected the Soviet Union to launch an attack on Pakistan after the December 1979 invasion of Afghanistan, the country's military chiefs have had to adjust their planning to account for this possibility in the future, as well as a host of lesser threats. We shall return to this issue in later chapters, but it need only be

25. Ibid., p. 2.

pointed out that in the area of air balances the Soviets have introduced about three hundred helicopters and fixed-wing aircraft into Afghanistan, where there were already one hundred Afghan planes.[26] As they have also greatly improved the airfields in that country, they would be capable of a large-scale attack on Pakistani airfields or other targets at very short notice. Ironically, because Pakistan has pushed its airfields farther to the northwest to protect them from Indian attack, they could now be reached within minutes—in some cases, seconds—by Soviet and Afghan aircraft.

Spreading this analysis a little farther, one additional factor makes it difficult to pin down exact force ratios between India and Pakistan—again, in the critical balance of aircraft. Both India and Pakistan might be able to introduce new aircraft rapidly, if allies or friends were willing. Several Middle East and Arab air forces fly the Mirage III or V—some with Pakistani pilots—and the MiG-21 is widely flown. Enormous technical and political difficulties stand in the way of such transfers, but they are taken as serious threats by the military staffs of both countries, as is the possibility of resupply from one or the other superpower.

Our analysis of the problem of relative-force ratios and balances has not told us much about the purpose of these forces. They can be used to deter, to attack, to create a conflict so as to internationalize it, and to attenuate a limited conflict by maintaining the capacity to escalate. The trouble is that military staffs and their civilian superiors cannot always be certain of the intentions of an enemy; thus, a force that is capable of and designed to deter an enemy, may—with some slight additions and changes—be capable of attacking and defeating it. This is the central concern of the Indian military when they look at Pakistan's inferior but still-potent forces; carried to the logical extreme, however, such a fear leads some of them to conclude that the Pakistanis should have *no* forces.

PAKISTAN'S UNCERTAIN FUTURE

All of these points of comparison of Pakistan's status and power would be of interest but not of any pressing urgency were it not for the fact that Pakistan shares one additional characteristic with a handful of states. Pakistan belongs to that class of states whose very survival is debated, whose legitimacy is doubted, and whose conventional security apparatus may be inadequate to cope with the pressures of hostile neighbors. Most

26. CRS, pp. 1–2.

of these states (Taiwan, Israel, South Africa) have or are likely to acquire some nuclear capability precisely because of their belief that neither external support nor their own security forces can ensure their survival. In the past, we have seen such states disintegrate and send forth a flood of refugees whose appearance is as inevitable as some kind of tidal wave generated by a disappearing South Pacific island. They may leave behind a flotsam of terrorism, but they are promptly swallowed up by neighbors and just as soon forgotten by the international community.

This is not likely to happen in the case of the new "pariah" states, and the international system will be subject to intense stress and strain because of that fact.[27] These states see nuclear weapons as the last chance they may have to ensure their survival; they are acquiring such weapons outside of traditional alliance systems and outside of the central strategic balance of terror. In the case of Pakistan we see an essentially prenuclear state taking a quite different strategic path from all previous nuclear powers, developing its own strategic nuclear doctrines that draw upon Islamic as well as neoclassical Western theories of deterrence and punishment. Pakistanis see nuclear weapons as a last-resort device that will deter an enemy from overrunning their territory; the possession of such weapons may make it difficult for an enemy to risk escalation of a border conflict, and to this extent they can substitute for expensive and difficult-to-acquire conventional forces. If the strategic situation of South and Southwest Asia does evolve to a point where the survival of Pakistan is in doubt, can either or both of the superpowers tolerate the use of nuclear weapons? If they are used, what will be the regional human consequences for the region, and what lessons will the other "near-nuclears" draw?

However, even aside from the potential use of nuclear weapons, the survival of Pakistan is of profound importance for two other reasons. First, the destruction of that country would create a shatter-zone of political instability in an area surrounded by the three largest states in the world, and which itself overlooks the Persian Gulf, even though there is little within Pakistan that is of commercial value to its neighbors. Some believe that this might lead to the expansion of stabilizing Indian power right up to the Khyber Pass, and that the strategic defense of South Asia would again reside in sure hands. But Pakistan's destruction might just as easily lead to further superpower intervention in the subcontinent.

27. For a rare optimistic view of the impact of proliferation, see Kenneth N. Waltz, "What Will the Spread of Nuclear Weapons Do to the World?" in John Kerry King, ed., *International Political Effects of the Spread of Nuclear Weapons* (Washington: Government Printing Office, 1979), pp. 165–95.

Secondly, the crushing of Pakistan—or even its enfeeblement—might have catastrophic repercussions throughout South Asia. Pakistan's heterogeneous population has close ties to various tribes and ethnic groups in every surrounding country. The volume of human tragedy resulting from a new partition would be incalculable and would continue for years, if not generations, because there is no clear way to divide Pakistan without creating dissatisfied, disenfranchised, and (in most cases) militant populations armed to the teeth. It requires little foresight or imagination, not to speak of a knowledge of recent subcontinental history, to appreciate the strategic and human interests at stake.

CHAPTER TWO

The Pakistan Army and Society

Oh, East is East, and West is West, and never the twain shall meet,
Till Earth and Sky stand presently at God's great Judgement Seat;
But there is neither East nor West, Border, nor Breed, nor Birth,
When two strong men stand face to face, tho' they come from the
  ends of the earth!

Rudyard Kipling

Kipling's famous "Ballad of East and West" was set in an area that is now Pakistan. It refers to a relationship in which "the twain" do meet: in this case, two men facing each other across the barrel of a gun. Kipling saw this equalitarianism of the strong and the brave as one of the redeeming features of the British presence in India; it certainly provided material for his pen.

Today the romance of imperialism is dead, but the suggestion in Kipling that there is something remarkable about two disparate cultures finding some sense of mutual respect in the hills of the Northwest Frontier Province has taken an ironic turn. In Pakistan (and in India) the grandson of Kamal has put on the uniform once worn by the colonel's son, and he is now an officer commissioned into a military tradition that traces its roots directly to Sandhurst.[1] Kipling would be upset at first but, like the British officers who have returned to India and Pakistan, he would undoubtedly acquire a grudging respect for the accomplishment of the two armies in preserving a cultural gap between officer and *jawan*.

This has been attacked by contemporary critics in both countries as both a feudal and an imperialist legacy, and they are of course correct. But

---

1. A large percentage of British officers of the British Indian Army did not think that "natives" could do their job and fought Indianization until the end. One of them, Enoch Powell, concluded in 1947 that British officers would have to stay on in India for twenty years; Auchinleck ignored this advice. Philip Mason, *A Shaft of Sunlight* (London: Deutsch, 1970), pp. 197–98.

such critics err in underestimating the complexity of the Pakistan Army, its relationship to Pakistani society, and, perhaps, the similarity of the two armies.[2]

All armies resemble each other to some degree. They assume some responsibility for national defense, they spend a great deal of time on self-maintenance, they play some role in the defense decision-making process, and they usually have an ancillary domestic law-and-order role. Yet—especially in an era of democratic and populist ideology—they also make claims to be national armies, representative of their societies.

In the case of South Asia the relationship between army and society is particularly complex, and in some ways unique. This relationship does affect the political involvement of the Indian and Pakistani armies, their military capabilities, and the way in which they perceive themselves, their societies, and the conduct of war. Although it is possible to make judgments about the fighting capabilities of the Pakistan Army on the basis of simple numerical data, such judgments can only be partial unless they are also based upon a working knowledge of an idiosyncratic military ethos. Nor is it adequate to lump the Indian and Pakistani armies together, and assume that their behavior will be similar because they share a common origin in the old British Indian Army. We cannot deal with all of the points of difference between the two armies, but these should be noted:

1. The periodic political involvement of the Pakistan Army has affected its relationship to the social system; when a uniformed army man strides into a room of civilians, the latter back away. The social status and power of the Pakistan Army are radically different from those of the Indian Army. It is not at all clear, however, that its greater status has meant an improvement in fighting ability.

2. The Pakistan Army was created from scratch in 1947: it inherited very few training institutions, it was seriously deficient in most stores, supplies, and weapons, and it received far fewer officers with Staff College or advanced training than did the Indian Army. This meant that it was dependent on British officers for its first four years, and this led to a mixed legacy of pride and bitterness at having to create a virtually new army in the face of active Indian hostility.

2. This is probably true of Bangladesh, which has retained much of the basic structure of its parent Pakistan Army and thus the old Indian Army. This adherence to traditional patterns was not unchallenged by some younger officers, who wanted to develop a form of people's army. For a survey see P. B. Sinha, *Armed Forces of Bangladesh* (New Delhi: Institute for Defense Studies and Analyses, Occasional Paper No. 1, 1979), and "Taher's Last Testament" in Lawrence Lifschultz, *Bangladesh: The Unfinished Revolution* (London: Zed Press, 1979), especially pp. 30–31.

3. Because Pakistan was created as an Islamic state, its army had to adapt to Islamic principles and practices while the Indian Army was accommodating itself to a professedly secular state.

4. Upon partition, India shed its responsibility for the defense of the north-west frontier, changing its entire strategic outlook; it inherited the much quieter northeast frontier, Ladakh, and other areas, although both armies had to adapt to a brand new strategic problem—their common Kashmir-Punjab-Rajasthan-Sind frontier.

5. The Pakistan Army developed quite early and close ties with foreign military establishments (especially that of the United States) out of necessity, whereas the Indian Army has been deliberately kept away from such contacts.

6. The Pakistan Army has been far more dependent on outside sources for equipment than has the Indian Army, and it has come to the idea of self-reliance much later than has the latter.

7. The complete reorganization of the Pakistan Army in the 1950s led to a special and distinct Pakistani approach to strategy and war; the Indian Army underwent an equivalent reorganization only in the middle 1960s after the war with China.

It is erroneous to conclude—because they paint their rocks and signboards in similar patterns, their officers carry swagger sticks and wear the same regimental ties, and the clipped accents bark out similar commands—that the Indian and Pakistani armies are very much like each other or that they are merely the last remains of the British Raj. The changes from the British Indian Army and from each other are sometimes subtle but are very important, and to speak of "the British tradition" as lingering on in India or Pakistan is to misrepresent both the degree to which that tradition was itself an adaptation to South Asian conditions and the influence of indigenous societies over a thirty-three-year period.

In this chapter we shall look at three important and distinctive facets of the Pakistan Army's relationship to its society. Each is of special interest to the sociologist or anthropologist, and they show how modern organizational forms are adapted to one of the most complex societies in the world. Each also demonstrates, however, how a distinctive army-society relationship can have important strategic and political consequences. The three facets mentioned are (1) the unique rank and class structure of the Pakistan Army; this structure, developed by the British, is found nowhere else in the world except India and is a key to understanding the way in which modern institutions accommodate themselves to South Asian society; (2) the representativeness of the Pakistan Army, which is a key to understanding the way in which the society itself is put together and how the military feel about their own place in society; and (3) the "aid to the civil power" role of the Pakistan Army, which is a key to understanding how the military originally acquired the confidence to intervene in Pakistani politics.[3]

RANK AND DISCIPLINE

It is widely recognized that a nation's military capabilities are dependent upon the linkage between available weapons and its strategic options. It is less widely recognized that the actual utilization of weapons is just as tightly linked to social structure. Pakistan is a society in gradual transition, and the Pakistan military has equipment which in some cases is among the most modern, yet its military-rank structure had its origin in the eighteenth century.[4] The nexus between military structure, equipment, and society is critical.

The distinguishing feature of the rank structure of the Pakistan Army is the existence of the Junior Commissioned Officer (JCO). This type of officer was developed first by the French and then by the British, as each sought to consolidate and expand their respective positions in South India. The JCO was and is a selected member in a particular class[5] of soldiers; he is more than a warrant officer but less than a regular commissioned officer, and his function is as much cultural as military. The British found that such an officer could bridge the gap between themselves and the other ranks; the JCO was something of an older brother or village elder, who disciplined and counseled the young peasant sepoy and served as a cultural transmission belt. When Indians were recruited to the officer corps in the 1920s and 1930s, the JCO still served a useful function, for such Indian officers were typically from highly Westernized families and were trained to be perfect copies of their British colleagues. The institution of the JCO has been continued in both India and Pakistan and continues to serve an important, although diminishing, role.

---

3. For an elaboration of these factors in an historical context, see Stephen P. Cohen, *The Indian Army* (Berkeley: University of California Press, 1971).

4. Ibid., p. 7.

5. The British-Indian military meaning of "class" referred to a particular ethnic, religious, regional, or caste group recruited to the military, not to the concept of "social class," e.g., upper, middle, or lower class. For the army (then and now) classes were evaluated in terms of their convenience for recruitment, trainability, and fighting qualities, and many low-status groups found their way into the military. Some, such as Jats, raised their social status through service in the Raj and some high-status groups such as Brahmins were derecruited for various reasons.

A bridge is useful, however, only if there is a gap and if it can bear the load. The utility of the JCO is debated in Pakistan. First, the average educational level of the jawan is slowly increasing, as is the ability of the commissioned officer to communicate with his men. More and more officers are themselves the sons of JCOs (although this process is probably moving faster in India than in Pakistan). Then, too, there are some problems associated with the JCO. He tends to be older (in some cases much older) than the jawan. This gives him the authority of age and experience, but may make him excessively cautious and mean that he is physically in decline. He may also lack the educational qualifications to acquire new technical skills, or to adjust to new and complex kinds of equipment.[6] In Pakistan the process of replacing the JCO with regular commissioned officers in armor and technical units is well under way; the only major problems are cost (the pay of three-and-a-half JCOs equals that of a single officer) and the fact that the JCO rank is an incentive for jawans. The description above of the JCO as an elder brother provides another clue to the distinctive feature of the Pakistan Army—the basis of its discipline. "Why do men fight?" is one of the fundamental questions to be asked of any army, and Pakistan has tried to devise an answer that is organizationally coherent yet compatible with broader social goals.

The old Indian Army motivated its soldiers through a complex blend of class pride, religious symbolism, unit tradition, the ideals of loyalty and duty, and liberal pay and service conditions as well as post-service-pension and land-grant programs. The British deliberately sought to bind the upper peasantry to the Raj by this judicious mixture of economic incentive and appeal to traditional values. For able Indians, a few limited opportunities for advancement and promotion existed, and the entire army was divided into a series of family-like regiments that emulated traditional village and caste loyalties.

The British trod carefully in religious matters. Recruits were bound to the unit through a religious oath (Hindu, Muslim, or Sikh priests and Maulvis were attached to the regiments for this purpose), but there were

6. Because the JCOs are drawn from the ranks, and because in these mixed units one class or ethnic group may have a major educational advantage over another, separate promotion cadres are maintained to enable Baluchis and Sindhis to acquire commissions. However, the troops are actually mixed in the field formations and may be commanded by JCOs of another ethnic group. The mechanization of the Indian and Pakistani armies (for example, when traditional infantry units are given armored personnel carriers) presents enormous manpower problems; there are simply not enough skilled mechanics to go around, and training a peasant with no mechanical background requires a major investment. Older soldiers and JCOs may find their leadership skills irrelevant in an environment dominated by the need to keep complex equipment in good repair.

thought to be two risks in emphasizing religion as a motive for fighting. The first was that the impression might grow that the British were favoring one religious community over another, or were tampering with religious customs and beliefs by creating a streamlined army version of Islam, Hinduism, or Sikhism. The second was quite the opposite, and somewhat relevant to Pakistan's present situation: concern was felt that as a result of emphasis on religion as a motive for fighting and group cohesion, outside religious movements might find greater receptivity within the military.

The suggestion that there should be a state religion, or a common religion for all soldiers (as is the case now in Pakistan), had been extensively discussed and rejected by the British after the Mutiny of 1857. In recasting the ideological basis of the Indian Army, some British officers advocated an all-Christian army. Because there were very few Christians in India, and these did not come from regions favored by the regiments, the idea was ultimately dropped, although it did further inflame that part of orthodox India that had suspected earlier that the British were trying to convert their Hindu and Muslim sepoys to Christianity by defiling them with cartridges greased with beef or pig fat.

Upon achieving independence, the Pakistan Army moved immediately to emphasize Islam as a unifying force. The Indian Army had had no all-Muslim regiments because of British fear of a recurrence of the 1857 Mutiny; the new Pakistan Army was, of course, almost entirely Muslim (a few non-Muslims have served in the Pakistan armed services, especially as officers). The professional journals of the military are filled with studies of the question of Islamization of the military, and all come back to the question of the degree to which traditional Indian Army patterns need to be altered according to Islamic principles. We shall return to this question in a discussion of the officer corps and shall note here only that the actual changes are quite modest. In the regimental training centers and in the units there is an "Islamic" presence, but it derives from the Indian Army tradition and is moderate in tone.

For example, the young recruits are still treated with firm paternalism and patience upon their arrival at the regimental training centers—a far cry from the psychological shock tactics thought necessary in some Western armies. The Frontier Forces Regimental Training Center, situated in a secluded Himalayan hill station, is typical. In the commanding brigadier's words:

When they come here they come on their own. There is no conscription, they are all volunteers. We keep them for thirty-six weeks; for a couple of weeks we clothe them, and acclimatize them. They don't even wear boots for a few weeks; we don't want to rush them along; this is a breaking-in period; first of all they get seven weeks of education before their military training starts; some of them are illiterates, quite illiterate, so we educate them immediately to enable them to pick up the instruction here. Then they go into drill, and only then military training, and it continues for a year after they leave, when they are in the units, where they are still known as "young soldiers." This is an *investment* we make.

The minimal educational requirement for a recruit is sixth class, but for promotion and additional pay benefits he must undergo additional schooling, provided free by the army itself. Special schools have been established around Pakistan by the army to provide education to potential soldiers and the children of soldiers.

Many of the young recruits are from remote districts and their lives have been geared to a peasant society. "They have been sitting on top of hills, watching sheep, and then they have to come here, with our regimented life. There are bathrooms, latrines, regular hours, fixed meals, perhaps not what he is used to in his village, so there is a little change, a drastic change in his life." These young recruits are also brought together with Pakistanis from other regions and ethnic groups—Punjabis with Baluchis, different Pathan tribes, Sindhis, and even members of various Islamic sects. The regimental training centers—which form the core of the system—continue the tribe-like or even family-like ambience that they had in the old Indian Army. The centers contain schools, hospitals, recreation centers, and housing for married officers and JCOs. The system, which greatly increases stability and continuity, binds officers and jawans together in a way rarely encountered in the West, and its British variant is being seriously studied by the United States Army.

In the regimental centers the recruits are given a brief history of Pakistan. They are taught that they are part of the Pakistan Army, not an Islamic army, although Islamic and Quranic injunctions are part of the training and indoctrination process. They are expected to take pride in the fact that they are Muslims and part of a broader world community.

It has been quite easy to blend traditional Indian Army patterns with Islam. The regiments have now been given distinctive Islamic battle-cries: "Nadar Hazar Ali!" ("I am Present before the Almighty!"), in commemoration of the Fourth Caliph, is the cry of the Pakistan Frontier Force. Recruits are reminded by signboards in the centers that "Life and death are the same thing: and when the experiment of life is completed, then the eternal life—which we call death—begins." Or that "Fighting in the name of Allah, fighting in the name of truth, is the supreme sort of worship, and anybody who does service in the armed force with the intention

of doing this job in worship, his life is a worship."[7] But they are also reminded that the following aphorism is quite British in origin.

> Sweat saves blood,
> Blood saves life,
> Brain saves both.

This pragmatism toward the mixing of religion and troop indoctrination is also seen in some unit mottos. That of the 25th Cavalry (an armored unit), for example, is "josh vahosh." A rough translation of the
Urdu would be "spirit and prudence." It was necessary to remind troops of
this in 1971, as in 1965 some had needlessly thrown away their lives in a
burst of enthusiasm.

The seriousness of the Pakistan Army's commitment to Islam does
vary. Until recently the unit Maulvis (religious teachers) were sometimes
comic figures. But one of the first changes made by Zia ul-Haq after his
appointment as Chief of the Army Staff was to upgrade the Maulvis, improve their status, and require them to go into battle with the troops.

Those responsible for military training do not feel that any heavy indoctrination is necessary and that Islam naturally supports the idea of the
military profession. One lieutenant-general involved with training at the
army level in 1980 points out:

Islam is a religion in which a certain amount of regimentation is germane. For
instance, you line up for prayers. You have a man standing up before you. You have
a system, a core, so basically therefore, for a Muslim, as I see it (maybe you see it
differently), he gets a certain orientation, a certain organization, and a certain
discipline. You have to wash your hands, your feet, your face before prayers. There
is a system of prayer: you stand, you bow, then you prostrate yourself. Even when
you are praying, you *stand upright* in dignity; even in prayer there is a discipline,
God does not want you to prostrate yourself all the time ... So this is prayer, and
soldiering; in our society it is easy to organize this way, towards the military side.[8]

7. These are rough translations from the Urdu, provided by officers of the PFF. At least
one respected general cautioned against dependence upon Islam as a motivating force when
he noted that the "fervor in our religion" is best expressed in short bursts of offensive movement over a bullet-swept battlefield. It is less effective in the trenches when "one is simply
being shelled from afar and can do nothing to retaliate," and Attiqur warns that: "We must
be extremely cautious, in our planning stages, not to make our religion our chief battle-
winning factor. The under-estimation of the enemy simply because he is not of our faith can
be dangerous. Of course, God will be on the side of 'the true.' But we are all a long way from
that. If we were all true, then we need worry about nothing."
    See M. Attiqur Rahman, *Our Defense Cause* (London: White Lion, 1976), p. 200. The
last sentence is a reference to the Quran: "Count not those who die in the way of Allah as
dead. Nay, they live and are nourished by their Lord." *Sura-Ali-Imran*, 168.
    8. Elias Canetti has made the same point and adds that there are other kinds of assem-
blies of Muslims as well: for "Holy war" (jehad) against nonbelievers, in Mecca during
pilgrimage, and an assembly during the Last Judgement when the dead meet before God and

And by inference, those who do not believe in the one true God are both inferior men and a natural potential enemy. In the words of a colonel directly involved in troop training at a regimented center:

Q: What do you teach the recruits about potential enemies?

A: As it happens, we don't have to teach them anything, everybody in this country knows who is the enemy! The threat, who is the enemy; we don't teach them this in the syllabus but somehow they all know!

Q: But what about the Afghans, or Russian Muslim troops?

A: Oh! There's no question, we will go wherever we have to—Arabia, Iran, anywhere—they have taken an oath, that is not the problem, but of course they would more readily and happily go to the other direction. As for the Russians, well, they [the other ranks] would have no hesitation; perhaps fighting the Afghans there would be some, but against the Russians there will be no hesitation. We all know they are atheists and, again, we group them with the Hindus—to us they are nonreligious. But the Iranians, they are not a martial race anyway. [This officer would probably change his judgment after the striking Iranian military victories over Iraq in 1982.]

To summarize, the Pakistan Army draws its manpower overwhelmingly from a peasant society in transition. It retains the Indian Army's cautious approach to troop-training; it encourages the jawan to regard his regiment and his unit as his home or substitute village; and it invests a great deal of time and effort in what has historically been called "man management," hoping to compensate in part for generally inferior military technology by very highly disciplined and motivated soldiers. Superimposed on this is a veneer of Islamic ideology that complements the indoctrination process and may yet come to dominate it.

REPRESENTATIVENESS AND RECRUITMENT

The question of the representativeness of the Pakistan Army has two aspects, the symbolic and the practical. The importance of symbolism is self-evident: a Pakistani who cannot share equally in the obligations and rewards associated with such a central institution as the military is not truly a citizen in the full sense of the word. Conversely, the dominance of a particular region within the military or any other important national institution is seen by the rest of the country as a potential threat, regardless

---

are divided into the believers on the one hand and the unbelievers on the other. The last is the most terrifying prospect of all to an orthodox Muslim, and the Quran repeatedly emphasizes the prospect of hope for the faithful and eternal damnation for the faithless. See Canetti, *Crowds and Power* (New York: The Seabury Press, 1978), pp. 141–43.

of the intentions of members from the dominant region. Although it is an error to associate the process of "nation building" exclusively with the eradication of provincial and local loyalties (and in a state as diverse and complex as Pakistan, a federal system with multiple allegiances is to be encouraged), when one province is so much more powerful than the others, as is the Punjab, even a "fair" representation of its members in the military may give the appearance of conspiracy.

The practical aspects of representativeness are no less important. In dealing with conflict within a region (such as Baluchistan) it is essential to have within the military and security forces individuals from that region who understand local languages, terrain, culture, and aspirations. Yet, enormous dangers are associated with such a practice. First, the military trains its members in the art and science of violence, and a continual flow of veterans from the army back to a rebellious area may strengthen the capacity of the rebels. Secondly (and apparently of great importance in the riots of 1977), disturbances in a particular region are quickly felt in military units drawn from there. These units cannot usually be trusted to control a crowd that might include their own friends and relatives.

The British who ran the old Indian Army strongly believed that "India" was made up of disparate, segmented societies, an agglomeration of "nations" with different characteristics and attributes. They concluded that not only were some ethnic groups inherently more martial or warlike than others but also, such groups had to be placed in mutual counterbalance to ensure that they would not unite against the British or exploit regions and castes and religious communities that were "weaker."[9] The idea of the "martial races" had complex origins (some of them mythical) but it did partially reflect actual regional, religious, and ethnic differences among Indians. It also led to a serious imbalance of recruitment in the old Indian Army and the dominance of Punjabis in the sepoy ranks. This dominance later spread to the officer corps, and by the beginning of World War II the largest single category in the Indian Army was Punjabi Muslims (PMs), just as they had been the largest category recruited to the Indian Army during World War I.[10]

9. There were no all-Muslim units in the Indian Army after the Mutiny of 1857, and Muslims were the only group in the army not to have their own regiment. The memory of this practice rankles many older Muslim officers who served with the British; they felt that their word as officers was suspect, although the British in fact worried more about Hindu officers from professional and political families.

10. In World War I, over 136,000 Punjabi Muslims were recruited (18 percent of the total); on the eve of World War II, almost 34,000 were in the army (29 percent), and during World War II over 380,000 came in (about 14 percent of the total). No other class came close

Upon achieving independence, Pakistan had to reconcile the fact of Punjabi Muslim dominance in both the officer corps and the other ranks with Islamic equalitarianism. Of the Muslims recruited to the old Indian Army, over 75 percent were from the Punjab before the war, and even during it they constituted more than half of all Muslims. Thus, the new Pakistan Army had something like 60 percent PMs as sepoys and in the officer corps, the second largest group coming from the Northwest Frontier Province (N.W.F.P.). From the beginning these officers claimed a special position in the new state of Pakistan: they stressed that the virtues of Pakistan were their virtues, that the Islamic character of Pakistan was reflected in the Islamic character of the military. In numerous popular publications as well as in the military schools, the history of Pakistan was traced to Muslim dominance in South Asia and Pakistanis were portrayed as the natural conquerors of the region by virtue of their purer religion and their martial characteristics. The British had repressed this religious spirit and these martial races, but they were once again liberated in Pakistan and found their proper expression within the military. In brief, the history of the Pakistan Army was the history of the Punjabi Muslim and the Pathan; this seemed entirely natural inasmuch as there were hardly any other Muslims in the army.

These assumptions led to the grotesquely inflated belief of the superiority of Pakistani martial classes over "Hindu India." The Indians had within their ranks some near-martial races—Sikhs, Gurkhas, and Rajputs were shown particular respect—but the Indian Army was "contaminated" by such nonmartial groups as Tamils, Telugus, Gujeratis, and, fatally, Bengalis.[11]

---

to these figures: 116,000 Sikhs and 109,000 Gurkhas were recruited during the war. In addition, 274,000 Muslims of other classes were recruited during 1939–45. Muslims as a whole constituted a quarter of the Indian Army as of 1947, but as noted above, did not have their own regiment. For detailed figures see Army Headquarters, India, *Recruiting in India Before and During the War of 1914–18* (Delhi: Army Headquarters, October 1919); unclassified printed volume in the Archives of the Ministry of Defense, New Delhi, and "Appendix H: Numbers of Major Classes Enrolled," in (India) *War Department History, Head 2, Expansion of the Armed Forces*, file in the Ministry of Defense Archives, New Delhi.

11. Efforts were also made to mythologize the role that Islam plays in maintaining discipline and providing a "cause" for Pakistan soldiers. This was particularly true in 1966–71, and a number of studies of the 1965 war grossly exaggerated the difference in fighting qualities between Muslim and Indian soldiers. Some studies boasted that one Muslim was worth a dozen Hindus, others asserted that the Indian soldiers were cowards, were raised in an atmosphere of irreligion and nonviolence, and were readily "foiled" by the tradition of "Terbiyat" nurtured in the homes of Muslim families—sound moral education based on principles and tenets of Islam. Such articles and books were to have a disastrous result in that they gave false assurance to Pakistan and diverted (or supressed) serious thought about the weaknesses that

No regular Bengali Muslim army units were formed during World War II, although over sixty thousand Bengalis had seen some service in pioneer (construction) units.[12] The Pakistan Army raised two battalions of the new East Bengal Regiment (EBR), partly from these pioneers and partly from Muslims who had served in the Bihar Regiment of the old Indian Army. Although these numbers were slowly increased, there was strong resistance within the Pakistan Army to greatly expanding East Bengal's representation in the military, as well as considerable distaste for the quality of Bengali officers and other ranks.

These Bengali units were organizationally significant because they were the only single-class units in the new Pakistan Army. After Independence the Pakistanis had systematically combined different West Pakistani Muslims (in varying proportions) in different army units—but not Bengalis.

We know the consequences of segregation and discriminatory treatment against Bengali officers and other ranks. They were the backbone of armed resistance to the Pakistan Army during the civil war; despite warnings, the Pakistan Army leadership never could make up its mind as to whether they should be taken into full partnership or completely eliminated. Because the army was running the country, the exclusion of East Pakistanis also had very broad political implications.[13]

This discussion of the military origin of the old Pakistan's destruction is offered as a reminder of the central symbolic and practical importance of representativeness within the military when it dominates the politics of a country. It raises the question: could it happen again? The present Paki-

---

were demonstrated in the 1965 war. For samples, see Lt.-Col. M. S. Iqbal, "Motivation of the Pakistani Soldier," *Pakistan Army Journal* (December 1966): 6–15, Maj. A. R. Siddiqi, "The 17-Day War: A PRO's Account," *Pakistan Army Journal* (June, 1966): 1–13, and Brig. Gulzar Ahmed (ret.), *Pakistan Meets Indian Challenge* (Rawalpindi: Al Mukhtar, 1967). The latter reprints the captured diary of an Indian Army general.

12. See Stephen P. Cohen, *Arms and Politics in Bangladesh, India, and Pakistan* (Buffalo: Council on International Affairs, 1973).

13. I had analyzed the problem in 1964 and concluded: "The peculiar relationship of the Pakistan Army with East Pakistan should be noted here, for it is extremely important. East Pakistan holds a special place in the military's image of Pakistani politics. Its politicians are in some ways the 'worst' as far as the model of a neat orderly political system is concerned. Also, East Pakistan is the one where the military is the weakest, in the sense of its claim to be an all-Pakistan organization, representative of the entire state. The military has tried to put a good face on the problem, but the fact remains that East Pakistan remains very un-represented, especially in the army, and the military seems very reluctant to materially make good the deficiency. There is no doubt that until East Pakistan can become more "trusted" the military would do everything it can to keep the East Pakistanis from acquiring the military skills and military organization which might be used against the dominance of the West wing."

stan Army is hardly more representative than the old one, and a few districts of the Punjab and the N.W.F.P. are still as dominant.

After Independence, it was determined that over 77 percent of the wartime recruitment from what became Pakistan had been from the Punjab, 19.5 percent being from the N.W.F.P., 2.2 percent from Sind, and just over 0.06 percent from Baluchistan (and of these total numbers, 90.7 percent• had served in the army). Today, the percentages have not changed dramatically: 75 percent of all ex-servicemen come from only three districts in the Punjab (Rawalpindi, Jhelum, and Campbellpur) and two adjacent districts in the N.W.F.P. (Kohat and Mardan), hence the army as a whole is still unrepresentative. These districts are part of or adjacent to the Potwar region of Pakistan—very poor, overpopulated, underirrigated, and on the path of countless invasions of South Asia. Between them, they contain only 9 percent of the male population of Pakistan.[14]

With the departure of the Bengalis, all regular units of the Pakistan Army are now integrated in that they are supposed to contain a fixed ratio of Pakistanis from several regions. The Air Force, Navy, and some scout or frontier-guard units have different patterns of recruitment. Each of the four major infantry regiments (Punjab, Baluch, Frontier Force, Sind) recruits on a national basis through a central system of recruiting officers. However, because of the large numbers of Punjabis, some units (even in the Baluch Regiment) have no Baluch and very few Pathans or Sindhis. The problem is further complicated in that quotas are by region, not by ethnic group. Thus a Pathan living in the Punjab is counted as a Punjabi, and a Punjabi living in Baluchistan is counted as a Baluch. There being no conscription, little can be done to press-gang reluctant or uninterested ethnic groups. Some regions of Pakistan have limited military traditions; others have cultural characteristics that are "martial" but make individuals difficult to subordinate to military discipline and routine. This is not a new problem: the British recruited Baluchis in the middle of the nineteenth century when they conquered Sind, and employed them in the Per-

14. A description of the Potwar plateau and surrounding regions (which also provide substantial recruits for the army) can be found in O. H. K. Spate and A. T. Learmonth, *India and Pakistan: A General and Regional Geography,* 3d ed. (London: Methuen, 1967), pp. 500–501. Pakistani officers have their own views as to why recruits from one region are better than those from another. The Potwar area is poor and underdeveloped, but it has been continually ruled by one power or another for most of modern history. It therefore produces surplus manpower of suitable toughness, but with some sense of loyalty to a higher political authority. The more settled and prosperous areas of Pakistan do not generate surplus sons in such great numbers, nor are they as tough. The Baluch do not lack for martial qualities, but because of the tribal nature of their society they are not quite as amenable to discipline as Punjabis or the more settled Pathan tribes.

sian Gulf, China, Afghanistan, Japan, Abyssinia, and India itself.[15] They
were then de-recruited and replaced by Pathans and Punjabi Muslims, so
that by 1910 the Baluch element of the 129th Duke of Connaught's Own
Baluchis ceased to exist. Punjabis took to discipline better, recruitment
was easier, and the nomadic Baluch had the disconcerting habit of de-
camping without notice.

The emphasis on the Punjab in Pakistan has also been justified in strategic terms. Officers attending the Staff College (Quetta) are taught in
their geopolitics course that every country has a core area, which contains
the strategic centers of population, political authority, and the basic sin-
ews of economic life, "the military loss of which would normally result in
the collapse of national resistance."[16] Of course, if Pakistan has a "core
area" it is the Punjab, and the other three provinces constitute "invasion
routes." The logic is similar to that of Ayub Khan's declaration that East
Pakistan could be defended by the maintenance of strong forces in West
Pakistan. No ethnic, regional, or cultural group likes to be told that it is
strategically second-rate, and the bitterness of Sindhis and Baluch today
toward the army's stress on the importance of the Punjab is reminiscent
of that of Bengalis in the mid-sixties.

There is now some awareness of the dangers of an unrepresentative
army. A predominately Punjabi army is particularly sensitive to political
unrest in the Punjab itself, yet large numbers of Baluch, or Sindhis (if
they could be persuaded or compelled to join the military), would eventually mean a better-trained and -disciplined population in two provinces
with separatist sentiment, and the memory of East Bengal remains. However, there is still Punjabi resistance to recruiting other ranks (and officers?) from the so-called nonmartial regions:

Q: Where do most of your soldiers come from?
A: (Armor Division commander in the Punjab): This area has its traditions; we
are armor, and a lot of our soldiers had their fathers, their grandfathers in the
cavalry, and they came from around here [Northern Punjab]. We have a large number still coming from Kohat, from Jhelum. You know if you go to the South, to
Multan Division, this is the area where there were no known soldiers, but because
of the war Bahawalpur State contributed some odd battalions; they were not

15. This information is from *Historical Retrospect of the Standing Orders of the 129th
Duke of Connaught's Own Baluchis* (Karachi: 129th DCO Baluchis, 1911). This is one of
many handbooks published by or about various regiments of the Indian Army; they contain
a wealth of information, not least about the attitudes of British officers toward their own
soldiers and India.
16. Command and Staff College, Quetta, *Staff Course: Background to Geo-Politics,
Edited Transcript* (ca. late 1970s).

known for their professionalism! They were known to be goody-goody, or they were known to be little, weak soldiers, you get my point? But the hard core, the fighters, the obstinate, motivated ones who can take the stress and strain, the ones with loyalties, a good name, certain traditions, belong to about five, six districts: 'Pindi, Jhelum, Attock, Kohat, Gujerat, a hundred miles around here, this is the place!

Because the disparity in recruitment within the army reflects real economic, cultural, and social differences in Pakistan, it is not surprising that the imbalance of regional representation within the army has not changed over a thirty-year period and is not likely to do so more rapidly in the future. This has given rise to some embarrassment and to suggestions for reorganizing the basic recruiting system. In a recent discussion of the fundamental structure of the infantry, one brigadier has advocated a "Corps of Infantry" that would mean the elimination of the regimental system and the present practice of maintaining quotas for different classes:

Class composition continues to sow doubts about the loyalty of men who have sworn to lay down their lives for their country; it continues to allow the inefficient and the weak to flourish under the protective garb of a quota; it continues to have large gaps in the ranks for enough numbers of a particular class are not available; it continues to deny a move directed towards national integration. It is an obvious British vestige from which we must rid ourselves.[17]

There have also been suggestions that the British-derived pattern of officer-jawan be altered in Pakistan and that the mass volunteer-army model be followed. Akbar Khan, once one of Pakistan's most senior officers and subsequently removed from the military after becoming involved in the 1951 Rawalpindi Conspiracy, has proposed a Vietnam-like people's army and the mobilization of millions of Pakistanis to recapture Kashmir once and for all and split up India.[18] He rejects the model of dependence upon heavy, expensive weaponry, and believes that a civilian militia and an armed populace would have enabled Pakistan both to defend itself and to remain free and independent of foreign powers, especially the United States. This is not a consensus view in the officer corps. More typical would be the comment of an anonymous officer who suggests that such a Corps of Infantry is "wishful thinking," and is "bound to cause more political trouble than it is worth at this stage of our political

17. Brig. Abdur Rashid, "A Case for Corps of Infantry," *Pakistan Army Journal*, June 1978, p.14.
18. *Raiders in Kashmir*, 2d ed. (Islamabad: National Book Foundation, 1975), pp. 182–83. Akbar Khan became Bhutto's Minister of State for Internal Security and was then appointed ambassador to Czechoslovakia.

development." But of greater importance is the fear that such steps would affect the quality of the infantry:

It is a pity that this [i.e., changing recruitment practices] was not done earlier . . . In our country . . . the general desire is to level everything regardless of merit. The good public schools have to be reduced to the level of others; efficient services have to be mixed with others so as to have mediocrity [referring to two measures undertaken by Bhutto]. Standards of education are lowered, and the time, it appears, has now come for the Infantry to be *leveled* off.[19]

A "people's army," which we shall discuss in chapter 5, would have the effect of putting many more people under arms but might not change regional imbalances; to my knowledge, no one has suggested conscription to increase representativeness. Most officers thus seem willing to accept the present situation for lack of a practical, economical alternative.

One final comment on representativeness is appropriate. As in the case of Bengali troops before 1971, there is an uneasy undercurrent in discussions of the martial or military qualities of Baluchis or Sindhis in Pakistan. If ordinary citizens, farmers, and peasants from these regions do not make good soldiers—or if they are not interested in participating in the defense of the country as soldiers—what does this imply about their loyalty to the state of Pakistan and about the loyalty and officer-like qualities of Baluchis or Sindhis who join the officer corps? To put this another way, what lesson is to be drawn by such groups in the face of Punjabi dominance? No less a figure than a former Chief Justice of Pakistan raised the issue in a lead article in the professional journal of the army. Justice Rahman reminds his reader that the main culprits in the corruption that led to the disintegration of the old Pakistan were invariably Punjabis, and that "this gave rise to a feeling of Punjabi domination which in its turn propelled into prominence regionalistic and parochial aspirations."[20] The dilemma was summed up by a senior retired lieutenant-general who had been a close associate of Ayub Khan and involved with recruitment:

The idea is to get more Sindhis in and the response is not there! It is like the Bengalis—the attempt to do it was there, the response was weak, but as I saw it, the attempt [to bring in Bengalis] was late—but there were those who could say, "See, if you had done it earlier, see what happened later?" Had we rushed it, would things have been worse?

19. Turk (pseud.), "Infantry Thinking," *Pakistan Army Journal*, June 1979, p. 46.
20. Justice (retd.) Hamoodur Rahman, "Ideology of Pakistan: The Raison d'être of Our Country," *Pakistan Army Journal*, June 1978, p. 9.

FROM DISORDER TO ORDER

A sure test of the integrity of any state is the role played by the military in maintaining law and order. If the military must be called out on a regular basis one or both of two things will eventually happen. The first is that the population will conclude that the government is incapable of dealing with its problems in a literally civil manner (and there will either be a successful move to change the government, or the latter will go on to more efficient methods of control and suppression of dissent). The second is that the army will rebel at being used in this fashion and will itself turn against civil authorities.

The British repeatedly had to use the Indian Army to maintain law and order, and they developed a standardized procedure called "aid to the civil power" in which authority was passed to a local military commander for the duration of the disturbance. A civil official would make the determination that force had to be employed and would formally authorize the military to restore order; when this task was completed, authority reverted back to civilians. During the British period, formal drills and exercises were developed by the military to enable it to deal with violent crowds or troublesome areas; the location of Indian Army units in cantonments adjacent to major cities was certainly no coincidence.[21]

With a few insignificant exceptions, the aid to the civil role had no impact on the loyalty of the Indian Army although very few officers or sepoys relished the task. They usually tried to employ the minimum amount of force, although the occasions where things got out of hand had profound political consequences.[22]

Because Pakistan was created in a burst of idealism and hope, it was particularly shocking to its soldiers when they were called out in aid to the civil authorities and were required to suppress or control their fellow citizens. Their assignment to such a task probably had more to do with the disillusionment of Pakistani army officers with their own political leadership than the alleged failure of Pakistan to pursue a military course in Kashmir in 1948.

The early aid to the civil establishment raised questions that still plague the Pakistan Army. The very fact of calling in the military implies civilian incompetence or a failure to apply corrective measures before

21. Indeed, the entire architecture and city planning of British India was dominated by considerations of security.

22. The most important episode was the Jallianwala Bagh massacre, a turning point in the history of the subcontinent. The local British commander firmly believed that a display of force would quiet down the entire Punjab.

things get out of hand. Is the military obligated continually to rescue civilian politicians and administrators from their own mistakes? Does the military dare to pick and choose the times when it will provide support, and if it does, will it then make the government dependent upon it? Will various groups in opposition or rebellion force military intervention in the hope that this will turn the military against those in power? How much aid to the civil can the military engage in before it comes to be associated with an incompetent or oppressive regime? What is the effect of aid to the civil authorities—or now, of martial law—on the training cycle of the military, on the morale of troops, and on the integrity of the officer corps?

The army did not object to being used to deal with natural calamities, such as floods or famine relief, and has developed a strong record in such activities. But

The more (the Army) wanted to stand aloof and devote its energies to the real duties of any army, the more it found itself entangled in civil tasks. Hard pressed governments were forced to call for its assistance in times of grave natural and man-made calamities, which became increasingly common in Pakistan.[23]

The natural calamities could be efficiently handled by the military; the man-made ones were another story. Three of the most important episodes occurred in East Pakistan, and in each of them the army was "obliged to participate, however reluctantly."[24] These were antismuggling and anti-famine efforts: Operation Jute (1952–53), Operation Service First (1956), and Operation Close-Door (1957), the latter originally named Operation Stable Door by the military. The first was a limited but successful operation but the next two were to prove more important for their effect on the officer corps than anything else. In both Service First and Close-Door the military was called off the job before a thorough clean-up was made; in both cases, army officers claim, politicians who were about to be hurt forced the government to recall the army. The leashing of the military in Close-Door was particularly traumatic, as Ayub Khan had asked for complete freedom of action for the army and was determined not to accept responsibility without it. Nevertheless, the military was recalled "in face of all popular opinion." Earlier, the military had been involved in the Punjab disturbances of 1953, which culminated in the imposition of martial law in Lahore. This was a vital issue to the army because it occurred near the central recruiting grounds; the agitation finally began to affect the troops themselves, striking

23. Fazal Muqeem Khan, *The Story of the Pakistan Army* (Karachi: Oxford University Press, 1963), p. 161.
24. Ibid., p. 167.

at the very heart of the army's cohesion, not least because the disturbances involved sectarian religious differences.

Such involvement in matters that were clearly the responsibility of civilian authorities was an important factor in the eventual take-over of Ayub Khan. He and other officers were persuaded that they would be continually used and abused by civilians, and that their own reputation, integrity, and fighting efficiency would eventually suffer.

One of the most-senior retired Pakistan Army generals, who was a key participant in these events, recounted his encounter with the politicians, an encounter that helped push the army towards direct intervention:

I went to his [Prime Minister M.A. Bogra of Bengal] office—I was only a major-general at the time [1953]. I sat down. I knew him. Young fellow, inexperienced, he got in because he was a Bengali. He turned to me and said, "General sir, general sir, do you know what happened? You don't know what happened?" I said no. "I'll tell you what happened. The Constituent Assembly has passed a resolution depriving the Governor-General of most of his powers. I have been told that when he comes back from Abbotabad he will declare a state of emergency and use the Army for intervention. Are you prepared to listen to him?"

Just think, the PM of the country, the defense minister consulting a very humble man, a major-general in the army, with such sensitive political questions. I had no brief from the Chief [Ayub Khan]. I said, "Sir, if this order comes to the C-in-C from the proper channels, then he will obey. It will then be a lawful command. If it comes from behind your back it will be an unlawful command and he cannot obey. If you tell us, 'come in,' we will obey." You know, he picked up a telephone and in my presence he talked to the Law Minister and told him, "No, you can't do it, General——says so." He also called the Intelligence people. I looked at this man. I thought he's like a child, and he's the Prime Minister of our country. I was so disillusioned and disgusted I went out, I went to my office and rang up the C-in-C on the securiphone and said, "Sir, see what has happened." He said, "You see, this bastard, this is what kind of person he is. You should have gone for him!" This is one of our main problems, the political chaos. The time came when we felt the army had to be protected, they were forming groups within the army itself.

Not surprisingly, when asked about the then current (1980) martial law, this retired general expressed his complete enthusiasm: "This martial law? I was so delighted when I heard it I called up Zia and told him, 'You have saved the country and you have saved the army—by cutting him [Bhutto] you have saved the army and the country.'"

Unlike their counterparts in India, Pakistan officers have not been able to let the politicians assume the responsibility for law and order, partly because they had virtually no faith in those politicians (especially after such events as those described above), but partly because they had begun to develop their own views on the reorganization and stabilization of

Pakistan. We shall discuss these views in later chapters, but it is important to note that they quickly became embedded in the very identity of the Pakistan Army officer corps. They grew out of a sense of pride in the military's own success at reorganization and integration in its first six years, and a pragmatic, technical approach to problems arising out of complex social changes and shifting ideological currents. These views are still widely shared. When, for example, a senior lieutenant-general was asked by Bhutto to assume control over the paramilitary Federal Security Force, he refused. "I told Mr. Bhutto that too many of our rulers have tried to rule with a stick; he was candid, he told me he wanted to use it as a stick, I said I am a professional soldier, I don't deal with these things—controlling groups such as the press and opposition parties!" And the general warned—prophetically, as it turned out—"if you [Bhutto] use a stick too often, the stick will take over—this has always been the history of the stick."

CHAPTER THREE

The Officer Corps

God, give us Men! A time like this demands
Strong minds, great hearts, true faith, and ready hands;
Men whom the lust of office does not kill;
Men whom the spoils of office cannot buy;
Men who possess opinions and a will;
Men who have honour, ... men who will not lie;
Men who can stand before a demagogue;
And damn his treacherous flatteries without winking;
Tall men, sun-browned, who live above the fog
In public duty, and in private thinking.

"A Prayer,"
issued by Military Intelligence Directorate, Pakistan Army[1]

Every year, throughout Pakistan, there is a search for approximately three hundred twenty young men between the ages of seventeen and twenty-two who can be taught to "live above the fog." They succeed where almost fifteen thousand fail: they are chosen to attend the Pakistan Military Academy (PMA) at Kakul. The selection process has several stages: an initial interview and written test narrows the field to about seven thousand hopefuls; a medical examination, a review by the Services Selection Board, and an intensive three-day examination/interview procedure yields the successful candidates. In thirty years these men will be filling the highest ranks of the Pakistan Army, and they may also dominate the politics of the state. Very few specifics are known about them. The 1979 group was about 70 percent Punjabi; the North West Frontier contributed 14 percent, Sind 9 percent, Baluchistan 3 percent, and Azad Kashmir 1.3 percent. The percentages have not changed drastically over the years, although there have been slight increases from poorer provinces and districts.[2] The heavy representation of Punjabis reflects the higher educa-

1. "A Prayer" was issued to all units by General Headquarters, Military Intelligence Directorate, Rawalpindi, in 1978 or 1979. The American origin of this "prayer" is described and its concluding lines are given in the subsection of this chapter headed "1972–82: The Pakistani Generation."

2. Applications dropped sharply in 1975 because of disturbances in schools and colleges but returned to normal by 1978, according to official sources.

tional achievements of that province, its military traditions, and its sheer size. There are no data on the social and class origins of these young officers, on their political preferences, on their ambitions and aspirations, or on their aptitude and competence. Although they constitute one of the elites of the state of Pakistan, virtually no scholar has studied them, in part, of course, because the military regards such information as a question of national security.

This lack of data has not prevented speculation about the social base of the officer corps. Eqbal Ahmed, an activist scholar of Pakistani origin working in the United States, divided the officer corps into two "classes." The first, he claims, was trained at Sandhurst and the Indian Military Academy (IMA) before World War II by the British, and dominated Pakistan until 1971. "Although excessively greedy and callous in the extreme, they were nevertheless moderate men in the sense that politically they were neither revivalists nor zealots. Belonging to an entrenched upper class ... these retarded tories had much stake in the old order; hence an inclination to eschew fascist solutions."[3] Ahmed argued in 1974 that they were succeeded by a second generation of "petit bourgeois origin" and "fascist outlook" who received their incomplete education during World War II. This generation is presumed to have been exposed to politics while they were in school during the height of the nationalistic movement, but they differ from their predecessors. In a characterization that verges on caricature, Ahmed claims that

having been trained and socialized in the old tradition, they share most of the authoritarian values and elitist attitudes of the old guard. However, being less acquainted with the liberal British tradition, they are more prone to viewing the world in straight lines, in terms of order vs. disorder, discipline vs. permissiveness, strength vs. weakness.[4]

Khalid Bin Sayeed's somewhat more restrained analysis is closer to the mark.[5] He correctly observed (in 1967 or 1968) that the army does not seem to attract men from the upper middle class to the officer ranks. Basing his conclusion on a brief visit to the PMA and some contact with the military, he speculated that "the great bulk of the cadets at the PMA come from either the lower middle class groups or predominately rural classes in West Pakistan ... The rural origin of the officer class seems to be a universal phenomenon in the army profession." Allowing for the ambiguity of such phrases as lower-middle or upper-middle class in the context of

3. Dr. Eqbal Ahmed, "Pakistan: Signposts to What?" *Outlook*, May 18, 1974, p. 11.
4. Ibid.
5. "The Role of the Military in Pakistan," in J. Van Doorn, ed., *Armed Forces and Society: Sociological Essays* (The Hague: Mouton, 1968), pp. 274–79.

Pakistani society, Sayeed's conclusion is essentially correct (and corresponds to a development that has occurred in India and in a number of Western countries). Sayeed goes on to point out some impressions that contact with the officer corps (and their writings) made on him: they tend to be unintellectual, they are ambivalent about religion, they are not from "political" families, they generally are "modernizers" in their outlook toward technology (especially in the Air Force), and they tend to be pro-Western in orientation.[6] Aside from such limited efforts, there has been no systematic analysis of the origin, ethos, and perception of the Pakistani officer corps.[7]

Without suggesting that "class" origins do not play an important role in the behavior of the military, it can be argued that such behavior cannot be explained even in large part by a class-based explanation. The primary reason for this is that the military is an intensely bureaucratized total institution that makes an explicit effort to mold and shape the beliefs of its members according to a formal ideology. However, there are other reasons as well.

The beliefs and attitudes of an entire officer corps are the product of at least four forces. The first is generational differences. As Eqbal Ahmed suggests, time does make a difference, and different age groups undergo varied and special experiences. The second force is also of great importance: officers may come from different social classes or different regions of Pakistan (this may or may not overlap with generational differences). A third influence on the officer corps is the character of professional education and training that an individual (or an age group) receives. Because armies are continually tinkering with their internal educational system, this is also subject to change, although most changes are minor in nature. Fourth, there is a procedural variable at work: in Pakistan, promotion beyond the rank of major is by selection and it is obvious that such promotions are supposed to winnow out the unfit and promote the best officers. This process also gives personal, family, or other connections a chance to exert some influence, especially at the higher ranks when political considerations may be important.

Although we may not yet have the data for a definitive study of the officer corps, there are areas where our knowledge is at least partial, and

6. Ibid., p. 284. Another distinguished Pakistani scholar, Shahid Javed Burki, comes to the same conclusion: the officer corps represents the "middle class" of Pakistan. See *Pakistan Under Bhutto,1971–1977* (New York: St. Martins, 1980), p. 202.

7. A partial exception is Hasan Askari Rizvi's excellent *Military and Politics in Pakistan* (Lahore: Progressive, 1974 and 1976) which examines the political role of the military but does not attempt an analysis of social origins, ideology, or professionalism.

we shall explore these below and in chapter 4 (where we examine the influence of Islam on military organization and thought in Pakistan). We begin with an examination of generational differences within the officer corps, and discuss the influence of certain major events.[8] This chapter concludes with a brief examination of three institutions that shape both the professional and political outlook of the Pakistani officer.

MILITARY GENERATIONS

It must be emphasized that although we have divided the officer corps into three major generations—with several subgenerations—these are not hard and fast distinctions. Certain events have had a profound impact on officers of all ages and generations (the 1971 war, for example), and often an earlier generation will "share" its experiences with later generations through the recruitment, training, and promotion process. Some of the major events that have influenced the Pakistan Army are correlated to an idealized promotion schedule in figure 6. Our generational classification is meant to highlight certain major trends, events, and influences that had a particularly powerful impact on one group of officers and in some cases on their superiors and subordinates as well.

THE BRITISH GENERATIONS

By the time the Pakistan Army was created, three distinct groups of officers had already received their initial professional training in the British Indian Army and had served in the 1939–45 war. Two of these groups had entered the army in peacetime and received their training at either Sandhurst or the Indian Military Academy (IMA), at Dehra Dun (after 1932). Ayub Khan belonged to the former group, and his friend and successor as Commander-in-Chief, Pakistan Army, Mohammed Musa, to the latter. It is often incorrectly assumed that the Sandhurst-trained officers were superior soldiers; there is substantial evidence to indicate that the IMA officers were better qualified and more professional in their outlook.[9]

All prewar officers have long since retired from the Pakistan Army, and very few who came in during World War II remain (Mohammed Zia ul-Haq being one of them). The older officers, however, did leave a perma-

8. See figure 6 for a rough chronology of entry and promotion in the officer corps, correlated with some major historical events.

9. Stephen P. Cohen, *The Indian Army* (Berkeley: University of California Press, 1971), ch. 5, "The Professional Officer in India."

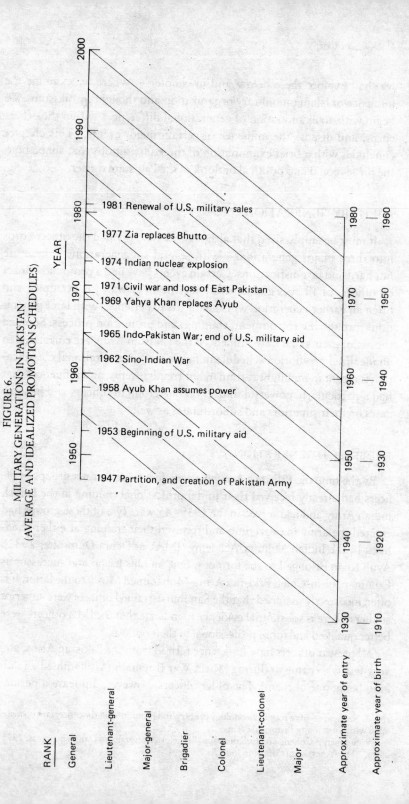

FIGURE 6.
MILITARY GENERATIONS IN PAKISTAN
(AVERAGE AND IDEALIZED PROMOTION SCHEDULES)

1981 Renewal of U.S. military sales

1977 Zia replaces Bhutto

1974 Indian nuclear explosion

1971 Civil war and loss of East Pakistan
1969 Yahya Khan replaces Ayub

1965 Indo-Pakistan War; end of U.S. military aid

1962 Sino-Indian War

1958 Ayub Khan assumes power

1953 Beginning of U.S. military aid

1947 Partition, and creation of Pakistan Army

YEAR

RANK
General
Lieutenant-general
Major-general
Brigadier
Colonel
Lieutenant-colonel
Major

Approximate year of entry

Approximate year of birth

nent impression on the present army in that they were responsible for establishing and commanding the major training and educational facilities; they also served as a model for younger officers. In their own writings they have stressed the importance of both tasks.

While quantitative data are not yet available, it is apparent that the social class origin of these three generations changed between 1930 and 1945. The British were extremely selective in whom they sent to Sandhurst and tried to choose from the most loyal, the most prestigious, and the most Westernized Indian families; but even then (especially among the Muslims) they tried to include sons of Viceroy's Commissioned Officers (VCOs) who had distinguished themselves in one way or another.[10] The most famous of these individuals was Mohammed Musa. Musa's father was an Afghan who had joined the Indian Army and had risen to be a senior VCO. Musa was selected for Sandhurst but did not go, because his father had angered the British CO of his unit; Musa then spent several difficult years as a sepoy and only then went on to the IMA. Another senior Pakistani army general (only a few years younger), commenting on officers such as Musa and Yahya Khan, categorized them as "the cruder types, unlike the more professional and rational type of officer" (in which group he placed himself). He is correct in that they were superficially more pugnacious, but they were not inferior officers because of that—except, perhaps when they were promoted to positions for which their experience and their temperament were ill suited, as in the case of Yahya.

During World War II, the British had no difficulty in persuading young Indians to join the army. Some were opportunistic job seekers but many were interested in the military and at the same time were sincere nationalists. The official British analysis of the quality of the Indian Emergency Commissioned Officers (ECOs) concluded that although, on the whole, they were inferior to both regular Indian Commissioned Officers and their British ECO equivalents, there were substantial numbers of very good Indian ECOs.[11]

Of some significance is the fact that about 12 percent of the Muslim officers in the British Indian Army were not from areas that were to go to Pakistan. These "Muhajirs," Muslims from Delhi, U.P., Eastern Punjab, and Central India were often better educated than their Western Punjabi or N.W.F.P. counterparts, and as a group were a prominent but now diminished component of the senior ranks of the army and air force. An

10. The title and rank of VCO has been replaced in both India and Pakistan by "Junior Commissioned Officer," or JCO.

11. Cohen, *The Indian Army*, p. 145.

officer who came to Pakistan in 1947 as a young captain was nearing retirement in 1980.

World War II exerted a major influence on all three subgroups of the British generation of Pakistan Army officers. Almost all of them saw service, and even though the ECOs received a rudimentary professional education, they did see combat duty as lieutenants and captains.

It has been argued that the war was the source of a division in the Pakistan Army between two schools of thought. These schools were based on whether one served in Burma or Italy: "The former believed in living to the point of discomfort and the latter to the other extreme, with the saying that any fool can remain uncomfortable."[12] Attiqur Rahman contrasts the acquisition of comfortable caravans for Pakistan Army generals and their armchair mentality with the austere simplicity of Generals Giap or Sherman. Other Pakistani generals deny the validity of the argument, but it is evident that the Pakistan Army lives quite well in its peacetime quarters, certainly better than does the Indian Army.[13]

My judgment is that the events immediately after the war had a greater effect on the future Pakistan Army than the war itself. When the decision to create Pakistan was taken, many Muslim officers had to choose between Pakistan and India (for others there was no choice: those from the areas that were to become Pakistan were not given the option of choosing service in the Indian Army, just as those Hindus and Sikhs from what became India were not given the option of joining the Pakistan Army—all this under the terms of the Partition). But for that group of extremely able Muslim officers of all ranks whose homes were in India (the Muhajirs), joining the Pakistan Army meant moving their families, leaving ancestral homes and properties, and starting over in a new country as well as a new army. As we have noted, this group was probably better educated than those officers who came from what is now Pakistan, and many have been among the ablest officers of the Pakistan Army. Why did they leave, and how did this decision affect their professional and political attitudes—and, in turn, succeeding generations of Pakistan Army officers?

A central, recurrent motive for choosing Pakistan was a sense of injustice and fear in relationship to the Hindu majority.[14] Even though religion

12. Lt.-Gen. M. Attiqur Rahman, *Leadership: Senior Commanders* (Lahore: Ferozsons, 1973), p. 38.
13. It should be emphasized that even if the criticism is valid it is not suppressed within the army; Attiq's books are required reading in several Pakistani military schools. He returned to government service as a civilian in 1979.
14. I have discussed communalism as a factor in regional foreign policy in several places. See "The Strategic Imagery of Elites," in James M. Roherty, ed., *Defense Policy Formation*

was rarely discussed in the British Indian Army messes, and Hindu and Muslim officers got on very well with each other (and many remain distant friends today), the vast majority of Muslim officers came to the conclusion that they could lead a better life in an Islamic state. One of the most-senior living Pakistan Army officers (who was with Mohammed Musa in the first batch at the IMA, and also served first as a sepoy) stated this view forcefully:

I am a pure Rajput; my family has been Muslim for only two or three generations. But I felt that India had to be divided, and told Messervey [the first commander of the Pakistan Army] that I would rather live in a small country as a free man than as a sweeper in a large country: my father, my grandfather, and I have all served under Christians: I did not want to see my children serve under Hindus.

Another very senior officer, who was a lieutenant-colonel in 1946 and private secretary to Auchinleck, also had to make the difficult choice of leaving his home. He saw Pakistan as an opportunity to escape Indian domination and to build a state according to true Islamic values:

I basically belong to India, Lucknow; all the people who belong to this part of the world [Pakistan], they came here automatically. We had the choice or option; but I think more than anything else it was a desire to have a homeland of your own where you could model it according to your own ideology, your own genius.

A third senior officer—very recently retired as a lieutenant-general and deeply committed to Islamic ideological concerns—was more vehement about his personal hatred of some Indians (or at least their attitude towards him), and told a story of his childhood to support his view:

I grew up in the Punjab. I thought Hindus were my friends. But one day I went to my friend's house, and they wouldn't let me in! They had come into *our* house, but I was unclean to them! Well, they are all like that; they'll take something, but they won't treat you fairly.

The experience of partition—the killing, the bloodletting, the random cruelty exceeded only by the organized variety—confirmed the worse suspicions of these officers. By all accounts, the Sandhurst-trained officers, the IMA products, and even most of the ECOs were not especially communal minded. Those who went into the army tended to be both secular and conservative in outlook, but Partition was a profound and determina-

(Durham: Carolina Academic Press, 1980), pp. 153–74, and "Image and Perception in India-Pakistan Relations," in M. S. Rajan and Shivaji Ganguly, eds., *Great Power Relations, World Order, and the Third World: Essays in Honor of Sisir Gupta* (New Delhi: Vikas, 1981), pp. 281–90.

tive experience for most of them precisely because they all regarded themselves as above crude religious communalism. In the Indian Army they
had willingly commanded Hindu troops of all castes and regions as well
as Sikh and Muslim troops. Even though the ethos of the army encouraged competition between such units, all officers were taught that ultimately it was the soldier-like qualities of a particular class that counted,
not its religion or territorial origin (in retrospect, many senior Pakistani
officers claim that non-Muslim troops were less competent, but there is
little evidence to support this). Partition taught the Pakistani officers one
fundamental rule, a rule that was compatible with the generally pessimistic outlook of a professional soldier: trust no one in a situation of Hindu
or Sikh vs. Muslim; take nothing for granted, except when you have the
force to defend yourself.[15]

This suspicion (but not fear) of communal enemies was engraved on
the psyches of almost all officers in the new Pakistan Army.[16] Their subsequent difficulty in obtaining a fair share of military stores from India,
Indian behavior in Kashmir and Hyderabad, and a thousand other examples of Indian duplicity—real or imagined—are part of their legacy to the
present-day Pakistan Army. For Pakistani officers of succeeding generations, this distrust of India is a fundamental assumption, no more subject
to question than is the very existence of Pakistan. As one of the Pakistan
Army's ablest major-generals stated, "Had they treated us fairly to begin
with, there would have been no need for Pakistan."

The three British-trained generations not only underwent the ordeal of
Partition but were also the generations that created the Pakistan Army.
Partition was a bitter experience for many officers, but it persuaded them
(especially those officers who had migrated from India) that their professional contribution to the new state was going to be vital. They were in
fact told this on several occasions by Mohammad Ali Jinnah himself.[17]
They undertook the exhilarating task of creating an army that tran-
scended its origins in the old Indian Army, and that was to be the institutional expression of a high ideal.

15. A favorite image is expressed in the words of a Pakistan Air Force officer: "I am
standing next to my friend. But he has a gun. Now, we are friends, but I cannot feel secure
unless I also have a gun."
16. It should be emphasized that this feeling exists within the Indian military as well,
although it is tempered by the fact that many officers are not from areas that suffered from
the violence accompanying partition or that experience communal conflict.
17. See Jinnah's speeches and addresses of April 13, April 15, and June 14, 1948, all to
various military formations and units, in *Quaid-I-Azam Mohammad Ali Jinnah, Speeches as
Governor-General of Pakistan, 1947–1948* (Islamabad: Ministry of Information and
Broadcasting, n.d.).

   While still under British tutelage, the army decided to modify slightly
the basic class and regiment structure of the old Indian Army, to central-
ize officer entry routes in a single training institution (the Pakistan Military Academy, founded in 1948), and to postpone any radical changes in
formation structure. It also moved to withdraw troops from the far-flung
system of forts on the North West Frontier.

   None of these steps except the last could be conceived of as a radical
departure from the past. The essential structure and relatively limited social role of the old Indian Army was retained in Pakistan, for most of the
new Pakistani officers continued to see their British predecessors as a worthy professional model. It was not, however, a foregone conclusion that
the army would take this path and not become more ideological and politicized. There is evidence that some Pakistani officers were influenced by
other patterns of military organization; the war had brought a number of
them into contact with the Indian National Army of Subhas Chandra
Bose, and the officers involved in the Rawalpindi Conspiracy of 1951
were influenced by more radical and socialist ideas.[18]

   From time to time the army has debated the question of a people's
army and the utilization of troops for social and nation-building tasks
beyond the traditional disaster-relief role. Within limits, the officer corps
was, and is, prepared to consider proposals to involve the army in such
"nation-building" tasks (because attitudes on this issue have not
changed), but they cite their already deep involvement in road construction, civil-engineering projects, and flood relief and point out that a number of firms and agencies are in effect run by the military already. These
include the Fauji Foundation and the military farms (the latter a legacy
from the British Indian Army, which developed its own system of animal
and grain supply).[19]

   Officers of the British generation, however, deeply resisted a greater
level of activity. They were familiar with the fate of one Indian Army general, B. M. Kaul, who used his division to build houses: Kaul claimed that
the military performance of his division did not suffer, but he was afterwards tagged with the nickname of "housebuilder," and a number of fellow officers used this against him when he ran into difficulty during In-

   18. On the I.N.A., see K. K. Ghosh, *The Indian National Army* (Meerut: Meenakshi,
1969). On the Rawalpindi Conspiracy, see "What Was the Rawalpindi Conspiracy Case?"
Outlook (Karachi), Nov. 11, 1972, and "Was the Rawalpindi Conspiracy a Myth?" *Outlook*
(Karachi), Jan. 13, 1973.
   19. The Fauji Foundation (Soldiers' Foundation) is located in Rawalpindi and has centers and facilities scattered throughout Pakistan. It employs retired officers and soldiers in
various economic enterprises, and in 1978–81 it was headed by a senior retired general,
Farman Ali Rao.

dia's 1962 border conflict with China.[20] Most Pakistan Army officers have the same aversion to any activity that might detract from the preparedness of their troops. One analysis by an officer of this generation points out that the average soldier is away from his unit for one hundred days a year on annual and casual leave; another hundred days are written off in Sundays, Fridays, and national holidays; at least a hundred days are dedicated to maintenance of equipment, festivals, ceremonial guard duties, inspections, and VIP visits.[21] This leaves sixty-five days in a year for actual hard training, "not too many to acquire instinctive, correct response to the circumstance of battle." Nor is the military profession compatible with the pursuit of another occupation, for example, having the military produce food:

There is a school of thought which wants the regular army to be engaged in the practice of agriculture during the days of peace. Of course, we shall get a lot of people carrying arms and growing turnips, but they would be nothing like professional soldiers. I have never heard someone suggesting that a barber, engineer, civil servant, stock broker or jockey devote his time to agriculture along with running his own profession.[22]

Riza points out that the ancestors of Pakistan's soldiers (the Scythian, Arab, Mongol, and Turkish horsemen who roamed Central Asia) did not engage in agriculture while fighting; their way of life was hardly different from life in war, and "professional soldiering has never, never been a spare time performance. With the sophistication of equipment the skills of a professional soldier become increasingly time-consuming." Riza and most other generals of his generation totally rejected a people's army, although they claim that Pakistan's army is a *national* army. Proposals for a people's army (or for the adoption of a people's guerilla-war strategy) were revived as a result of contact with American and Chinese officers, and we shall consider such efforts below, as well as in chapter 6.

Although qualified by a new interest in Islam, this concern with professionalism is one of the central beliefs of the officer corps today. It has also been a factor in the army's internal debates over intervention in politics and the expansion of martial-law activities, in the past and the present.

Officers of the British-trained generation were very sensitive to doubts about their own professional competence and the way in which they were

20. One can also cite the fate of Col. Abu Taher of Bangladesh, who tried to involve his troops in food production, alienating some of his more traditional colleagues. See Lawrence Lifschultz, *Bangladesh: The Unfinished Revolution* (London: Zed Press, 1979), p. 85.

21. Maj.-Gen. Shaukat Riza (retd.), "For the Defense of Our Land," *Defense Journal* 2: 7–8 (July–August, 1976), p. 14.

22. Ibid.

rushed through to higher rank.[23] One of them—a 1935 IMA graduate who retired as corps commander in 1971—defended his generation against the charge that they lacked professionalism:

Wait a minute. Generals are not produced overnight. Our first crop became major generals from major in a matter of one or two years. The professional grooming which an army should get wasn't there. From that point of view, yes, we weren't professional. But so far as the attitude towards soldiering was concerned, the five years of war that we had been through counts for something.

This officer, and virtually every other member of the prewar generation, was deeply involved in training succeeding generations in the art and science of soldiering. If they had to be rushed through the upper ranks (and this meant that some were not fully qualified and that some incompetents did reach higher rank), there was an awareness that a full range of training establishments had to be created immediately and made to work so that the army would survive. They did this with some success, and we shall examine three important training facilities later in this chapter.

The final important contribution of the British-trained Pakistani officer was the development of extensive military links with countries other than Britain. These links, particularly with the United States, contributed to the material and technical growth of the Pakistan military, but they did have their tragic aspect. They postponed a critical examination of a number of politically explosive ideas that received their fullest expression in the next generation of Pakistani officers, the "American generation."

THE AMERICAN GENERATION

Three things set the 1950–65 generation of military men apart from their predecessors and successors. First, they were exposed to the full weight of the American military. Many of them received some training in America or from Americans, whereas their predecessors had received most of their professional training from the British in India and Pakistan; later generations of Pakistanis (with scattered exceptions) have been entirely trained in Pakistan. Along with American equipment and training came American military doctrines, American approaches to problem solving, and—a mixed blessing—American pop culture. Secondly, these officers had no direct experience with the Indian Army and came to have

23. The same anxiety existed among senior Indian Army Officers. It is difficult for an outsider to conclude whether or not the rapid promotions they experienced allowed incompetents to rise to the top. See Attiqur Rahman's forthright critique of the Pakistan Army in the first pages of *Leadership: Senior Commanders*.

an exaggerated view of the weakness of both India and the Indian military. For this generation the events of 1965 were puzzling and disturbing, and some came to believe that a conspiracy in Pakistan was responsible for the failure to achieve a clear-cut military victory over India. Needless to say, the events of 1971 were utterly devastating, although even that war fed the habit of conspiratorial thinking. Thirdly, officers of the American generation came to acquire an overblown estimate of their own and Pakistan's martial qualities, and some came to believe implicitly the myth that one Pakistani soldier was equal to five, ten, or more Indians.

Although there is no indication that they differed greatly from their predecessors in terms of social-class origin, region, or commitment to professional duty, the generation of officers that entered the military (especially the army and air force) after independence were more intensely exposed to American influence. Pakistan joined the Baghdad Pact and SEATO, and developed bilateral ties with the United States. It received substantial amounts of equipment from the United States, and along with the equipment came training and—most important in the long run—exposure to the most current and prestigious military tradition. The United States connection led to the complete revision of tables of organization, the addition of several entirely American-equipped divisions (and tables of organization that were approximately two-thirds of current Pakistani levels, which were, in turn, based on British tables). Under the aid program, Pakistan was to be provided with materiel to equip one additional armored division, four infantry divisions, one armored brigade group, and support elements for two corps. Pakistan, "to its lasting disadvantage," had to agree to American tables of organization, and there was considerable suspicion on both sides about Pakistani efforts to increase the number of fighting units within the terms of the agreement.[24] And United States equipment and organization having been accepted, the adoption of American techniques (in gunnery, for example) was inevitable.

Almost as important as material aid was the new standard of comparison that the Americans offered. In artillery alone, over two hundred Pakistani officers attended American schools between 1955 and 1958. There they competed against students from Asia, Europe, and the Americas, and some went on to tours with NATO.

We acquired confidence in absorbing new equipment and carrying out a two-fold expansion within seven years of our birth. The reorganization of the army stimu-

24. Maj.-Gen. Shaukat Riza (retd.), *Izzat-Q-Iqbal: History of Pakistan Artillery, 1947–1971* (Nowshera: School of Artillery, 1980), p. 114.

lated critical thinking; a questioning of "sacred scrolls" [and] an awareness that complacency is a symptom of hardening of [the] arteries.[25]

The same point was emphasized by a close associate of Ayub Khan, who summarized the way in which he helped to bring about changes in field formations, training centers, military schools, and even the Army headquarters.

The process [of planning the expanded army] was: I used to make out a report and it went to Ayub, and in the margins he would say yes or no. Very quick. The Americans affected everything—the scales were completely different, hundreds of our officers went to America, and we had new standards of comparison. Also, the experience the Americans gained in World War II and Korea, it couldn't have been bought, it was offered to us on a plate. We wouldn't have done so well in '65 without it—not just the material aid, but the training.

Even in the Staff College (Quetta), the oldest military institution in Pakistan and the one that retains its British qualities to this day, there was an important American contribution in the form of periodic visits by American nuclear experts. As the official history of the college notes, a 1957 visit by an American nuclear-warfare team "proved most useful and resulted in modification and revision of the old syllabus" to bring it into line with the "fresh data" given by the team.[26]

There were also other important American contributions. After long exposure to British and British-Indian patterns of organization—a way of war that emphasized caution and the conservation of men and material and the formal adherence to tradition—the Pakistanis were exposed to a military philosophy that stressed mechanization, the lavish use of ammunition and stores, and an informal personal style. To be "modern" was to emulate the Americans in their breezy, casual, but apparently effective ways. Only in the 1970s, with the awareness that the American approach might not always succeed, was there a renewed search for a particularly Pakistani strategic and organizational style.

The American contact also led to a more detached study of guerilla war and people's war than had been earlier attempted. The American doctrine was primarily concerned about *suppressing* such a war, but Pakistanis also studied it in terms of *launching* a people's war against India, or developing a people's army as a second line of defense.

25. Ibid., pp. 122–23.
26. *1905–1980: Command and Staff College, Quetta* (edited and compiled by Command and Staff College, Quetta, Pakistan, Sept. 1980; printed at the Command and Staff College Press, Quetta), p. 79.

With United States assistance, a Special Forces unit was established in 1959, and the professional military journals explored the concept in some detail. Studies were made of Algeria, Yugoslavia, North Vietnam, and particularly China; several of them concluded that guerilla war is a "strategic weapon," a "slow but sure and relatively inexpensive" strategy that is "fast overshadowing regular warfare."[27]

Maoist military doctrine was particularly attractive to many Pakistani officers because of Pakistan's long and friendly connection with China and that doctrine's apparent relevance to Kashmir. The prerequisites for people's war were thought to be there: a worthy cause; difficult terrain; a determined, warlike people (the Pakistanis); a sympathetic local population (the Kashmiris); the availability of weapons and equipment; and "a high degree of leadership and discipline to prevent (the guerillas) from degenerating into banditry."[28]

Indeed, some of these tactics and strategies were employed in 1965, without much impact, as they had been tried in 1947–48 in Kashmir. The concept was put aside for a number of years until it again emerged during the course of the civil war in East Pakistan. Ironically, several Bengali officers who had been in Pakistan's Special Forces took the lead in organizing guerilla units in what was to become Bangladesh, often facing those Special Forces officers with whom they had earlier served. As we shall discuss in later chapters, a variant of people's war has been developed under General Zia, in the form of a national militia, although the philosophy behind these new *Janbaz* forces is considerably less political or radical than is Maoism.

On a personal level, the new tie with the United States made a deep impression on thousands of Pakistani officers who came to professional maturity during these years, as any contact with the Pakistan Army will show. The views of a young colonel with extensive American—including Special Forces—training sums up the emotions of his generation:

Q: Why did America let us down? We were friends—I made many friends in ——. Didn't you know we were the best friends and allies you had in the area, the

27. Three representative articles are Maj. S. A. El-Edroos (Frontier Forces Regiment), "A Plea for a People's Army," *Pakistan Army Journal* 4:1 (June 1962): 19–25; El-Edroos, "Afro-Asian Revolutionary Warfare and Our Military Thought," *Pakistan Army Journal* 4:2 (Dec. 1962): 35–41; and Maj. Mohammed Shafi, "The Effectiveness of Guerilla War," *Pakistan Army Journal* 5:1 (June 1963): 4–11.

28. Shafi, "Guerilla War," p. 11. Additionally, the increasing American interest in India after the development of Sino-Indian conflict (culminating in a war in 1962) led many Pakistanis to search for an "equalizer" between their own forces and the growing Indian military establishment. The latter received American, British, and Soviet support after 1962, whereas the American arms program to Pakistan was virtually completed by 1959.

only dependable one? Why don't you realize that? Our two countries are so much alike, we think alike, we like the same things—there could be a new alliance to hold back the Russians.

A: But Pakistan is nonaligned.

Q: That doesn't make any difference; when two countries are as close as ours were, alliances don't make any difference.

This officer, and many like him, long for a lost world; they have no doubt who their enemies are but are less than certain about their friends, and feel—largely because of the disappointment of the earlier relationship—a personal interest in renewing an American connection. As realists and professional skeptics, they are consciously aware of the difficulties of a new grand alliance with the Americans; but on a private and perhaps subconscious level they retain affection for the country that was so intimately involved with their professional and personal development.

Pakistani officers even today emphasize the historical "friendship" between the United States and Pakistan; this friendship is based on a common belief in democracy, a staunch anticommunism, and Pakistan's reciprocal loyal support in matters such as the U-2 and in international forums. Such officers must, however, confront the question as to whether Pakistan has changed for the worse or America has changed in such a way as to lead to the erosion of a relationship that meant so much to them; to escape such a choice, many tend to blame the devious Indians, the liberals and Zionists of American politics, or their own politicians.

The negative aspects of the American connection have been commented upon by several distinguished officers (who are not in any sense anti-American). M. Attiqur Rahman observed that one institution inherited from the British, the officer's mess, was modified, and not for the better. It was and is vital in developing unit *esprit* and a sense of comradeship in peacetime that would be invaluable during war. It also serves as the home for unmarried officers. But then,

Some of our messes, against clear Army orders, admitted ladies, perhaps imitating some aspects of the American Officers' clubs. From the introduction of ladies it was but a step to providing singing girls, presumably under the influence of some cultural motive. Not very edifying for the up and coming young officer.[29]

What in retrospect seems to have been particularly insidious was the American public-relations operation within the Pakistan Army, which weaned the officers away from their "old and favorite" British periodicals, only to substitute American ones. One officer who dealt with them de-

29. M. Attiqur Rahman, *Our Defense Cause* (London: White Lion, 1976), p. 44.

scribed how the U.S. Information Service extended its operations in Pakistan under the Motivation (later Troop Information) Program, as part of the military-aid program. A separate cell was created in the (Pakistan) Inter-Services PR Directorate to handle the collection and distribution of American journals, books, and films throughout the Pakistan Army, Navy, and Air Force. In retrospect, he concluded that "the so-called Motivation Program was an elevation of normal PR to a higher sphere of intellectual education and indoctrination."[30] Worst of all, this officer claims (and others support the argument) that the American military presence compromised the "purely national image" of the armed forces:

It appeared as if the Americans had taken over where the British left off. The progressive or the anti-West elements in the country did not approve of the American infiltration. Foreign hardware was one thing but foreign personnel was quite another. The attitude of the American aid personnel to an average Pakistani was anything but desirable by native standards. In the beginning the Americans mixed well with the Pakistanis; but as their numbers increased they became more aloof and distant. It seemed as if there were two military establishments in one country: one national, the other foreign.[31]

Officers who make this point are neither anti-American nor Anglophiles of an earlier generation. They wholeheartedly participated in American training programs but have since come to realize the negative aspects of a relationship that has rarely been criticized in public or within the military.

Underlying some of the bitterness toward the Americans was the fact that American estimates of Pakistan's defense needs were often sharply at variance with those of senior generals. After the American build-up of the Pakistan armed forces was completed (roughly by 1960), American interest in India grew steadily, as it declined in Pakistan. This was due not only to a change in administration but to a revised estimate of threats to the subcontinent from the West (against Pakistan from Russia) and from the East (against India from China). Some Pakistanis have indicated that the American view was that Pakistan needed only 3½ divisions for its defense.

Pakistani Army officers are today on their best behavior with visiting

30. Unpublished manuscript by a retired army officer associated with public relations, p. 141.

31. Ibid., p. 145. The question of the "national image" of the Pakistan Army can be traced back to the formation of the state. Jinnah was concerned about the need for retention of British officers as commanders-in-chief of the three services, and used this to support his argument that Pakistan must have its own Governor-General, a Pakistani, not a Britisher shared with India. He became Pakistan's Governor-General, and Lord Mountbatten served as India's. See Sharif Al Mujahid, *Quaid-I-Azam Jinnah: Studies in Interpretation* (Karachi: Quaid-I-Azam Academy, 1981).

American dignitaries and officials (and often these Americans have been so predisposed to the idea of a staunch, vigorously pro-American Pakistan that their hosts are reluctant to disillusion them). But in the 1970s, Pakistani officers, even those trained in the United States, came to a cautious and skeptical appreciation of American intentions and what a new American presence in Pakistan would or should look like. One of Pakistan's best strategists and most widely known military writers cautioned a visitor against a repetition of the 1950s and 1960s style of American aid to Pakistan and offered very sound advice:

When there was an aid program the Americans drove around in enormous cars, they lived apart, they had a standard of living—it was the whole "ugly American" complex. People questioned this, they thought, "what is the value of American aid if most of it is plowed back into a high standard of living for those who are dispensing it." No, if you do come back, look at what the Russians are doing in Karachi, or even the Chinese. We don't expect you to live like them, but it is a bad influence on our own people to live the way you did.

Two other experiences of the "American" generation must be noted briefly, for they were of crucial importance in shaping attitudes and beliefs. One was the evident success (until 1970, at least) enjoyed by the military in its attempt to structure and control Pakistani politics. The other was the self-delusion of the military and the belief that it not only had mastered Pakistani politics but could master the Indians as well, despite India's size and increasing military preparedness after 1963. Pakistanis were to be told that the 1965 war demonstrated their martial superiority over Hindu India, and some of the worst racism and cultural arrogance seen since Partition emerged under official sponsorship in a number of articles and books. This self-delusion was fostered by a powerful and effective public-relations machinery under the control of the commander-in-chief. This PR apparatus was aimed at the outside world—particularly at the Americans—but it also influenced the military's judgment of its own competence and raised civilian expectations to excessive heights. When the military did falter (in 1965), the PR programs were intensified, but when the army was broken (in 1971), it collapsed, only to be revived in modified form under Bhutto.

One senior army PR official has written of both Ayub's and Yahya's rule:

After the seizure (of power) military image-building becomes more blatant and intensive. A sort of an image-craze grips the top military echelons and they seek to gratify it by any means, by persuasion if possible, and force if necessary ... PR, towards the end of the Ayub era seemed to have badly affected Ayub's perceptions and sober judgement. He appears to have become a hopeless addict to the allurement of his tailor-made publicity and its remarkable capacity for making the black look white ... In a country such as Pakistan, where for many years the armed forces have been at the helm of civil affairs, the influence of adulatory publicity on them cannot be overlooked. It appears to have affected them deeply enough to change their professional attitudes and standards and to breed in them the unfortunate belief that the armed forces could do no wrong.[32]

Much the same point is made by Fazal Muqeem Khan in his semiofficial study of the events leading up to the disaster of 1971. Although no friend of India, he contrasts the ability of the Indians to learn from the mistakes of 1962 and 1965 with Pakistan's deliberate suppression of public criticism of the army's performance.[33] At the time, he and others were producing a stream of books and articles designed to raise morale, not question policies; clearly, the close association of the military with the leadership of Pakistan (in the form of Ayub Khan and then Yahya Khan as president) had a damaging effect on the professionalism of the military itself, and this remains one of the major lessons for this generation of officers.

1972–82: THE PAKISTANI GENERATION

Q: Why did you join the PAF and not the army?—all your relatives are in the army.
A: [PAF flying officer] Well, I was going to join the army, but then the war came [1971] and the army wasn't so popular anymore. I didn't want to go through that, so I joined the air force.
Q: Go through what?
A: Oh, people laughing at you, insulting you—the army wasn't very popular then, you know.

The outstanding characteristic of those who have joined the Pakistan Army in the past ten to fifteen years is that they are the most purely "Pakistani" of all. They are more representative of the wider society in class origin, they have been least subjected to foreign professional influences, and they are drawn from a generation with no direct contact with India. More problematically, they have joined during a period in which the reputation and prestige of the army had plummeted. None of this implies that they will not become as good professional soldiers as men of earlier generations. That kind of judgment is very difficult to make without much more detailed knowledge of the military than is now available, or by waiting twenty years or more and seeing how they perform in war and politics.

32. Unpublished manuscript, p. 140.
33. *Pakistan's Crisis in Leadership* (Rawalpindi: Ferozsons, 1973), pp. 3–4.

It has been suggested that the most dramatic military event of the 1965–80 period, the defeat of the Pakistan Army in East Pakistan, has created a mini-generation of its own.

When the Pakistan forces surrendered to the Indian Army, over ninety thousand officers and men became prisoners of war. These troops were removed to POW camps scattered throughout India and held until mid-1973. Their fate was linked to negotiations over the postwar relationship between India, Pakistan, and Bangladesh and came to rest in the hands of Indira Gandhi and Zulfiqar Ali Bhutto (who had succeeded Yahya Khan).[34]

Of the POWs held by India, some eventually moderated their views toward their captors. A few had friends in the Indian officer corps, and many captured Pakistanis came to blame their own leaders for their defeat and imprisonment. Yahya Khan and his close military advisors are held responsible for the initial error of mistaking the true sentiments of the Bengalis, and for later failing either to fight effectively or to pull out in time. Not a few officers believe that they were sacrificed by Yahya. Bhutto has also been criticized by both the former and the latter for his role in the outbreak of war in East Pakistan and for having unduly delayed the prisoners' return to Pakistan because he was afraid that they would turn to political action at a time when his own position was unsteady.

However, other officers are known to have hardened their attitude toward the Indians as a result of their captivity. This group has been described as seeking revenge not only on their military chiefs but also against the Indian military. When confronted with this proposition, one brigadier, a hero of the POW camps (he had organized several escape attempts, and refused to acknowledge the authority of his Indian captors), offered an alternative explanation. "It is true that when we came back we were angry and bitter, and felt that we were being treated separately," he admitted, "and there was the odd report of an individual who had trouble with his commanding officer, or could not fit in, or who left the service." But the collective hatred toward both the Indians and the responsible Pakistani officials dissipated:

We did not constitute a separate age generation, because we were of all ranks, from lieutenant to lieutenant-general. We are not going through the army together as a *group;* if we were, then you could talk of a separate generation, one with a grudge. We were accused by some of not having fought to the death, and that somehow we

34. For the best account of the war by one of those captured, see Siddiq Salik, *Witness to Surrender* (Karachi: Oxford University Press, 1977), and for a version of the release of the POWs sympathetic to Bhutto, see Salmaan Taseer, *Bhutto: A Political Biography* (London: Ithaca Press, 1979), pp. 143–44.

did not uphold our military honor, and we were corrupted or dishonored both by surrendering and our captivity, but we did not feel this. No, in time our feelings have diffused somewhat, although I certainly will never trust the Indians—how can we after what they did? One day saying that they will never use force, and the next day invading?

Such feelings are widespread within the army's upper ranks, but are probably no more intense among those who had been POWs than those who had not. Yet their influence may be substantial as they move upward to general-officer rank and come to hold key positions in the important training commands and military schools. After the debacle of 1971 there was a changed atmosphere in the military. The authority of senior officers was no longer accepted without question, and was openly challenged on several dramatic occasions.[35] The 1965–71 period came to be known as the "sawdust years," in which military honor and professionalism slipped away from the Pakistan Army. The experience of 1965 was not subject to analysis, and this professional failure contributed to the disaster of 1971, as did the military's involvement in "the mire of politics."[36] The myth of invincibility of the army was shaken in 1965 and shattered in 1971, and its corollary, the corrupt ineptitude of the Indian Army, embodied a reproach that was increasingly applied to the Pakistan Army itself. It was also evident that Pakistan stood alone. The military had no special relationship with the United States or with any other powerful state except China. The military's failure to provide effective leadership and to keep Pakistan together led to a radical deterioration in its public image. As one of the most-senior serving Pakistani officers has put it, "after 1971 I was ashamed to wear my uniform, I was ashamed of my army."

The officers who joined the military after 1965 are now (1982) reaching the rank of colonel; those who joined after 1971 are now captains and majors. Very few of them have had contact with American military personnel, although they have all attended various professional military schools and a limited number of foreign officers have received training in Pakistan. Intense self-study has marked the early years of their professional careers (1972–80). This reexamination of the principles upon which the state and the army are based may yet lead to a renewed professionalism. Two main reasons for this critical self-study can be adduced.

35. One of these episodes is described by Salmaan Taseer: "Suddenly the atmosphere [at a meeting in which a senior general was trying to explain the events surrounding the 1971 disaster] had become defiant and rebellious. The air was thick with cigarette smoke, and it was beginning to look more and more like a 'people's court' during the French Revolution. Overt respect for senior rank had vanished. The younger officers were shouting 'Bastards!', 'Drunkards!', 'Disgraceful!', and 'Shame!'" Taseer, *Bhutto*, p. 130.

36. Riza, *Izzat-O-Iqbal*, p. 298.

After the disaster of 1971, Bhutto systematically attempted to point out the failings of the senior military leadership and at times to ridicule those responsible. Yet Bhutto did not undertake a general purge of the army or even of those involved in the events of 1971. His goal was to create in Pakistan the kind of professional but docile military establishment that the Indians had by reducing the power and prestige of the army without reducing its fighting capabilities.[37] Bhutto also emulated the Indians when he tried to build up a paramilitary force—the Federal Security Force —that would stand between the army and the police but would also serve as a counter to the military if necessary.

Bhutto's efforts were at first welcomed by most officers. They realized that the professionalism and integrity of the army had badly deteriorated and were themselves trying to restore it. One of the officers interested in the reprofessionalization of the military was General Mohammed Zia ul-Haq. His tenure as Chief of the Army Staff has again seen the military come to power, but his primary military interest has been to restore the integrity of the army and improve the quality of its officer corps.

Zia encouraged a number of reforms and changes at all levels. Under Zia, a program of sending combat officers to universities in Pakistan for postgraduate higher education in such nonmilitary subjects as history, psychology, and political science as well as strategic studies has begun; before 1978 only the Army Education Corps did this. Several officers have also gone to foreign civilian institutions for such training. The new National Defense College, at present located in Rawalpindi and extremely well equipped, has two courses. One is purely professional, dealing with higher military strategy; the other, which lasts for ten months, is the senior joint civil and military course. Pakistani officers also have close contact with the many foreign officers who attend Pakistani training institutions such as the Staff College and various technical schools. Special, if not lavish, attention is being given to the selection and initial professional training of young officers, as we shall see later in this chapter. Finally, a number of actions have been taken that are weighted with symbolism. A new camouflage battle tunic was ordered, and was worn by all officers, including Zia. It conveyed an alert and combat-ready attitude. Another gesture was the publication and circulation of "A Prayer" by the Military Intelligence Directorate, quoted at the beginning of this chapter. Its praise

37. Bhutto discusses this at length in his death-cell testimony, *If I Am Assassinated* ... (New Delhi: Vikas, 1979). In it he argues that the military, especially Zia, have been "soft" on India and are incompetent to boot. The *Defense White Paper* (see ch. 5) clearly bears his hand; what was resented were his attempts to attack the reputation of Ayub Khan and some other generals.

of men with "strong minds, great hearts, true faith," who possess integrity and honor and who will "stand before a demagogue/and damn his treacherous flatteries," clearly refers to the army's relationship to the just-executed Bhutto, and more broadly to the politicians of Pakistan. Such symbolic actions hardly guarantee either that the older officers of the Pakistan Army will undergo a professional regeneration or that the new, post-1972 generation will somehow be men of greater integrity or competence than their predecessors. This is doubly true when such gestures are examined more closely. According to one Pakistani officer, the camouflage battle tunic does not, in fact, conceal the wearer any better than the old garment when both are tested under infrared light, and as of 1982 it was being phased out. More poignantly, "The Prayer" distributed by the Intelligence Directorate was in fact written by an American writer and poet, probably in 1859–65, and refers to the United States during its civil war. Most Pakistani officers who have read it assumed that its author was an anonymous British Army or British Indian Army officer.[38] Furthermore, the version as printed in Pakistan omits the last four lines of the original:

> For while the rabble, with their thumb-worn creeds,
> Their large professions and their little deeds, —
> Mingle in selfish strife, lo! Freedom weeps,
> Wrong rules the land, and waiting Justice sleeps!

These dropped lines might well be applied to Zia's Pakistan by critics of the martial-law regime.

Many thoughtful officers in Pakistan are fully aware that even if wide-ranging reforms are implemented and the quality of the officer corps does improve, there is no assurance that the problems that they will face in years to come will not overwhelm them—problems such as the inability of the military to separate itself from politics, the deep division within Pakistan over the army's attempt to transform and Islamize society, and the strategic encirclement of the country. It may be that competence will not be enough to ensure the survival of the army as we know it today. What we can evaluate with some precision, and provides us with additional clues about the future, are the institutions that have been created by the military and that in turn re-create it year after year.

38. Josiah Gilbert Holland (1819–81) was a popular New England poet, writer, and editor whose writings sold more than a half-million copies. "A Prayer" is excerpted from Holland's brief poem, "Wanted." See J. G. Holland, *The Complete Poetical Writings* (New York: Scribner's and Sons, 1883), pp. 472–73, and his entry in the Dictionary of American Biography.

INSTITUTION BUILDING AND PROFESSIONALISM

The Pakistan Army has literally hundreds of training institutions. Each combat unit trains separately and in conjunction with other units in accordance with a fixed annual cycle. Such training begins with the individual in his section and goes up to the platoon, company, battalion, brigade, division, and corps. Finally, interservice training exercises are conducted frequently.

The three institutions described below are not combat formations but "pure" training centers. As such, they are concerned not only with preparing individuals at various stages of their careers but also with developing and applying doctrine. Their directing staffs and instructors have the responsibility of reflecting on *why* as well as *what* is taught. All are vital to the functioning of the Pakistan Army: one serves as the gateway to the military profession, another imparts various levels of technical education, and still another is the gateway to promotion to the upper ranks of the army.

PRESERVING INSTITUTIONS: THE STAFF COLLEGE, QUETTA

A heavy, brass bell decorates the entrance hall of the college building of the Pakistan Army's Command and Staff College in Quetta. Appropriately, as Quetta faces northwest towards Afghanistan and the Soviet Union, the bell is a war trophy salvaged from a Russian battleship.[39] It was presented to the twenty students and two instructors who were members of the fledgling Staff College by the Imperial Japanese Navy, as a memento of their visit in 1907 to battle sites in Manchuria. The bell is a reminder both of the age of the Staff College—it had been founded only two years earlier—and the persistence of strategic alignments.

Although many of its buildings have been replaced or transformed (Quetta suffered a devastating earthquake in 1935), the institution still serves many of the functions expected of it by the British, and can still boast of a long and glorious history. Although, curiously, it no longer offers instruction in "strategy" or "law," as it did when it opened its doors in 1905, it is still the oldest (and in some ways the most vital) institution in the Pakistan Army.

The Staff College was established to supplement the British Staff College, Camberley, for British Indian Army officers. Strictly speaking, it

39. For a history of the Staff College see *1905–1980: Command and Staff College, Quetta,* cited in note 26.

owed its creation to Lord Kitchener, whose reorganization of the Indian Army in 1902 established a number of new staff appointments. The practice of sending six officers annually to Camberley was inadequate, and in any case, Camberley would not increase the positions available to the Indian Army. In addition to training selected officers for staff appointments in the Indian Army, the college was to provide them with the background required for higher command. The present (1980) mission of the college is to "train officers for war and in so doing fit them for grade-2 staff appointments and, with further experience, for command."[40]

The Staff College's distinguished graduates were three British field marshals (Auchinleck, Montgomery, and Slim) and Sir Douglas Gracey, one of the two British officers who served as commander-in-chief of the Pakistan Army (and one of nine students in the class of 1928 to rise to the rank of general). Quetta offered a two-year course of study until World War II forced a cut to twelve months in 1939 and six months in 1940. In the latter year the first two "Pakistani" (i.e., Indian Muslim) officers, K. M. Idris and Nazir Ahmed, attended it, and the then Captain Ayub Khan was a student from December 1940 to June 1941. Two years later an Indian Muslim officer joined the directing staff. With the end of the war, the college course reverted to one year, and the institution survived Partition intact.[41]

Very little change was made in the Staff College after Partition. Indeed, it retained a British commandant until 1954 and five British officers remained on the directing staff for an additional year. The college continued to be a small institution for a number of years; it graduated only fifty-eight students in 1958. Because of the need to stretch available officer material at the middle ranks of major and lieutenant-colonel, the course of study remained conservative to make it somewhat easier for those who took it (and also because the army of the chief enemy—India—was in some ways a World War II force). Strategic conservatism, with young and untried officer material and a known and equally conservative opponent, made good sense. Pakistani officers who had been through the Staff College when it was run by the British could come back and fit into a familiar regime.

After Partition, the College organized "senior officers" courses, partly to fill in some of the educational gaps of those Pakistanis who had been

40. Ibid., pp. 4–5.
41. School legend has it that Yahya Khan slept in the library at night to protect its ten thousand volumes from pilferage.

rapidly promoted after Independence. Ayub Khan attended one such course as a major-general in 1950; the courses were later replaced by the comprehensive National Defense College. The first generation of Pakistani officers received a competent if conventional training at Quetta. That Quetta functioned at all was both something of a surprise and evidence of the professional dedication and commitment of this early Pakistani generation.

The Staff College's curriculum is very much as it was before World War II, and such changes as have occurred largely followed developments at Camberley, still regarded as the "parent" institution. A foreign officer, writing in the 1970s, could note that "the curriculum is based on that inherited by the college in 1947, and appears to have undergone minor modifications. Tactics are essentially WWII ... The program of instruction has changed very little over the years ... One can gain some insights into the British system as it was practiced in 1947."[42]

The Staff College's special strengths are in the analysis of terrain, conventional tactics, and the beginning of a broader professional education for those who pass through it. It takes its title literally, and stresses the preparation of its students for staff work on the brigade or divisional level. Foreign officers who have attended Quetta are critical of this: they contrast it with equivalent schools in the West, where students are encouraged to engage in more speculative analysis. Some have also been critical of the college's relative neglect of logistics and of the overall neglect of logistics in the Pakistan Army itself. One analysis points out that only 3 to 4 percent of the students at Quetta are logistics specialists, compared with a quarter of those at the Australian staff college.[43] If true, this may reflect not only a distaste for the less glamorous branches but also the Pakistani expectation that future wars will be very short and fought with material on hand.

In addition to courses and exercises devoted to staff training, the Command and Staff College continues the process of strategic education begun at the Pakistan Military Academy (and later resumed in the National Defense College). In chapter 6 we shall describe the strategic doctrines of the Pakistani officer in greater detail, but it is worth contrasting the sys-

---

42. Communication to the author from a former student.

43. Maj. Marcus Bromet (Ordnance, Australian Army), "Career Planning and the Logistic Officer," *The Review, 1979* (Quetta, Command and Staff College), pp. 27–33. Bromet's figures, taken from the honor boards posted at the Staff College, show an increase of 460 percent in students from 1950; there were 215 in 1980. Forty-four percent (94) were from the infantry, only two students were from Ordnance, and four were from the Army Service Corps. In 1979, none of the 31 members of the directing staff was from a logistics corps.

tematic syllabus dealing with technical matters, geopolitics, and tactics with the Staff College's instruction on Indian strategy.

As of a few years ago, these were the weakest elements in the entire course of study. Indian strategic objectives are presented as a fixed doctrine, rooted in communal attitudes and pretensions to great-power status. The syllabus is often factually inaccurate, and course instructors do not encourage debate or discussion on the subject.[44] A mixture of suspicion, awe, and contempt emerges in a prelude to an analysis of Indian nuclear plans:

In no field is the inquiry into Indian "intentions" more revealing of the intricacies of the Indian mind than in the field of her nuclear development. The official line that India is developing her nuclear power potential for peaceful uses only is well known. The instinctive Pakistani reaction to it, shaped by centuries of close association with the Hindu mind from Chanakya and Kautilya to Panikkar and Subrahmanyam, is equally well known.[45]

The analysis itself is superficial and often inaccurate, but drives home one important point: that Indian intentions are subject to rapid change, hence the Pakistani military planner must deal only with the already substantial (and growing) Indian capability:

From this brief review of Indian grand strategy, there is hardly any need to strain ourselves to draw any "conclusions" about Indian intentions. The "intentions" show through without so much as a "Pardon, my slip is showing!". . . This axiom must be borne in mind while attempting to evaluate India's relentless drive towards big-power status and regional hegemony through careful orchestration of political, economic, psychological and military means.[46]

In contrast with this insecure and inadequate appreciation of India, the quality of strategic analysis in other areas is quite good. Of special note is the section on geopolitics, which freely draws from the work of Western, Asian, and Islamic thinkers in an eclectic but informative blend. These lectures were for several years delivered by Professor Abdul Qayyum, a retired army colonel of Bengali origin and a favorite of Zia ul-Haq.[47] He challenged his students to analyze critically the past and Pakistan's strategic identity, and to study carefully a diverse range of theorists. These

44. Communication to the author from a former student.
45. Command and Staff College, Quetta, Staff Course, *Military System: India*. This mimeographed document is issued to students and revised annually. The quotations are from a set distributed in the late 1970s.
46. Ibid.
47. Prof. Col. Qayyum expanded his lectures on Islam for print at Zia's request, and the latter wrote a foreword to them. See *On Striving to Be a Muslim* (Lahore: Islamic Book Centre, 1978).

lectures contribute to a professional military education: the briefing papers and analyses dealing with India simply perpetuate stereotypes, transmitting them from one generation to another. The rigidity of thought of many Pakistani officers concerning India is now less a product of their experiences before Partition—current students of the Staff College had not even been born then—than of crude images of India that have become a part of their formal and informal military education. We do not wish to imply that Pakistan does not have a real security problem vis-a-vis India, but rather that the Staff College teaches an inadequate, reductionist theory of Indian motives and strategy. As a matter of fact, the syllabi dealing with Pakistan that are used at Indian service schools are not much better. We shall return to the implications of these respective misperceptions in our final chapter.

CREATING INSTITUTIONS: THE ARTILLERY SCHOOL, NOWSHERA

Whereas the Staff College has certain intellectual shortcomings, the Artillery School at Nowshera is an example of successful institution building and adaptiveness. It is perhaps more typical than Quetta of the dozens of new establishments created immediately after Independence to replace regimental training centers, technical training centers, and other facilities that had been situated in India. Many of these new institutions were built upon facilities that had been part of the old Northern Command of the Indian Army. They were short on space, resources, and staff, but those who built them remain proud of their accomplishment.

Nowshera (about 10 miles due east of Peshawar) was a prewar gunnery station. It was one of the oldest permanent installations of the Indian Army, having been established as a gunnery range in 1907. There is a separate Artillery Center in Campbellpur, on the northwestern edge of the rugged Potwar plateau. The center serves as home for the entire artillery regiment. The school was founded in 1948 and followed British doctrine and techniques for several years; its instructors were trained in Britain until 1952, after which they were trained at Ft. Sill, Oklahoma, and increasingly at Nowshera itself. Despite the existence of an R. & D. cell in the mid-1950s, the school encountered major problems of standardization of procedures and doctrine when American equipment started flowing to Pakistan. These problems were not uncommon in other components of the Pakistan Army, as well. For example, it still had a number of British Model 62 wireless sets in the 1965 war, and they were sometimes incompatible (i.e., no frequency overlap) with the American PRC 10. The retrospective history of Pakistan artillery notes that these and other handicaps could have been anticipated, but "no remedial action was taken before, during, or after the 1965 war."[48] New problems arose after 1965 when the supply of American equipment ceased and Chinese, Italian, and even North Korean artillery was acquired. Each system had a different table of ballistics and different firing and density tables, and each nation produced different kinds of sighting and calibration mechanisms. The Artillery School was forced not only to train its own instructors, but also to initiate and formulate a single set of table and firing systems peculiar to Pakistan but adaptable to a wide variety of foreign equipment. One senior gunnery officer pointed out to a visitor that

You thought you were punishing us for going to war in 1965 but the cut-off was a big favor for us . . . We had to stand on our own for the first time, we couldn't tap into your supply system for parts, and so forth. It was difficult, but it actually made us better, for we had to combine all these weapons from all these countries and come up with our own system.

This view is expressed in many Pakistani training facilities, although it is often accompanied by expressions of hope that a new American program might be started (at least in the wake of the Soviet invasion of Afghanistan). Several cases can be cited (especially in the defense-production field) where the military was hurt by the termination of major American arms shipments and has had to adapt, and in doing so may have improved its self-sufficiency if not always the quality of equipment. The necessity of self-reliance and self-sufficiency was an important and difficult lesson for officers who were particularly influenced by the American relationship.

Among other things, Pakistan has expanded its program of training foreign officers at Nowshera (for a number of years it has sent training teams to other countries). Nowshera offers the full range of gunnery courses from basic through specialist and advanced instructor to foreign as well as Pakistani students. One additional comparative advantage of Pakistan is displayed on some of the classroom buildings—relevant sayings from the Quran.[49] Nowshera is thus one example of Pakistan's success in mastering basic military technologies and in institution-building, and there are many others. This capacity to improvise and to build on a slender base greatly impressed Pakistan's allies in CENTO and SEATO in

48. Riza, *Izzat-O-Iqbal*, p. 140.
49. For example, prominently displayed on the front of Tactics Hall is the following Quranic saying (in English): "Oh ye believers take your precautions tactically and either go forth in parties or go forth all together."

the 1950s, when Pakistan was widely regarded as a pillar of these Western-sponsored defense alliances.

THE NEXT GENERATION: THE PAKISTAN MILITARY ACADEMY

The Himalayan hill station of Kakul, nearly 80 miles from Rawalpindi, has been and is the setting for one of the most interesting processes of cultural change in Pakistan. It is the site of the Pakistan Military Academy, founded in 1948 to turn "gentleman cadets" into junior officers modeled on their counterparts at West Point or Sandhurst. The very idea of such an institution (and others like it at Dehra Dun and Khadakvasla, in India) was ridiculed in the early part of this century. Most British officials were convinced that Indians could not become gentlemen or officers. They later recruited what they took to be gentlemen—the sons of the professional classes and landed aristocracy of India—and did turn them into professional officers, but for many years this group has not offered itself in large numbers. These academies must therefore attempt to duplicate the Western professional officer by training young men who are more truly Indian or Pakistani than they are cultural outriders of Western civilization. They do know English (or learn it), but their reference points are largely in the subcontinent, not outside of it.

This is a critical point. Can an individual who is entirely the product of Pakistani society become a professional officer comparable with his Western equivalent? If so, through what processes and with what personal consequences? The issue was formulated by Arnold Toynbee in the context of an examination of the cultural origins of war:

The secret of the West's superiority to the rest of the world in the art of war from the Seventeenth century onward is not to be found just in Western weapons, drill, and military training ... It cannot be understood without also taking into account the whole mind and soul of the Western Society of the day and the truth is that the Western art of war has always been one facet of the Western way of life. Hence, an alien society that tried to acquire the art without attempting to live the life was bound to fail to master the art; while, conversely, a Russian, Turkish, or other non-Western military officer who did succeed in his profession up to the normal Western standard could achieve this only by acquiring much more of the Western civilization than was to be found in the textbook or on the parade-ground.[50]

Toynbee is mistaken. Adopting the "Western art of war" is related to a "Western way of life," but it is possible to retain and live a Pakistani or an

50. Arnold Toynbee, *The World and the West* (New York: Oxford University Press, 1953), p. 26.

Indian way of life. This is not only because some of that way of life (at least for sectors of the middle and upper classes) is permeated by Western ways, but also because young officers have been able to compartmentalize their lives and still harmonize demands from profession and society.

But what is such an officer to do when such demands cannot be harmonized? Many Pakistani officers are quick to point out the danger of allowing "acceptable" practices (in the context of traditional social values) to erode professional values. Accepting token or substantial bribes; allowing relatives to profit from inside knowledge; treating soldiers as servants or menials rather than with respect and dignity—these are all practices in the ambiguous grey zone between cultures. They may have increased in recent years as officers have been preponderantly drawn from what Pakistani officers call the "same stock" as the rest of the country and are subject to the same temptations and corruptions. Admonitions addressed to the young officer or commander are filled with warnings about such temptations.

The point is also made that even the highest officers of the Pakistan Army, Ayub Khan and Yahya Khan, for all their greatness and professionalism, fell when temptation came, and their subordinates emulated them in corruption:

Openings for personal aggrandizement were, of course, available only to the few, but the many used to note such things as cheap loans and cheap housing, trips overseas, availability of cars, and the provision of rest houses together with all the necessary comforts with which to pass the long night.[51]

At the beginning of this chapter we presented recent figures on the number of applicants to the PMA. Those responsible for recruitment and for training of young officer-cadets are satisfied with the quality of applicants.[52] Given the relatively slow growth of the Pakistani economy in the 1970s, the limited opportunities open to educated young men, and the strong regional traditions of military service in Pakistan (especially in Punjab and the N.W.F.P.) this comes as no surprise. Still, the present cadets are a far cry from those that entered the Indian Army in the 1930s.

---

51. M. Attiqur Rahman, *Our Defense Cause*, p. 41.

52. Those involved with selection to the PMA have two criteria for determining the "right type" of candidate: whether an individual is willing to make the army his career "with determination," and whether an individual is "trainable," i.e., amenable to the discipline of the academy and the military. In their words, the recruiters are looking for a person willing to wake up early, work hard, and not complain; it is no wonder that the sons of officers and JCOs, who are already familiar with the requirements and routine of the army, are preferred; the other two armed services are perceived as less Spartan and also better places to put a technical education to work.

Their English is much worse, and they typically come from middle-class families (or are the sons of JCOs), although each class has a sprinkling of sons from the great military families of Pakistan, whose males have served in the army for two, three, or four generations and before that may have seen service in a Mughal or Afghan army.

The PMA is today undergoing a series of reforms and changes as part of the broader interest in improving professional military education in Pakistan. In contrast to the situation in India, where there are several entry routes into the army, the PMA is virtually the only way to become a Pakistan Army officer, although it offers several different courses: for the few jawans who become officers and for technical graduates, as well as the main course.

Proposals to change this system of getting young men and molding them according to Pakistan Army requirements have been consistently rejected, although there are provisions for the entry of a limited number of individuals with a B.A. or B.S. degree who attend a short course at Kakul.[53]

The pattern of education at the PMA is quite different from that at Sandhurst (where a briefer technical military education is offered) and more like that of West Point, where military and academic subjects are combined. The entrant to the PMA is a matriculate (tenth year of education) and is trained up to the equivalent of the Pakistani B.A. or B.Sc. degree in two years. These degrees are awarded (as in India) by a cooperating university at a ceremony held just after the cadet is commissioned.

After a series of studies, the main course at the PMA has now been modified. The current plan is to emphasize academic studies for two semesters (one year) and military ones for two semesters. The idea of a semester system is a recent one, borrowed from the American pattern.

Those responsible for the PMA have to deal with a basic fact: their cadets come from regions and families with very low educational standards, and must be given a heavy academic curriculum. As one senior PMA staff member pointed out:

At Sandhurst they get boys who already know English, who have had a good grounding in science, and so forth; in Pakistan we have a national army, anyone may join, and that means that we get boys who are not only from public schools, but from all over, from villages: and they have to be disciplined into a particular pattern of communication, and that is primarily English. And English is spoken only in educated circles, so we have to bring them up educationally in the Academy, and we have to emphasize science.

53. Lt.-Col. Ihsanul Haq, "System of Recruitment and Initial Training of Officers," *Pakistan Army Journal*, December 1964, pp. 34–36.

More than half of the PMA course therefore deals with purely academic subjects taught at a basic level, and there are plans to extend the course by one semester to enable the staff to teach additional academic subjects. The goal is to produce an officer who is not only technically competent to handle a platoon or command a tank, but one who is able to continue his professional education in years to come and to assume the responsibilities · of an informed citizen. In the opinion of the same PMA staff member:

We are in some ways like a Western army, in that rigid patterns of obedience and command will not work. A change is a must, and it has to come pretty soon in view of the Russians now being on the Durand line, which is a de facto Russian-Pakistan border. There's no way to undo it: I think we have got to have more educated, widely educated officers than what we have before. A boy reads a book, or a newspaper, or even a *Newsweek,* and he sees something about "credible defense"; he need not know the details of it but he must know what it is: the same thing is true of "deterrence." We cannot get along with the "Koi Hai" officer type anymore.

In the past there has been resistance to lengthening the PMA course. Some officers have argued that the whole concept of isolating the young cadet for several years is wrong: that the PMA should be cut back to one year because it is producing "semi-educated and immature officers."[54] Another (and opposite) objection to the trend in increasing educational requirements in the army is a fear that young officers will be overeducated—which for a soldier may not always be a virtue. Despite such concerns, however, it is likely that the trend to increased educational requirements for the PMA and for senior officers will continue.

In addition to professional military training and academic subjects, the PMA, like other total institutions (especially those serving as feeders to structured bureaucracies), attempts to mold and influence the character of its members. Personality and character account for half of the weight in an internal evaluation scheme (academic and military subjects each carry 25 percent), and PMA staff speak of this in terms of "leadership, power of decision, initiative, will-power, character, organizing ability, intelligence, imagination, moral courage, sense of duty, sense of responsibility, self-discipline," and so forth. In all, the personality of the cadet is analyzed and evaluated on twenty or more different attributes. Moreover, cadets selected at random are studied throughout their academy careers. This evaluation scheme follows the cadet through his years at the PMA and includes participants from the Inter-Service Selection Board (which made the original se-

54. Ibid.

lection to the PMA) and, beginning in 1980, evaluations of PMA graduates by their unit commanders. The hope is that by gathering together the peer evaluations of PMA cadets, their unit-commander assessment, and assessments made by the ISSB and the PMA staff itself there will be a number of tests of whether the PMA is acquiring and producing the "right type" of officer.

Another indirect measure of the success of the PMA in attracting and training types of individuals who fit their model is the effectiveness of the internal disciplinary system at Kakul. The PMA has a "partial" honor system, in which cadets are required to inform on those discovered cheating or even turn themselves in to authorities. Such honor systems have not always been effective at West Point and the other American military-service academies; in both cultures there is tension between traditional and personal social ties, the fear of failure, and the injunctions of the honor code. This in turn has led a few officers to think about the meaning of the honor system (largely derived from comparable Western institutions) for an army that has a quite different code available to it—that of Islam.

CHAPTER FOUR

Islam and
the Officer Corps

The professional soldier in a Muslim army, pursuing the goals of a
Muslim state, CANNOT become "professional" if in all his activities he
does not take on "the color of Allah."

General M. Zia ul-Haq, 1979[1]

Several widely held images of the Pakistan Army have tended to blur our
understanding of the relationship between Islam and the military. These
images verge on stereotypes: that the Pakistani soldier goes into battle
dreaming of death and heaven or that he pursues an "Islamic" strategy in
conjunction with Muslim brethren in other states. Neither statement is
wholly true, although there have been occasions when the cry of Islam has
been given by the military. The argument that the Pakistani soldier is an
Islamic fanatic is not entirely without basis, but neither is it an accurate
characterization. The army does employ "Islamic" slogans, some of
which were quoted in chapter 2 ("Fighting in the name of Allah, . . . is the
supreme sort of worship, and anybody who does service in the armed
forces with the intention of doing this job in worship, his life is a worship"). In this way the military uses Islam as a motivating force. During
the fight for East Pakistan, for example, the local commander, Lt.-Gen.
Tikka Khan, quoted freely from the Quran and the Sunnah in his talks to
the beleaguered East Pakistan garrison:

As Muslims, we have always fought against an enemy who was numerically and
materially superior. The enemy never deterred us. It was [by] the spirit of *jihad* and
dedication to Islam that the strongest adversaries were mauled and defeated by a

1. From Zia's foreword to Brig. S. K. Malik, *The Quranic Concept of War* (Lahore: Wajidalis, 1979).

handful of Muslims. The battles of Uhud, Badar, Khyber and Damascus are the proof of what the Muslims could do.

And, drawing from Sir Mohammed Iqbal, he recited to the troops:

Allah exalts the *mujahid* whether he lives or dies. He is a *ghazi* [crusader] if he lives, and a *shaheed* [martyr] if he dies. The *mujahid* seeks Allah's grace. He does not covet wealth and property.[2]

At the same time, the Commander-in-Chief and President of Pakistan, Yahya Khan, urged his soldiers on with the message that in the Mukti Bahini (the Bangladesh guerilla movement) they were fighting an anti-Islamic "Kaffir" army, and that they (the Pakistanis) were upholding the highest traditions of *mujahiddin*—soldiers of Islam. As one senior officer recalled, "expressions like the 'ideology of Pakistan' and the 'glory of Islam,' normally outside a professional fighter's lexicon, were becoming stock phrases . . . The Service Chiefs sounded more like high priests than soldiers."[3] Such exhortations, particularly when uttered by less than distinguished generals during a stupendous military fiasco, brought ridicule to the army and to Islam. These grandiose statements are hardly representative of the role that Islam plays within the military of Pakistan.

In almost every case it can be shown that there is considerable "Islamic" divergence within the officer corps, a divergence that has its roots in the very origins of the state. Pakistan itself contains within it many Islamic traditions. South Asian Muslims not only had diverse contacts with the rest of the Islamic world, but also made important contributions of their own to Islamic thought and doctrine.[4] But three aspects of the relationship between Islam and the military are of particular interest. These are (1) the way the military view Pakistan as an Islamic state, (2) the application of Islamic principles within the military, and (3) the reconciliation of Islamic and contemporary strategic doctrine.

THE ARMY AND AN ISLAMIC PAKISTAN

The movement for a homeland for South Asia's Muslims was not led by the extremely orthodox, but by middle- and upper-class Muslims. These lawyers, politicians, and doctors, most of them from the educated

2. Quoted in unpublished manuscript, p. 217.
3. Ibid., pp. 208–10.
4. For a useful survey of modern Islamic thought, see Aziz Ahmad, *Islamic Modernism in India and Pakistan, 1857–1964* (London: Oxford University Press, 1967).

Muslim communities of northern India and Bombay, saw their struggle in historical and practical terms, not as a theological quest. Many were not particularly religious in their private lives (Mohammad Ali Jinnah was notorious in this respect), but they thought of Pakistan as a state where they would be free from the domination of their more numerous Hindu counterparts. Although the Muslim League was dominated by such men, revivalist Muslim groups such as the Jamaat-i-Islami did not favor an independent Pakistan but rather sought to preserve the unity of the Indo-Muslim community.[5]

The shift from a concept of an Islamic Pakistan as a state run largely along British Indian secular principles (albeit with an external Islamic personality) to a Pakistan that became a laboratory of Islam occurred after independence. This shift reflected the increased influence of traditionalists and conservatives, deferred and delayed because of the great power of the highly westernized bureaucracy and officer corps during Ayub's and Yahya's regimes.

By and large, the young officers who formed the Pakistan Army tended to be more Westernized, more educated, and more sensitive to Hindu slights, and less concerned about building a perfect Islamic state. This came much later. The supreme irony of Pakistani politics is that when the state did come into existence, its semisecular leaders then came under pressure from orthodox and conservative Muslim groups. Ever since, they have had to make the necessary concessions to appease those groups, until now, perhaps for the first time, there is in Zia a leader who takes Islam seriously as a guide for Pakistani society.

In the years prior to the creation of Pakistan, little if any attention was given to the problem of the Islamic character of the future Pakistan Army. Jinnah had had an early interest in military affairs, and spoke out with considerable expertise on the Indianization of the Indian Army officer corps. However, his interest in military affairs flagged and no other prominent advocate of Pakistan took it up. After independence there was little detectable concern about the relationship of the military to Islam and the Islamic state; in his few talks to various army units, Jinnah stressed the necessity for obedience and dealt in generalities, as in his speech to two antiaircraft regiments in 1948: "Now you have to stand guard over the development and maintenance of Islamic democracy, Islamic social justice, and the quality of manhood in your own native soil."[6] The primary.

5. Ibid., p. 208.
6. Address on Feb. 21, 1948, reprinted in *Quaid-I-Azam Mohammad Ali Jinnah, Speeches, 1947–1948* (Islamabad: Ministry of Information and Broadcasting, n.d.), p. 63.

concern of both the political and the military leadership was to establish a basic military structure, not to dwell on ideology.

Other than relatively trivial steps, such as gradually replacing British-inspired symbols and slogans with Islamic ones, there was no outward change in the rather un-Islamic appearance of the officer corps and various installations in the Pakistan military. Primary attention had to be given to building an organization and to the development of strategic doctrine. The close relationship with first the British and then the American military encouraged deferral of the issue of Islam and the military: it was enough that the army served an Islamic state; after all, even Jinnah had encouraged the non-Muslim officers and men in the Pakistan military to "serve the ideal of Pakistan"; if Christians and Hindus could be good Pakistanis, then there was no need to press the question much further.[7]

This laissez-faire attitude suited most officers of the British generation and many who came to professional maturity during the American connection. Slowly, however, things began to unravel. The successive political and military failures of Pakistan, coupled with officer recruitment from more and more traditional sectors of Pakistani society, gradually increased the salience of the question of the relationship between army and state in an Islamic country. Officers began to ask what international models might be more relevant to the Pakistan Army than the secular British or American patterns. Because the Indian Army practically embodied a variation of these, and there had to be a sharp differentiation between India and Pakistan, how could Pakistani soldiers come to view their state correctly in an Islamic way, and how could the military reflect or contribute to that Islamic character? It took many years for this transition to occur, but the surprising contours of an "Islamic Pakistan Army" are now clear.

If the Pakistan movement and the first twenty-five years of the history of Pakistan can be characterized as a struggle to turn Indian Muslims into Pakistanis, the years since 1972 have seen an extension of the process: a struggle to turn Pakistanis into good Muslims. This great transformation has its parallels elsewhere in the world, and Pakistanis are aware of them. For example, when asked "what other army and country does Pakistan

---

There had been a more careful analysis of strategic problems, as will be discussed later in this chapter and in chapter 6.

7. Ibid., p. 154. In an important speech to the officers of the Staff College, Quetta, just before he died, Jinnah noted that "every officer and soldier, no matter what the race or community to which he belongs, is working as a true Pakistani," and he made similar references on other occasions.

most resemble?" a group of colonels and brigadiers answered almost in unison, "Israel." They support the Arab cause, and would fight against the Israelis if necessary, but they regard the Israeli pattern as nearly identical to their own, and are deeply impressed with Israeli military capabilities. They point out other similarities. Israel was also created by a partition; it also has a strong British military legacy moderated by extensive contact with American forces; and it also exists to provide a homeland for coreligionists who fled persecution. Above all, the Pakistani military admires the tenacity and skill of the Israeli Defense Forces and has carefully studied the major Middle East wars. Pakistanis would like to think of their country as another Israel, with a tough, small, outnumbered, but ultimately triumphant army that draws its strength from a shared religion and modern military technology. On one point the similar backgrounds of Pakistan and Israel are divergent, and this has worked to Pakistan's disadvantage. Israel has a territorial identity that goes back several thousand years, and there is no question (for Israelis at least) that the state has a right to exist, although opinions differ as to the degree to which that state should be Jewish. The idea of Pakistan is quite recent, and was not accepted by all South Asian Muslims. A distinguished retired army general, however, draws another parallel (possibly because he has served as ambassador to a Middle East Arab state). "Pakistan," he argued, "cannot have an army and a political system which is derived from secular, Western models. The comparison should be with the Catholic states of Europe: how long did they take to work out a relationship between the army and the state?" Answering his own question, he cautioned against any assumption that Islamic principles provide firm, clear-cut guidance: they have to be developed and worked out in each Muslim nation.

This view is essentially that held by Sir Mohammed Iqbal, the Indian poet-philosopher who was so influential in developing the idea of an autonomous Muslim state. Iqbal's address to the All-Indian Muslim League in 1930 was his most important political statement; in it he dealt at length with the strategic prospects for a future Pakistan and with its structural identity. "In Islam," Iqbal told his audience, "God and the universe, spirit and matter, Church and State, are organic to each other."[8] The problem with the West was that it had lost touch with its spiritual Christian moorings; in a future Muslim state in South Asia this could not be allowed to occur:

8. Wm. Theodore de Bary et al., comp., *Sources of Indian Tradition* (New York: Columbia University Press, 1958), p. 722.

The religious ideal of Islam is organically related to the social order which it has created. The rejection of the one will eventually involve the rejection of the other. Therefore, the construction of a policy on national lines, if it means a displacement of the Islamic principle of solidarity is simply unthinkable to a Muslim.[9]

There is no doubt that under President Zia's leadership this "construction" is being tackled seriously by the military for the first time in Pakistan's history. In the five years since he came to power, Zia has systematically extended and reinforced the Islamization of Pakistan itself. He has introduced a number of banking and commercial practices based on Islamic law and tradition; he has introduced punishments, such as lashing and amputation, drawn from the Quran (although the latter has not been carried out), and he has begun "Islamic" reforms in many areas of Pakistani society. Office workers, professors, and others are required to come to work in indigenous dress; new women's universities are proposed so that men and women will be separated in higher education. Strict regulations on the sale and consumption of alcoholic beverages have been retained, and careful social censorship of the press and TV is in place. At times this process of Islamization has verged on the savage. Many educated Pakistanis are deeply offended by public floggings, or emulation of Saudi practices that they consider barbaric. They—and not a few officers—are unnerved by exhortations to "live and die with honor," and to identify the enemies of Islam "within and without" Pakistan, who must be hunted down and killed like snakes, "even when he was offering prayers."[10] It should be emphasized that many of these steps were initiated by Zulfiqar Ali Bhutto, under pressure from orthodox elements in Pakistani society, but they were vigorously extended by Zia and his advisors.[11]

This activist policy towards the Islamization of Pakistan by the military is only tentatively supported by many officers. They retain an earlier view that there was great danger in becoming too deeply involved with social change in any area. This position is not now heard, as it implies criticism of official policy that has been pursued with some vigor since 1977. Privately,

9. It might also be added that the Turkish model (a state with a predominantly Muslim population, governed by a secular political authority) that is favored by some Pakistani officers was explicitly rejected by Iqbal as un-Islamic. The Turks had rejected both the concept of Islamic rule and pan-Islam, and were doubly in error. Ahmed, *Islamic Modernism*, p. 140.

10. Remarks by Lt.-Gen. Faiz Ali Chishti, Islamabad, Jan. 19, 1980, reported in *Sunday Morning News* (Karachi), Jan. 20, 1980. At the time, Chishti was regarded as one of the powers behind Zia and commanded the army corps responsible for the capital city; he was speaking in his capacity as Federal Minister for Labor and Manpower; a few months later Chishti was removed and was retired from his government positions. His views seem to be closer to those of Jamaat-i-Islami than even Zia's.

11. For a discussion, see Stephen P. Cohen and Marvin G. Weinbaum, "Pakistan in 1981: Staying On," *Asian Survey* 22:2 (February 1982).

they wonder how seriously Islamization is really being pursued or whether it is merely a political device to pacify religious extremists. Conversations with a range of officials with some influence in the decision-making process indicate that the army's attempt to reform the state is taken quite seriously. One official, a recently retired senior lieutenant-general with close ties to Zia (and still active in public affairs in Pakistan) provided a full elaboration of the way some officers view the weaknesses of Pakistani society and how Islam is both a goal and a corrective:

We [the leadership] are progressive and enlightened individuals. But Islamic laws have been brought in [chopping off hands, lashes]. Are we hypocrites? Well, there *are* good laws, but they require a good society, the two things have to go side by side. The development of the world has not been uniform: within certain countries also the development has not been uniform. In the West, for example, a law can be enforced uniformly, it will be acceptable practically to everybody as being the law at that time, because the whole society has grown upward simultaneously. In the East it is not so. In Pakistan, for example, you find people who live in caves! You can find people living by centuries, till the twenty-first, leave alone the twentieth. So, a law which a man of the twentieth century considers to be modern and civilized is considered to be uncivilized for a man living in the fourteenth century. And there are people here living in caves, in a prehistoric period!

I think we are trying to civilize people here, whereas in the West the people are becoming animals, going towards the other direction; for me, homosexuality is such a big crime against humanity. Chopping off hands for stealing in Pakistan, *I* do not consider to be against humanity. You consider such things [liberalization of laws concerning homosexuality] to be a step forward, we consider it to be against human nature.

And expressing the view of virtually the entire leadership of Pakistan in the Zia years, he concluded:

We do not accept that the West goes out to impose its views on us. We do not cry or shout about what Sweden has done—they have authorized their children to go to court against their parents—now this is destroying human civilization which has been developed by this race of human beings over centuries. It is wrong, totally wrong, but if we had done it, the whole of the West would have started shouting "Look how uncivilized and backward those Pakistanis are." You people have a friend in Pakistan. You can always find fault, but you will destroy us, with what result? The West is looking for an ideal society, but is an imitation of that ideal for us? I think it would depend on the situation: you cannot impose a proper type of culture, civilization, without considering the basic structures of that society.

The inner tensions and contradictions in this view are clear. The typical officer is highly Westernized in appearance and values, yet he is truly Muslim and Pakistani and rejects much of what he believes is the degradation of the West. Nevertheless, Islam does not provide a complete model or pattern, certainly to these highly informed and cosmopolitan individuals. The Pakistani leadership is trying to work for an amalgamation of two cultures, but it is doing so under enormous pressure and without a clear understanding of the difficulty of the task. The Pakistani leaders' approach is to draw upon their own professional experience and careers: if good government works within the military, if it can be imposed by adherence to regulations, law, and tradition, then the broader society should be amenable to the same kind of ortho-social control. By 1983, after several years in power, those around Zia who hold these views know that they have not been able to persuade many Western-educated Pakistanis of their correctness, but this in the view of some of Zia's advisers only confirms the degree of un-Islamic rot in Pakistan and the need to persevere.

ISLAM AND MILITARY ORGANIZATION

We have discussed the way in which Islam is invoked in the Pakistan Army to enhance the fighting spirit of the other ranks. This is hardly a Pakistani or peculiarly Islamic practice, and is merely an adaptation of the British Indian Army system of using class, caste, and religion for the same purpose (and that was a refinement of practices already in existence when the British developed the armies of the Bombay, Madras, and Bengal presidencies). But what of the officers? Is their recruitment, training, and behavior regulated in some special way by Islam? There is no short answer to this question.

The officer corps cannot be characterized as "orthodox" or literalist in their view of the Quran, but individual officers can; others, however (probably the great majority), are devout Muslims and would, on a pragmatic basis, like to adapt their professional lives to Islam, and they do so where it is professionally convenient. Meanwhile, they live as reasonably orthodox Muslims within the military. A group of officers may be sitting in the officers' mess in the late afternoon with a guest. Of a dozen officers, one or two officers may excuse themselves or just slip away for prayer. Their departure is not remarked upon; they return quietly and rejoin the conversation. There is no mass compulsory praying in the military (except for one unit prayer each Friday, a practice that dates back to the British). This might be just as well, for a certain percentage of officers are quite irreligious in the sense that they used to drink alcohol freely in the messes and in their homes before prohibition was imposed in 1977 by Bhutto.

Generally, however, the Pakistan Army has never been a hard-drinking army, and there is evidence that, with some flamboyant exceptions, this was true of Muslim officers in the British Indian Army. As one Muslim Sandhurst KCO pointed out:

I was with the British, but I never drank, the first time was in Italy, when I asked for some water—*aqua*—and the farmer said to me, "only animals drink water in this country." So he brought wine, and that is what we had, but the majority of us were not that type. In our people the troops don't like the officers drinking. To keep up their confidence it was essential for Muslim officers to at least not drink openly—quietly was okay, not openly—I was commanding Muslim troops.

Pakistan Army officers regard with some derision the debates in India over supplying rum to Indian Army jawans at high altitudes. Periodically an Indian M.P. demands that prohibition be imposed on the army and that rum rations cease; the government invariably replies that because of "military necessity" such rations must continue. Pakistani troops are at the same altitude, facing the Indians, and are not supplied with liquor; one general recalls that he issued *gur* (raw sugar) to his troops in such a situation, and that they survived nicely. For most Pakistani officers, not drinking is a sign of self-restraint and morality, yet they are reluctant to condemn openly their colleagues who do (or did) drink.

The recent emphasis on prohibition is not unrelated to the reprofessionalization of the Pakistan Army and the disaster of 1971. It is widely known that Yahya Khan was a heavy drinker and some officers suggest that he used drugs. Their view of alcohol is derived from their broader view of religious and moral guidance: once an individual begins to deviate from the correct path he may be on a slippery slope to moral and physical destruction, ruining his own life, and placing the lives of his men in jeopardy. While there is reluctance to tell a fellow officer how to live his life, renewed concern is felt in Pakistan over the dangers of excess.

A recurrent theme of the military literature of Pakistan is that the officer should be careful about his religion; it is one way he may preserve his honor. This view was argued by Attiqur Rahman in his comprehensive critique of Pakistan's military and security policy. Although otherwise he had very little to say about Islam, he did assert that

As a beginning [to framing a code of honor for the military] what better source have we at hand than our Holy Book? It should not be difficult to codify certain aspects of military honor from these sacred pages. Those verses that pertain to the duties of man to man—the treatment of prisoners—telling the truth regardless of consequences; uprightness; the treatment of women ... Once these are known by all cadets passing out of their parent institutions—and if those who disregard them are punished severely—then some idea of honor will find its place in the armed forces.[12]

12. M. Attiqur Rahman, *Our Defense Cause*, p. 187.

There has been a limited attempt to introduce Islamic teachings in the Pakistan Military Academy, but only as a complement to regular professional and academic subjects. The Director of Studies of the PMA has written extensively on this matter and is careful, as are most other writers, to separate the domains of military science and academic subjects, on the one hand, and Quranic inspiration and guidance, on the other:

In the domain of military psychology we try to understand external behavior and in the domain of religion we try to find out the inner nature of that reality. The psychological and religious processes are in a sense parallel to each other . . . Both are directed to the purification of experience in their respective spheres.[13]

Islamic training and thought has also been introduced as part of the curriculum at the Command and Staff College, with the strong encouragement of Zia ul-Haq. Most of the themes discussed above have found their way into various courses at Quetta. Of particular note are the lectures of Prof. Col. Abdul Qayyum (ultimately printed in book form with a foreword by Zia), which provide the intellectual basis for these changes.[14] Qayyum is an officer-scholar of enormous range. He is adept in dealing with Islamic theology and doctrine but is remarkably open and rationalist in his approach. Qayyum points out that those educated in a Western tradition are in an especially difficult position in Pakistan—they are caught between being Muslim and being non-Muslim. This basic dichotomy in their life means that they must push forward or retreat; there can be no split between life and faith, career and religion.

Furthermore, the professional soldier should not look scornfully upon the "Mullah." The Mullah is a bridge for the officer between his Westernized profession and his faith:

For he, the Mullah, has kept at least the husk of Islam alive, and we (the so-called "educated") have neither husk nor substance. And if some day (and I pray that that day may come soon) we should get to the substance of Islam, we shall do so rising on the shoulders of the Mullah . . . The keeper of the base is not any the humbler than the climber who climbs to the summit.[15]

In words that have been echoed by Zia and other officers, Qayyum insists that the gift of Western education is not an end in itself and that the Pakistani must not be merely "a professional soldier, engineer, or doctor" but

13. Lt.-Col. S. M. A. Rizvi, "Men and Motivation," *Pakistan Army Journal*, December 1978, p. 4.

14. *On Striving to Be a Muslim* (Lahore: Islamic Book Center, 1978). In his range of scholarship and his approach to the linking of Islam and career, Qayyum most clearly resembles Iqbal.

15. Ibid., p. 16.

must use this to become "Muslim soldiers, Muslim engineers, Muslim doctors, Muslim officers and Muslim *men*."[16]

As we have noted above, Islamic writings have been introduced into the syllabus at the Staff College and other military-training centers. Students at the Staff College are now advised to intensify their studies of Western strategic and military doctrine, but to do so in a way that strengthens their Islamic core values.[17] In a discussion of strategic methodology, Professor Qayyum urges his students to make the Quran their base and from there to move in any direction in search of strategic and historical truth. Thus, an officer may safely explore the writings of Western, non-Muslim, and Asian writers; indeed, Qayyum argues that the Quran itself demands such a liberal approach: "Say: Travel ye through the earth and see for (for yourself) the nature of the consequences for those who rejected the Truth (6:11)." The Quran, according to Qayyum, is the "Furqan" (the criterion to distinguish right from wrong), and provides a guide to investigation; such investigation "will enable us to grasp with increasing comprehensiveness the meaning and the spirit of what the Quran so tersely, compactly presents." In this way Qayyum attempts to meet the argument of the literalists who claim that if all truth is contained in the Quran, there is no need to look elsewhere. The Quran itself justifies such a search, and is in turn more clearly understood by it.

Colonel Qayyum's own lectures in the 1970s on geopolitics at the Staff College were an example of this effort to integrate Western and Islamic thought. Although much of the contemporary Western literature on geopolitics is cited and analyzed approvingly, a long introductory section dealt with the great Islamic scholar, Ibn Khaldun (b. 1332).

Others, however, would like to accelerate the Islamization of the military. From time to time, criticisms have appeared in the professional literature urging the abandonment of practices that dated back to the British days. One young officer, then a student at the Staff College, criticized the college itself and the rules and regulations of the entire army as having a "distinct aroma of subjugation suited to a colonial power," and as not reflecting a true Islamic equalitarianism.[18] The "colonial rubbish" still (in 1977) present at the Staff College had to go; this included the college's symbol (an owl), restrictions on Pakistani officers wearing indigenous clothes in public, and the requirement of Western formal dress at dinner.

16. Ibid.
17. The following text is drawn from Command and Staff College, Quetta, (recent) *Staff Course, The Historical Approach to Geopolitics*, edited transcript of the talk (lecture 1).
18. See, for example, Maj. Muzaffar Ahmed, Punjab Regt., "Challenge of Change," *The Owl* (Staff College Yearbook), 1977, p. 28.

The owl was originally chosen by the British as a symbol of wisdom, but in South Asia it is regarded as a particularly foolish bird, not a wise one.

These criticisms may have been officially inspired, for within the next few years they were reflected in certain changes. The *sherwani* has replaced Western-style formal civilian dress, and in 1979 *The Owl*, the professional magazine of the Staff College, was renamed *The Review*. Carefully reflecting Zia's desire to see the creation of an officer who was both Muslim and professional, the first issue of *The Review* carried these two excerpts on successive pages: "In the military profession, as in any profession, self-criticism is an essential prerequisite in effecting change. But, if it is to be more than self-castigation, self-criticism must have significant intellectual content," and "Let those fight in the way of Allah who sell the life of this world for the other. Who so fighteth in the way of Allah, be he slain or be he victorious, on him we shall bestow a vast reward." The latter is, of course, from the Quran (4:74), the first a quote from Morris Janowitz's *The Professional Soldier*.

It remains an open question as to whether these efforts to create an officer who is both professional and Muslim will succeed. The dangers that Abdul Qayyum and others worry about (that excessive Westernization will create an essentially secular officer) may not be as real as their obverse. Although no systematic sampling is possible, contact with a number of younger officers (major and below) indicates a more simplistic approach to such matters. Drawn increasingly from rural Pakistan, or from smaller towns and cities, such officers begin with a distorted image of the West. The lack of contact between the Pakistan army and Western military establishments has exacerbated the problem. Many younger officers are extremely curious about the "evils" of Western civilization: drugs, sex, alcohol, and deviant behavior. Officers from traditional or conservative families are exposed to such phenomena through their limited access to the Western press and news magazines and by word-of-mouth accounts from fellow officers. Given the opportunity, they demonstrate an insatiable curiosity about premarital encounters between boys and girls in the West, whether Jews and Christians believe in one God (and if it is the same God that Muslims believe in), and how Westerners manage to avoid looking at a girl who is "pushing out all over." Their usual failure to do so, one Pathan major concluded, was evidence of the ultimate decadence of the West. Raised in a conservative Pathan family in Rawalpindi, he could not reconcile the obvious power of the West (and the United States in particular) with such decadent practices as open pornography, premarital sex, and homosexuality. These are evil practices (according to the Quran), and Pakistani officers who are fully Westernized in appearance and demeanor and are professionally competent hold this to be true. But it is clear that their lack of direct contact with Western societies has led to a misunderstanding of the apparent contradiction between spiritual poverty and material power, and it is not certain that any amount of advanced military education will alter such deeply held beliefs.

ISLAM AND STRATEGIC DOCTRINE

Before Partition there was no serious study of the *Islamic* character of a hypothetical Pakistan's strategy. The debate that did occur revolved around conventional strategic questions: Would India be adequately protected by the existence of a separate Muslim state between it and Afghanistan and the Soviet Union? Would such a state be able to maintain a suitable army? And, would a strategic problem arise within South Asia as a result of the creation of Pakistan?

Jinnah and Iqbal both believed that a new Pakistan would strengthen the defense of the subcontinent precisely because of its Muslim and Islamic nature. Iqbal himself observed (in 1930) that

Possessing full opportunity of developing within the body politic of India, the North West Indian Muslims will provide the best defenders of India against a foreign invasion, be that invasion the one of ideas or bayonets. The Punjab with 56 percent Muslim population supplies 54 percent of the total combatant troops in the Indian army and (if the Gurkhas are excluded) the Punjab contingent amounts to 62 percent of the whole.[19]

Iqbal rejected the suggestion that such a concentration of armed Muslims would lead to pressure on India itself, but this was precisely the fear of a number of his coreligionists who supported Congress. In a prophetic analysis of Pakistan's probable strategic problems, Dr. Shaukatullah Ansari pointed out in 1944 that Pakistan would have insufficient resources to defend itself without outside help; that it would have *two* two-front conflicts (in the West, with the Russians and Afghans, and in the East, with Japan and China), and in both, with India; that a united India would be a great power, whereas a divided one would be as weak as Egypt, Burma, or "Siam," and that if an independent Pakistan were created the British would use it to control India through Pakistan (this idea was later to resurface in India, albeit with the United States replacing Britain).[20] Ansari

19. Presidential address to the Allahabad Session of the All-Indian Muslim League, Dec. 29, 1930.
20. *Pakistan: The Problem of India* (Lahore: Minerva Book Shop, 1944), p. 105.

unsuccessfully urged his fellow Congressmen to concede a substantial degree of autonomy to the Muslims of a united India, along the lines of a confederate or even Soviet pattern.

These arguments revolve around the strategic implications of a new Muslim state in South Asia, not how that state's internal Islamic character could shape its strategic doctrine. This is a relatively recent question, although one of great importance for Pakistan and other Muslim states that are avowedly "Islamic." As Muslim states have won independence, they have invariably inherited a Western-trained military establishment; even where these armies have made adaptations to Islamic tradition in their internal organization, they have rarely abandoned the doctrines of deterrence and warfare taught at Camberley and Ft. Leavenworth. There is an historic logic to this: the Muslim states lost their independence to the British, French, and others not because their soldiers lacked martial qualities but because they were saddled with inferior military technology and lacked a "modern" doctrine of warfare. There is considerable reluctance, therefore, to abandon the theories of Clausewitz, Liddell-Hart, and Schelling. Most Pakistan Army officers would not do so, but a movement to develop a synthesis of Islamic and Western theories of warfare has begun, and some go so far as to reject or radically reinterpret basic tenets of Western strategic thought.

Such Pakistani strategists face several problems. The first is that Western theories of deterrence and war have worked, or at least are fully developed. The Quran's guidance in these matters is not entirely elaborated in any single Sura, but must be pieced together and supplemented by the study of significant battles in the early history of the survival and spread of Islam. Secondly, it is not evident that the modern state system (in which Muslims live apart from each other with different armies) is an entirely legitimate creation. As A. K. Brohi has written,

Even Iqbal ... went so far as to suggest that Muslim states, to begin with, be treated as territorial states and that, too, only as an *interim measure* since these are later on to be incorporated into (a) commonwealth of Muslim *states*. Each one of these states has first to acquire strength and stability before it is able to prepare the ground on which a unified state of Islam can appear on the historical scene.[21]

Despite these and other problems there have been several noteworthy attempts in Pakistan to interpret the Quran so as to develop an Islamic doctrine of war and strategy.[22] In the 1960s a series of textbooks were prepared

21. In the preface to Malik, *Quranic Concept of War*, p. viii.
22. For more general analyses of Islam, war, jehad, and military doctrine, see Majid Khadduri, *War and Peace in the Law of Islam* (Baltimore: Johns Hopkins, 1955); Bernard

for use in Pakistani colleges and schools. More recently, military officers have regularly written on various tactical and strategic aspects of famous Muslim battles, and occasionally on the relationship between Islam and Pakistan's strategic doctrine. These efforts are sanctioned by the Quran and have been encouraged by General Zia. They are not entirely abstract exercises; in at least one area, the use of nuclear weapons, they may provide the conceptual framework for a Pakistani nuclear-arms system.

One important contribution of this new literature on Islamic strategy has been to clear away a number of accumulated misconceptions about such concepts as Jehad and just war. Jehad has long been misrepresented as a "religious duty inculcated in the Quran on the followers of Mohammed to wage war upon those who do not adopt the doctrines of Islam."[23] Contemporary Pakistani writers and most scholars reject this. A. K. Brohi stresses that the Quran commands man to struggle against the forces of evil and to defend the interests of believers by Jehad, "a word which is untranslatable in English but, broadly speaking, means, 'striving,' 'struggling,' 'trying to advance the Divine causes or purposes.'"[24] There are many aspects of Jehad, and force is only the most extreme and intense form; in fact, while urging Jehad, the Islamic tradition also proclaims that "The ink of the scholar is more holy than the blood of the martyr."[25]

To some Pakistanis, this is an important issue because it leads them to conclude that Islam does not promote a doctrine of total war and, indeed, urges upon its followers reconciliation with its enemies. Brohi, a lawyer, stresses the limited circumstances in which a Muslim can go to war: to uphold His law and the honor of His name, and for the defense of legitimate interests of the believers; war is permitted only in defined circumstances and "is a highly controlled affair; indeed, it is totally regulated by law."[26] A textbook (published by the Islamic Military Science Association of Karachi) stresses this point and attacks the theories of unlimited war and "pure war" developed by Clausewitz and other—especially American—military theoreticians.

Lewis, "Politics and War," in Joseph Schacht, ed., *The Legacy of Islam*, 2d ed. (Oxford: Oxford University Press, 1979); and Ahmed M. Rifaat, *International Aggression: A Study of the Legal Concept* (Stockholm: Almquist, Almquist and Wiksell, 1979).

23. The Encyclopedia Britannica, quoted by "Rangrut," (Maj.-Gen. M. Akbar Khan), *The Islamic Pattern of War—Planning and Training*, vol. 1, *Theory*, rev. ed. (Karachi: The Islamic Military Science Association, 1968), p. 118.

24. Malik, *Quranic Concept of War*, p. ii. This closely follows the argument and tone of several earlier Indian Muslim thinkers, including Sir Sayyid Ahmed Khan and the Islamic socialist, Ubayd-Allah Sindhi. See Aziz Ahmed, *Islamic Modernism*, pp. 50, 195.

25. Rangrut, *Islamic Pattern of War*, p. 118.

26. Malik, *Quranic Concept of War*, p. iii.

The "Islamic pattern of war," however, is a humane and honorable alternative to mass slaughter and nuclear annihilation. [It] not only prohibits total war and encourages to negotiate honorable peace but makes it, therefore, not necessary as a rule to proceed to the total conquest of the enemy's territory. It thus recognizes that war is an evil which may in certain circumstances become unavoidable. Even then, every effort must be made to limit the mischief and horror of war.[27]

A number of passages in the Quran support this interpretation. The believer is also instructed that enemies need not be permanent: "But if they [infidels] be inclined to peace, incline thou too: and trust in Allah. Verily, He is the One who Knows. And if they should thereby intend to outwit thee, then, verily, Allah doth suffice thee!"[28] And "It may be that Allah will [in time] establish friendship between yourselves and those whom you now hold as enemies: Allah [over everything] hath power; and Allah is Forgiving, Merciful!"[29]

The most recent and comprehensive Pakistani study of war and Islam states many of these same conclusions. Written by a serving brigadier and with a forward by President Zia, it is both an analysis of Islamic strategic doctrine and a study of early Muslim battles. Brigadier Malik also concludes that "The checks and controls imposed by the Holy Quran on the use of force have no parallel. In practice, there were but few isolated instances where the Muslims transgressed these limits but the Holy Prophet (peace be upon Him) disapproved of them." However, he adds that the exercise of restraint in war is essentially a two-sided affair:

It cannot happen that one side goes on exercising restraint while the other keeps on committing excesses. In such a situation, a time comes when the very injunction of preserving and promoting peace and justice demands the use of limited force. It would be sinful to withhold the use of force under those circumstances. Islam permits the use of the "sword" for such a purpose. Rather than be apologetic about it, a Muslim should be proud of the fact that, when used, his sword is meant to subdue the forces of tyranny and repression, and to bring peace and justice to mankind.

Malik's emphasis is clearly that of a serving soldier with a belief in the unhappy necessity of the occasional use of force, not of a civilian looking for ways to avoid its use. His most interesting argument, however, pertains to the way force is used.

For Malik (and for many other officers) the concept of terror is central to the Islamic conduct of modern war:

27. Rangrut, *Islamic Pattern of War*, p. 160.
28. Hasim Amir-Ali, *The Message of the Qur'an* (Tokyo: Charles E. Tuttle Co., 1974), p. 38 *(Sura Anfal)*.
29. Ibid., p. 7 *(Sura Mumtahinna)*.

Terror struck into the hearts of the enemies is not only a means, it is the end in itself. Once a condition of terror into the opponent's heart is obtained, hardly anything is left to be achieved. It is the point where the means and the end meet and merge. Terror is not a means of imposing decision upon the enemy; it is *the decision* we wish to impose upon him.[30]

Malik derives this conclusion from a reading of a number of Quranic passages which use the word "terror." For example, Malik's translation of *Anfal*, 12, is: "Remember, the Lord inspired the angels (with the message), 'I am with you: give firmness to the Believers: I will instill terror into the hearts of the Unbelievers.'"[31] This is not dissimilar to N.J. Dawood's translation: "Allah revealed His will to the angels, saying: 'I shall be with you. Give courage to the believers. I shall cast terror into the hearts of the infidels.'"[32]

Yet, in a recent comprehensive edition of the Holy Quran, praised by some of the most senior generals in Pakistan, the word "terror" is often replaced by "awe," or in the example of *Anfal*, 12, "fright," which gives the passage a different emphasis: "Remember how thy Lord (appeared to) urge the angels: 'I am with you—hold ye fast the Faithful; anon, I shall instill the hearts of infidels with fright!'"[33]

Other examples could be discussed, but this is not the appropriate place for a textual analysis of militant passages in the Quran. What is of interest is the linkage that Malik (and, in private conversation, other officers) make between the concept of terror and Pakistani strategy. They insist that a strategy that fails to strike terror into the heart of the enemy will suffer from "inherent drawbacks and weaknesses; and should be reviewed and modified." Furthermore, this standard must be applied to "nuclear as well as conventional wars." The strategy of nuclear deterrence, "in fashion today," cannot work unless it is capable of striking "terror into the hearts of the enemy." To do this, his faith must be weakened, whereas the Muslim soldier must adhere even more firmly to his own religion. Neither nuclear nor conventional weapons are to be used on a random, haphazard basis, but they must support and strengthen this central objective of Islamic war. Terror will weaken the enemy's faith in himself, and that in turn will lead to his destruction. War is a matter of will and faith, and even instruments of mass destruction have a clear-cut and (in one sense) a limited, pin-point role in war. Some Pakistan Army of-

30. Malik, *Quranic Concept of War*, p. 59.
31. Ibid., p. 57.
32. *The Koran*, 4th rev. ed. (Harmondsworth: Penguin Books, 1974), p. 315.
33. Hasim Amir-Ali, *The Message of the Qur'an*.

ficers therefore strongly object to characterizations of their nuclear program as "crazy" or irresponsible. They see a Pakistani nuclear weapon (albeit still a "hypothetical" one) in these terms:

What do you think we are? Do you think one man will make that decision? [to use a nuclear weapon] No! There is not a single person with his finger on the trigger, not for regular war or nuclear war, if that should come. Islam provides the *conditions* and criteria which will make it impossible to launch nuclear weapons without a just cause. Nuclear weapons are modern terror weapons, and Islam enjoins us to strike terror into the heart of the enemy, it provides moral guidance, a set of principles for going to war—such a decision would not be irresponsible!

Although one can appreciate this interest in developing a rationale for the controlled use of nuclear weapons as well as conventional force, it is not clear that the officers who make these arguments fully comprehend the destructiveness of even the smallest nuclear weapon. Nor have they thought very carefully about the contradiction between the use of nuclear weapons (even tactical battlefield weapons) and Quranic injunctions about sparing the lives of innocent women and children. To do so, however, would weaken the credibility of a strategy of deterrence based on terror or mass destruction. If Pakistani generals acquire nuclear weapons, they will not be rid of the inherent dilemmas of a nuclear war, dilemmas faced by all nuclear powers, present and future.

CONCLUSION

The accomplishments of the Pakistan Army over the past thirty-five years are considerable. It virtually created itself out of very few material resources, albeit with strong British support. Under American influence, the Pakistan Army reached a considerable level of technical and professional competence. It is second only to the Indian Army in this respect among military establishments between Israel and Vietnam—indeed, in some ways, it may be superior to the Indian Army. This is demonstrated by the quality of many of its training programs, its élan, and its professionalism, although not always by success in combat.

The Pakistan army officer is not distinguished by strategic brilliance. He is increasingly drawn from sectors of Pakistani society in which reflection, contemplation, and analysis are not outstanding characteristics. A modern military establishment needs such talents, however, as much as it requires the presence of the heroic virtues; success in war is not simply a function of tactical brilliance and skill in handling machinery and weapons.

It is in the examination of alternative strategies, in a clear and accepted understanding of the role of the military in society, that the deficiencies of the Pakistan Army are most evident. Although Pakistani officers seek military education, there is some resistance to military intellectualization, and perhaps even some fear of too great a self-scrutiny. Some attempt has been made to remedy this by appealing to Islamic teachings on education (which, indeed, urges one to go "even to China" for knowledge), but even this is resisted by some officers; one of Pakistan's ablest young brigadiers expressed this suspicion with the comment that "the trouble with education is that it allows you to think about the other side." This has two profound implications: that education may lead to indecisiveness in battle, and, even more disturbing, that in certain matters (such as relations with India) it may lead to the questioning of the cherished assumptions of an earlier generation. Such assumptions, long since frozen into doctrine and hitherto unchallengeable, may be wrong; if they are, then the basic strategic premises of the Pakistan Army may now be defective, as some think they were in 1965 and 1971. If the retrospective criticisms of 1965 and 1971 are allowed to reach their logical end, will they result in challenges to the present strategic assumptions of the present generation of the upper military leadership? Our earlier analysis of military generations in Pakistan suggests caution in attempting to answer these questions without a more careful scrutiny of the political role of the military and its strategic doctrine. The attitudes and beliefs of the officer corps are not the product of a single variable or influence; they resemble a marble cake more than a layer cake.

Nevertheless, although each succeeding generation has been stamped by one or more particularly vivid experiences, some events have had a cumulative effect on the officer corps as a whole. There is a more realistic assessment of India as a military foe: no longer do Pakistani officers boast that one Muslim is worth five or ten Hindus. There is a better understanding of the difficulties inherent in relying upon others for vital military equipment. There is an appreciation of the virtues of self-reliance. There is (as we shall examine in the next chapter and the succeeding one) a more realistic appreciation of the limits inherent in military rule in Pakistan. History has been a strict school for the Pakistani officer; that he still functions as a professional is a remarkable accomplishment in itself, although no guarantee that he will not lead the state of Pakistan into a new and uncharted cataclysm.

CHAPTER FIVE

The Army, Politics, and the Higher Direction of War

I have praise and respect for the Armed Forces of Pakistan. I am proud
of their valor. I fail to understand why the Respondent [Zia ul-Haq]
considers himself to be the symbol and spokesman of the Armed Forces
of Pakistan merely because a year ago, I made the biggest mistake of my
life by appointing him Chief of the Army Staff.

Zulfiqar Ali Bhutto[1]

I said to him, "Sir—I still called him that—Sir, why have you done
all these things, you whom I respected so, you who had so much?"
And he only said that I should wait, and he would be cleared.
It was very disappointing.

Zia ul-Haq[2]

THE PAKISTAN ARMY AND POLITICS

There are armies that guard their nation's borders, there are those that are
concerned with protecting their own position in society, and there are
those that defend a cause or an idea. The Pakistan Army does all three.
From the day Pakistan was created, it has been active in helping to establish internal order and in protecting Pakistan's permeable and often ill-
defined borders; during this period it has used its power and special position within Pakistan to ensure that it be supplied with adequate weapons,
resources, and manpower. Moreover, it has always regarded itself as the
special expression of the idea of Pakistan, and a few officers have advocated an activist role in reforming or correcting the society where it has
fallen below the standard of excellence set by the military.

The contrast between the Pakistan Army's many roles and the absence
of doctrine to justify such activism presents an even more acute dilemma
today during the heady days of Ayub Khan's rule. The army is in a
figurative salient: the "enemy" is on three sides, and it runs a risk with

1. Supreme Court of Pakistan, *Constitutional Petition No. I-R of 1977*, Begum Nusrat
Bhutto, petitioner, vs. The Chiefs of the Army Staff, etc., respondent. *Rejoinder to the Reply
of the Respondent.*
2. *The Times*, Sept. 8, 1977.

further political involvement; yet the road back to the barracks is also closed, for an immediate retreat would bring down the wrath of an embittered civilian population, tired of martial law.

The contrast with civil-military relations in neighboring India is a permanent reminder to Pakistani civilians and soldiers alike of what might have been. In India, strategic decisions are essentially made by civilian politicians and bureaucrats, the military is under tight fiscal control, and it certainly has no broader sense of mission or purpose.[3]

Most senior Pakistani officers have a grudging admiration for the Indian accomplishment, but quite typically—as in the case of an armored-division commander—attribute the difference to the Indians' being lucky in their leadership:

The thing is, India had a very big advantage [over Pakistan] in the leadership of Pandit Nehru over these twenty years. You have seen that in spite of the fact that his daughter had a reverse and the Janata Party had seen her out, the people of India, because of the outstanding leadership of Pandit Nehru, once they saw that the other party is no good, then they ran back to her. So they have a very big advantage, whereas we have been a little unfortunate. You know, at the time of Partition our political leaders—we had a reversal. The Quaid-I-Azam [Jinnah] had died, the other Prime Minister, Liaquat Ali had gone away [he was assasinated] and then the cult was mediocrity; the politicians were not trained and we had political confusion for ten to twelve years. People thought the country is gone! And that is the reason this professional army was called in, because there was some leadership in it. These martial laws have come in and they have been very hard on the army, but there was no way out. Gradually, now, these politicians know that to be a leader, you have to be a leader—but there have been lapses. But India has had a family; God almighty was very kind to them!

Other senior officers and a number of scholars have tried to develop a coherent theory to explain the difference in behavior between the Indian and Pakistani armies, and one that might even point the way toward the restoration of effective civilian control.

These theories are worth examining for two reasons. First, most contain an element of truth, in that the persistent political intervention of the Pakistan Army is the consequence of an array of factors. It is true (as the military like to believe) that their political activity has at times been the result of a political vacuum, but it is also true that some parts of the military leadership have been excessively eager to seize power and that this seizure at times reflects broader regional, class, and other interests as well

3. For a comparison of the Indian and Pakistani patterns of civil-military behavior from 1947 to 1970, see Stephen P. Cohen, *The Indian Army* (Berkeley: University of California Press, 1971), ch. 5.

as civilian encouragement. To these factors we shall add one that has been virtually neglected in the extensive literature on the Pakistan Army's political involvement: intervention as a consequence of military organizational and doctrinal characteristics.

Secondly although some of these popular theories of intervention are more useful than others, all have their adherents in Pakistan. This is clearly a case where belief in a theory is a political fact of great importance in its own right. For example, non-Punjabi politicians, students, intellectuals, and journalists often believe that the army intervenes because it is protecting Punjabi interests. They continue to believe this in the face of evidence that other considerations may motivate the military.

Before addressing ourselves to the organizational and doctrinal compulsions that have led the Pakistan Army to intervene repeatedly in politics, we first turn to some theories that offer at least a partial explanation of such intervention.

THE RELUCTANT PROFESSIONALS

The theory of military intervention most widely held in the military itself (and shared by some, but not all, Pakistani civilians) is that the major responsibility for intervention "falls on the shoulders of the political leadership." This is the conclusion reached by Dr. Hasan Askari Rizvi, the author of the only full-length study of the Pakistan military in politics.[4] The failure of civilians "to keep a balance between the diverse forces working in the political system" led the military into intervention by default. "If the civilian institutions are not capable of asserting themselves on the military, the military by virtue of its qualities dominates the civil institutions. Therefore, it is the root which must be cured first. The sooner we realize this, the better." If only the politicians would make the system work, then democracy would flourish in Pakistan. If it has failed, according to one distinguished retired general officer, Lt.-Gen. A. Hamid Khan, writing shortly after Bhutto's execution, "it is only because it has never been tried out."[5] Even then, the standard of government need not be very high; the people of Pakistan did not require a new "Quaid" or "Sher," but only honest and selfless service. The answer lay not with the military, but with the politician, who "must clean and reorganize his own field to serve

4. *The Military and Politics in Pakistan*, rev. ed. (Lahore: Progressive Publishers, 1976), p. 296.

5. Lt.-Gen. Abdul Hamid Khan (retd.), "Organization for Defense," *Nawa-i-Waqt*, Lahore, Apr. 10–11, 1979. English translation provided by Gen. Hamid.

the people and give the country the political stability it needs." General Hamid contended that this in turn was vital for the military itself, so that it could return to its prime role as defender of the country.

These are hardly new arguments. From Ayub's days onward, the military has justified its intervention in politics because of the incompetence of civilians, but there are recent variations on the theme. A brigadier, who in 1980 commanded an important training institution, contrasted coups in Africa and Latin America with what had repeatedly occurred in Pakistan. In African and Latin American states it was the military that was ambitious; in Pakistan, however, there had been a complete "political vacuum." He recalled the years just before Ayub took over (when he was a young officer) and there was economic and political chaos in Pakistan, including the death of the speaker of the East Pakistan Assembly.

I was a security officer then: I saw people kissing the ground where Ayub had stood! So it was not a coup as in the banana states, it was a coup brought about by the people, forced onto the army. "We want you to stabilize things," they said, and then the army has come in and stabilized things—it will take a little time to stabilize, institute political institutions once again.

The metaphor of a political vacuum that is filled by the military by default is popular and widely held and has been applied to the 1977 military intervention. Indeed, Zulfiqar Ali Bhutto was warned that the military was being inadvertently drawn into politics in Baluchistan, where he had used them to supplement the local police. His own secretariat cautioned him that this was infecting the officer corps, whose middle ranks were acquiring a "taste" for power. Bhutto was also warned that the officers were also developing contempt for politicians and the feeling that only they, the officers, "could deliver the goods." His advisors urged him to begin withdrawing the military from Baluchistan, and to divest it of the powers of arrest, house-search, and detention:

The withdrawal of the army, which may be gradual, might lead to more incidents but that risk should be taken . . . It is time that the experiment of gradual withdrawal of the army from the law enforcement is given a trial. The impression amongst the junior army officials that the army is a panacea for all ills, which had received a severe blow after the debacle in East Pakistan, is again gaining ground. It can be very infectious and cannot remain confined to one province. This infection may not be allowed to spread.[6]

6. Memorandum of Rao A. Rashid Khan, Special Secretary, Prime Minister's Secretariat, July 13, 1976; reprinted as annexure 64, pp. A-266-73, of the *White Paper on the Conduct of the General Elections* (Rawalpindi: Government of Pakistan, 1978).

The White Paper issued by Zia's government implies agreement with Rashid's argument:

Despite Rao Rashid's justified reservations about the role of the army in civil affairs, it is a matter of record that Mr. Bhutto's regime did not follow a policy of gradual withdrawal of the army in Baluchistan. On the other hand, in the wake of nationwide upheaval in the post-election period, he imposed selective Martial Law in the cities of Karachi, Hyderabad and Lahore and the army was thus once again called out "in aid of civil power," in areas other than Baluchistan as well.[7]

This implies that the warnings about "middle rank" officers were accurate, and tends to support the argument that the final move against Bhutto was instigated by such officers, who pressured their senior commanders. However, the evidence for this is incomplete, as it was Zia and his supporters who determined which documents were to be included in the White Papers: some senior officers involved in the coup were themselves known to have broader political ambitions.

One final variation on the theme of "political vacuum" was proposed by a senior retired lieutenant-general with extensive international experience. Comparing the Punjab with the rest of South Asia, he noted that it had always produced "great soldiers" but never any "great politicians."

The soldier class has the highest status in Pakistan, the trades like carpentry and politics are taboo! Part of this was the fault of the British: they encouraged the Hindus after the Mutiny of 1857 [in which Muslims were prominent], but not the Muslims, and our Mullahs kept us from learning English. There is also something in our minds which makes us unable to have a democracy—the idea of opposition is foreign to Islam.

Q: But Bhutto was a brilliant politician.

A: Bhutto! Why did he go wrong? Why do our politicians do things that fail?

Q: What about the military entering politics?

A: No, they're not better. They fail because they do not recognize that they have to start from the bottom, not from the top. Ayub, Asghar Khan, the others, they don't want to work their way up. There's something about us which makes us unable to have a democracy—perhaps the idea of opposition is foreign to Islam, probably the Turkish model would suit us better than the parliamentary model.

Although deeply pessimistic, this general, in fact, reflected Zia's own thinking quite accurately, and a search for alternatives to parliamentary democracy was begun in 1980. Bhutto's alleged failure was widely regarded as a national disaster, even among those generals who detested him personally; they acknowledged his capacity to inspire, lead, and give

7. Ibid., pp. 74–75.

some sense of purpose and direction to Pakistan. A measure of their desperation—not ambition—is that such officers concurred in his removal and execution.

The above argument that the Punjab (indeed, all of what is now Pakistan) is not fertile territory for politicians has some historical basis. In his careful study of Bhutto's rule, a distinguished Pakistani economist (Shahid Javed Burki) traces the incapacity of Pakistan to organize itself to the schism between "insiders and outsiders." The first were the Pakistanis who lived before partition in what is now Pakistan. They were a largely rural, conservative population with little interest or experience in modern political institutions, let alone democratic processes. The second group were epitomized by the generally better educated, more urban, and "modern" newcomers from India, who were concentrated in the great urban areas of Karachi, but also lived in Lahore, Hyderabad, Lyallpur, and Rawalpindi.

Pakistan society was, therefore, born polarized. On the one side were rural people with their own customs and traditions, their own history and institutions. On the other side was an urban population with relatively more modern institutions and with goals and aspirations that were completely different . . . The conflict between these two groups determined the course Pakistani society was to take on the road to economic and political development.[8]

As we have noted in chapter 3, the military itself is no monolith and is as diverse in its attitudes as the society it seeks to defend and protect. Many young officers had come from India in 1947, or were from relatively Westernized families, but succeeding generations have more accurately reflected traditional Punjabi, Sindhi, and Pathan values: they represent and respond to the very divisions that have made it difficult for Pakistani politicians to "make democracy work." When the general cited above said there was "something about us which makes us unable to have a democracy," he was referring as much to the officer corps as to the broader society.

THE AMBITIOUS GENERALS

These interpretations of Pakistan's coups view the military as guided by its own professional concerns but drawn into politics because of incompetent politicians. Other interpretations of Pakistan's three martial-law regimes are less sympathetic to the generals.

For a number of years it has been widely believed by some Pakistanis

8. *Pakistan Under Bhutto, 1971–77* (New York: St. Martin's, 1980), p. 11.

and most Indians that the domination of the military is closely related to its outside linkages. It has been an axiom of Indian foreign policy—first expressed by Nehru and later revived by Indira Gandhi—that the Pakistani generals are unrepresentative dictators who have forced their way into power in order to prevent a rapprochement with India. This is also a convenient justification for refusing to take Pakistan seriously so long as the military does hold power.

A 1980 interview of Indira Gandhi repeats the theme: "India was not afraid of Pakistan," she said, "but what is worrying is that when they receive massive arms supplies, the military gets entrenched, fortifying those people in Pakistan who do not want friendship with India or want to take revenge." India's receipt of military equipment from the Soviet Union was different as it was not "paid." Rubbing it in, she added that Pakistan had no enemies, as it was friendly with China and would not be attacked by the Soviet Union, Iran, Afghanistan, or India.[9] It is hard to tell whether such statements are intended as a goad to the Pakistanis or reflect an astonishing naïveté about a close neighbor. It is probably the former; Mrs. Gandhi was deeply angered with the generals for eliminating Bhutto (whose career paralleled hers in many ways) and for getting along so well with her own domestic political opponents, Morarji Desai and Atal Behari Vajpayee.[10]

One full-length study, by a prominent Indian scholar, traces this connection between the generals, foreign policy, and military rule.[11] Dr. Aswini Ray attempts to document the thesis that unstable civilian governments in Pakistan have always turned to foreign policy as a way of shifting the context of political debate in their favor, that this in turn has led some Pakistanis to argue for the serious reconsideration of a hostile policy towards India, and that, sensing this as a threat, the military has then intervened in politics to ensure that the civilians would not lead Pakistan towards rapprochement. Ray sums up his analysis in this way: "It had been a series of vicious circles for successive Pakistani governments. Internal instability goaded the leadership to shift emphasis upon foreign policy, which . . . led to further instability." But when Prime Minister Feroze Khan Noon sought "to take initiatives in the direction of removing the

9. *India Abroad* (New York), Aug. 1, 1980.
10. They had admired and been astonished by the efforts of Desai and Vajpayee to normalize relations with India's neighbors; they feared, but also respected, Mrs. Gandhi as the woman who dismantled Pakistan in 1971, lost power in 1977, and regained it in triumphal fashion in 1980.
11. Aswini Ray, *Domestic Compulsions and Foreign Policy* (New Delhi: Manas Publications, 1975).

only remaining alibi for Pakistan's military alliance (the 'threat' from India) by offering a no-war alliance," Ayub intervened. Ray acknowledges the domestic disruption existing in Pakistan at the time but correctly identifies foreign-policy concerns as one factor that motivated the military.

Bhutto made a similar argument from his death cell. The central thesis of his last political testament is that the generals moved against him because of pressure from the United States to refrain from going nuclear.[12] It is the linkage between the Pakistan Army and foreign governments (especially that of the United States) that Bhutto said was an alien force within Pakistan. Bhutto may have believed this, but there were still compelling reasons for the military to remove him other than their allegedly antinuclear views; they certainly do not seem to have slowed the pace of nuclear-weapons development in Pakistan after his death.

Without denying the importance of the army's link to foreign governments, especially the American, there is substantial evidence to indicate that this has not invariably worked against regional accord. Furthermore, the current variant on the argument implies a negative correlation between outside military adventurism and domestic military dominance.

Ayub himself came under criticism from many Pakistanis in 1962–63 and in 1965–66 (when Bhutto led the attack) for being too soft on India. In 1962–63 some generals had urged Ayub to attack India while that state was distracted by the Chinese; he refused, and instead offered a joint-defense arrangement, which was rejected by India. In 1965–66 Ayub was accused of not prosecuting the war against India with enough energy, and Bhutto broke with him on this issue. Indeed, Bhutto leaked a distorted version of Ayub's meeting with the then British High Commissioner to Pakistan, purporting to show that Ayub had yielded to Western pressure to end the war.[13] The correlation between military rule and bellicosity in Pakistan does not seem to be supported by events that have occurred during Zia's rule. He reversed years of stalemate by offering to India what that state had demanded for years, a "no war" pact.[14] Although this offer may never mature into a formal agreement, it is strongly opposed by Bhutto's supporters because they believe that this would strengthen the military's freedom of maneuver at home—a result exactly

12. Zulfiqar Ali Bhutto, *If I Am Assassinated . . .* (New Delhi: Vikas, 1979), pp. 135–38.
13. This extraordinary attempt to denigrate Ayub is contained in the *White Paper on the Jammu and Kashmir Dispute* (Islamabad: Ministry of Foreign Affairs, 1977). Bhutto was later attacked by the military for releasing state secrets.
14. This has a long and complicated history, and we shall discuss the issue in the next chapter; various Pakistani officials have claimed responsibility for the idea of a "no war" offer; it was suggested to Zia as early as April 1978 by one foreign visitor.

the opposite of the one that Indira Gandhi and others have perceived. In private discussions after the no-war pact was offered, many Pakistani civilians opposed to the military claim that a no-war agreement would enable the military to devote their full energies to domestic matters; they assume that the Pakistan army cannot "fight" on the domestic and foreign fronts at the same time, and that their own chances of overthrowing Zia's government would be enhanced if it were threatened by India. Moreover, they are prepared to attack Zia (as Ayub was attacked) for being "soft" on India and on the Kashmir issue, even though Bhutto himself virtually negotiated a settlement of the dispute in 1972.[15]

PUNJABI DOMINATION

A third theory of military intervention maintains that this has been a cover for continued Punjabi domination of the rest of Pakistan. This view is strongly held by politicians, intellectuals, and journalists, in Sind, in Baluchistan, and (somewhat less) in the North West Frontier Province. We have discussed the relatively unrepresentative nature of the Pakistan Army, which is slightly more Punjabi than the overall population. Not only are Sindhis and Baluchis underrepresented in both the officer corps and the ranks but there are important differences in regional style and historically considerable tension has existed between the Punjab and these other areas. Then, too, there may be strategic considerations that unwittingly reinforce the impression of Punjabi dominance.

It is easy to induce non-Punjabis to complain about Punjabi dominance. In the past few years some important Baluchi politicians have begun describing the Punjabis as "foreign colonialists," a term reminiscent of language used by the separatist Bangladesh movement. Sardar Ataullah Mengal (in London exile) has made this his central political theme:

I am simply a Baluch nationalist. I have got no ifs, ands, or buts about me. All we want to see in the country is our people liberated from the yoke of the Punjabi colonialism, or neocolonialism, or any new colonialism—whatever it is. Because now, within countries, the bigger nationalities, they exploit the smaller nationalities.[16]

15. Bhutto attacked Zia himself for being soft on India in his final political testament, *If I Am Assassinated...*, pp. 130, 218, 220. Perhaps to show that it is not yielding on Kashmir, the Pakistani government has, under Zia, raised the question of Kashmir on several occasions, most notably before a UN meeting on human rights and refugees in March, 1982. This led to India's breaking off talks on a treaty between the two states. *Far Eastern Economic Review*, Mar. 5, 1982.

16. Interview with Mengal, June 1981. For a comprehensive study of Baluch subnationalism and a brief discussion of regional breakaway, see Selig S. Harrison, *In Afghani-*

Mengal feels there is little difference between Bhutto's rule and Zia's (Bhutto was a Sindhi, Zia a Punjabi born in what is now India). For him, Bhutto entered into a "hot" phase against the Baluchis, and was pressured to do so by the Punjabi military; Zia has entered into a "cold phase," but behind this relative moderation remained "the mind of the Punjabi":

I have seen the mind of the Punjabi, how it is working. I have seen what object the Punjabi has before it, what is the goal of the Punjabi, and there is no difference [between Bhutto's military attacks on the Baluchis and Zia's withdrawal]. The army will leave no stone unturned to save its colonies.

The last point is widely believed by many Sindhis. They also regard the army as an alien force, holding on to power to ensure that Punjabi domination and its own perquisites and status remain unchallenged.

A few politicians, such as Sardar Mengal, Khair Bux Marri, and other Baluchis, proclaim that they have finally broken with "Pakistan" as it now exists. They cannot trust the military and are too weak to defend their interests within Baluchistan, so many have sought exile abroad, particularly in Afghanistan. Mengal, who remains in London, presents their dilemma this way:

Q: You don't see any way in which Zia or a successor could take conciliatory steps to bring you and others back as part of the system?

Mengal: I will just act as a well-wisher of the Punjabis. You come to me with a proposal from the diehard Punjabis, and I come back with a maximum demand short of independence. Can you accept me as a nation but within Pakistan's concept? Can you guarantee my rights? You will say "yes," but what rights do you want? And I will say, "I want rights in my province." You will say, "write it down and sign it," and I will, and you or General Zia will sign it, it will be in the constitution. But what guarantee is there that the constitution will remain! In the history of Pakistan three constitutions have been completely obliterated—in '56, '62, and '77.

. . . (Pakistan) is not my country, it is the country of the Punjab. The Punjabis are determined to retain the rest as a colony. I know that the Punjabis were determined to outnumber us in Baluchistan—they will take people from the outside and settle them in Baluchistan.

Their strategic doctrine requires the Pakistan military to maintain relatively high force levels. These same high force levels also enable the military to suppress domestic opposition. It is thus not surprising to find that

_____
stan's Shadow: Baluch Nationalism and Soviet Temptations (New York: Carnegie Endowment, 1981), and also Robert G. Wirsing, *The Baluchis and Pathans*, a report of the Minority Rights Group, no. 48, March 1981, for an excellent brief study.

many Baluchis, Sindhis, and others disagree with the army's strategic policy. They argue that a looser confederated Pakistan would be a more patriotic Pakistan, and would better be able to resist Soviet or Indian pressures; indeed, many deny that the Indian threat is as severe as the Punjabi-dominated army considers it to be.

This vision of a decentralized Pakistan (in which each province would have some capacity to defend itself) runs counter to the fundamental strategic assumptions of the army. For the army, such decentralization is strategically foolhardy, and they have little faith in people's armies or militias; indeed, much of their history has revolved around the control, through suppression, of armed tribal populations, some of which had ties with foreign powers. A strategic lesson taught at the Staff College is that state power rests on industry and population, for these are essential to support a modern military establishment. Thus, the Punjab is regarded as Pakistan's "heartland," and other regions are merely "gateways."[17] Such doctrine is reminiscent of Ayub's and Yahya's assurances to East Pakistan that the defense of the east was in the west; as we have discussed in chapter 2, no region likes to be told that it is strategically second-rate or insignificant, especially when the message comes from an unrepresentative army.

The theory of Punjabi domination via the military is the product of the actual numerical imbalance between the Punjab and the other provinces and the bluff, rough Punjabi style (which has an undercurrent of treachery, according to Mengal and others), complicated by a Punjabi-centered strategic orientation. For their part, many in the military find Baluchis and Sindhis as "foreign" as they found the Bengalis; exacerbating the problem for some generals is the fact that, whereas the original movement for Pakistan was not very strong in Punjab itself, it was quite weak in Sind, the N.W.F.P., and Baluchistan (which comprised largely semifeudal tribal elements kept well out of the mainstream of Indian politics). The Muslim League had been most powerful in Bengal and the United Provinces, and the idea of Pakistan was greeted with lukewarm interest elsewhere.

As Selig Harrison and others have pointed out, this tension between the dominant Punjab—symbolized for many Pakistanis by military rule—and the other three provinces may yet tear the state apart, as con-

17. In one Staff College study of geopolitics, Pakistan is described as having two "population-cum-economic core areas," Karachi in the south and Lahore in the north (Staff Course, Modes of Approach to Geopolitics, Lecture 1). The analysis concludes with the remark that "as for under-developed problem units, one has only to think of Baluchistan: its isolation from the two economic core areas, its distance from the seat of the federal government, its vast spaces and poor communications, its soil poverty, lack of water, sparse and scattered population."

flict between Bengal and West Pakistan erupted into civil war in 1971. Although Baluchistan is a much smaller province than East Bengal, it is adjacent to Soviet-controlled Afghanistan and also to Iran, and Baluchis live in both countries. Moreover, the more populous Sind is almost as disaffected. Sindhi bitterness has greatly increased since the execution of Bhutto by the military, and the Sindhis feel totally unrepresented in the central group of military administrators who continue to dominate Pakistani politics five years after Bhutto's arrest.[18]

If a future division of Pakistan should occur, it will probably come about as a result of incompetence, not destiny. Several multiethnic societies have managed their affairs in such a way as to counterbalance the military predominance of one region or another. In Yugoslavia, the Serbs dominate the military and also fear Croatian separatism; in Nigeria, the north dominates the military by virtue of its size; and even in neighboring India, the Punjab provides a disproportionate number of officers and men. In each case a mixture of concessions to regionalist sentiment and the development of representative political structures counterbalances a powerful military, although a necessary condition for this is restraint on the part of the military itself.

It may be that Pakistan is well beyond such a solution. Gerald Heeger has characterized Bhutto's Pakistan as a "postmilitary" state in which repeated military intervention has led to the breakdown of political institutions and the general deterioration of political discourse.[19] Writing after the 1977 martial law, William Richter shared Heeger's view and concludes that Pakistan has developed a "praetorian tradition" of repeated military interventionism, which Bhutto's "patrimonial" rule did little to change:

The persistence of the present martial law regime thus contributes to the reinforcement and extension of Pakistan's praetorian tradition in the broader sense as well. Pakistani political parties have historically been weak; elections, when not avoided altogether, have been preludes to disaster; succession has generally come about through mass agitation and military takeover rather than through ballot box; and no ruler—civilian or military—has relinquished power voluntarily. The conduct and contradictions of Pakistan's third military regime point strongly to the probable continuation of this tragic political tradition.[20]

18. Even the Governor of Sind in the Zia years was not a true Sindhi, but came from the region between Sind and Punjab, as Sindhis are quick to point out.

19. See Gerald Heeger, "Politics in the Post-Military State: Some Reflections on the Pakistani Experience," *World Politics* 29, 2 (January 1977): 242–62, and William E. Richter, "Persistent Praetorianism: Pakistan's Third Military Regime," *Pacific Affairs* 51, 3 (fall, 1978): 406–26.

20. Richter, "Persistent Praetorianism," p. 426.

It is hard to find fault with this description, and indeed some of the generals (even at the highest level) would find it accurate. But if intervention has become a tradition in Pakistan, it is not a popular one. From 1969 onward there has been substantial disagreement within the military about the wisdom of its interventions. The army's quite complex attitude towards politics is not merely the product of a reaction to political incompetence or of its own ambition, or even the combined push and pull of both factors. It is also derived from the very organizational ethos of the Pakistan military and the legacy embedded in its structure.

SEPARATE SPHERE AND MILITARY INTERVENTION

The Pakistan Army remains hostage to its origins. It inherited much of the British view of civil-military relations, and this view is transmitted to each succeeding Pakistani generation at the Pakistan Military Academy, the Staff College, and in informal discussions in the messes. The British (in India) liked to envision the "proper" relationship between military and civilian as that between two "separate spheres" of military and civilian influence, while acknowledging that ultimate responsibility lay in the hands of duly appointed (or elected) civilians.[21] British India was seized and originally ruled by the sword, and was governed for many years by military proconsuls. But by the end of the Raj the role of the military had been limited and elaborate administrative and fiscal mechanisms were devised to control it. The military's sphere of influence was recruitment, training, discipline, and strategic planning; the actual use of the military, from the most minor "aid to the civil" operation up to the strategic deployment of the Indian Army in the Persian Gulf, Southeast Asia, and elsewhere was a political—hence a civilian—decision.

A few of Pakistan's earliest political leaders were aware of the army's proconsulate tradition, and made some effort to ensure that it would not reemerge in an independent Pakistan. On the day of Pakistan's independence, August 14, 1947, Mohammad Ali Jinnah (who had just become Governor-General) scolded one young Pakistani officer. This officer, according to Asghar Khan (who was to become an Air Marshal in the Pakistan Air Force), had complained that

Instead of giving us the opportunity to serve our country in positions where our natural talents and native genius could be used to the greatest advantage, impor-

21. Cohen, *The Indian Army*, pp. 29–30.

tant posts are being entrusted, as had been done in the past, to foreigners. British officers have been appointed to head the three fighting services, and a number of other foreigners are in key senior appointments. This was not our understanding of how Pakistan would be run.[22]

Jinnah was deliberate in his answer. He warned the officer concerned not to forget that the armed forces were the "servants of the people" and that "you do not make national policy, it is we, the civilians, who decide these issues and it is your duty to carry out those tasks with which you are entrusted." He continued by stressing the need for "moderation" in thought and action, not extremism. This story cannot be independently verified, but Jinnah repeated his warning in almost the same language ten months later during his first and only visit to the Staff College. He expressed his alarm at the casual attitude of "one or two very high-ranking officers." After praising the defense forces as "the most vital of all Pakistani services," he warned the assembled students and instructors (the latter being largely British) that some of them were not aware of the implications of their oath to Pakistan, and promptly read it out to them.[23] And he added,

I should like you to study the constitution which is in force in Pakistan at present and understand its true constitutional and legal implications when you say that you will be faithful to the constitutions of the dominion. I want you to remember, and if you have time enough, you should study the Government of India Act (of 1935), as adopted for use in Pakistan which is our present constitution, that the executive authority flows from the head of the Government of Pakistan, who is Governor-General, and, therefore, any command or orders that may come to you cannot come without the sanction of the executive head.

The supreme irony of the event is that the constitution of Pakistan was to be suspended and altered by some of the officers in his audience, including Yahya Khan, then the only Pakistani on the directing staff. They moved from the military "sphere" to the civilian in 1958, although Ayub had been asked on several earlier occasions to step in and intervene.

The metaphor of separate spheres implies a division of responsibility, and the complaint of the Pakistani generals about the deterioration of political leadership is also a complaint that the civilians have failed to fulfill their responsibility to the military and to the state. For the military

22. Air Marshal M. Asghar Khan (retd.), *Pakistan at the Crossroads* (Lahore: Ferozsons, 1969), reprinted in *Defense Journal* 4, 11 (1978): 9–10.

23. Mohammad Ali Jinnah, address to the Staff College, June 14, 1948, reprinted in several editions of Jinnah's speeches and the official history of the Staff College, 1905–80, pp. 70–72.

this is vital, even if there was no fear that civilians might pursue foreign policies that were anathema to it.

The importance of legitimate and effective political leadership as a prerequisite for civilian control cannot be overemphasized. Relative power is not the decisive factor. If it were, military governments would be far more widespread than they are today. Rather, the Pakistan military is concerned that incompetent civilian leadership might hurt the quality and sometimes the very existence of the military as an organization and thus threaten what it believes to be the only real line of defense against India and one of the main forces holding the state together. Continued intervention in politics only strengthens this feeling: if the military lets one politician weaken the army (or establish a paramilitary force such as the Federal Security Force to balance or counter it), is it not shirking its obligations to the state as a whole? Politicians come and go (as some generals say), but the military is permanent; it damages the long-term survival of the state by weakening the army's capacity to step in and set things right. Setting things right, of course, is the preferred model of intervention, and the generals would like to see their involvement in politics as a glorified "aid-to the civil" operation.

They are less concerned about the initial intervention (which by definition is necessary when things have gotten completely out of hand) than about hanging on to power too long. One of Ayub's close associates presented this argument, which is still widely shared:

Some people would say that the army, to save itself, wanted to come in, I would say it's not the question of the army—nobody is going to destroy the army—these people were not going to destroy their own army. It was a question of saving the country, and sorting out the situation. Now, it is different *after* that. When General Ayub went on for eight or ten years, *that* is different—but when he took over, the intention was to clear the mess. It must be remembered that as far as the army is concerned, it is a professional army and an ordinary officer doesn't care about politics. People have relations in politics, but it doesn't make any difference— when I commanded the PMA, we used to stress these things from the beginning, "the army is completely aloof from politics," lots of stress on this.

But there is a second and much-neglected motive for intervention at work in Pakistan that derives from the idea of separate spheres of responsibility. In addition to the practical question of civilian incompetence hurting soldier and state, a moral dimension is embedded in this issue. Professional soldiers take human life and destroy property in the name of the state. They are taught in their service academies that the moral responsibility for their killing lies with the government, and that decisions

concerning life and death are morally neutral if they are politically legitimate. If the legitimacy of political leadership deteriorates, the officer must
reassess the morality of his own actions. A government that lacks legitimacy can no longer presume to be the arbiter of morality; those who
perform tasks on the margin of moral behavior—the military and police—rapidly find themselves in an untenable position. Thus, all of the
Pakistani generals who have seized power have been concerned about the
legality of their initial action and of subsequent acts that they and their
subordinates commit under the rubric of martial law. This was an important issue for Ayub Khan, who ensured the passage by the Pakistan National Assembly of legislation retrospectively legitimating his actions.
Yahya Khan would have asked for such legislation from the Assembly if it
had met after the 1970 elections, and in fact he was found to be a usurper
by the Pakistan Supreme Court in 1975.[24] President Zia and his close
advisors are no less concerned about the legitimation of their actions, and
have therefore hesitated to abrogate the 1977 constitution of Pakistan.
Even if Zia were to decide that he wanted to give up power, he cannot do
so until there is clear-cut settlement of the moral and legal responsibility
for the acts of violence that his government authorized—including the
hanging of Bhutto. The hesitation of Zia and his aides to give up power or
transfer power to civilians in the absence of any such settlement may only
further complicate or harden civilian opposition to military rule, but it
does indicate that they are highly sensitive to their legal and moral status.
Their training and indoctrination has emphasized the legitimacy of civilian, not military rule, and the generals therefore lack a clear-cut theory of
military intervention that would permit them to undertake sweeping
changes in Pakistani society; Islam now provides some guidance, but extreme Islamic practices divide the officer corps as well as the broader population, and very few officers would be inclined to pursue a Maoist or
revolutionary course of action.

To sum up our argument, the Pakistan Army, like any massive bureaucracy, is constrained by its own past. This heritage tells the army that intervention may be necessary but that it must be limited in scope and time; yet

24. The best account of constitution building in the Ayub and Yahya years is in the three
studies by Herbert Feldman: *Revolution in Pakistan* (London: Oxford University Press,
1967), *From Crisis to Crisis* (London: Oxford University Press, 1972), and *The End and the
Beginning* (London: Oxford University Press, 1975); for texts of a number of documents
pertaining to the 1977 martial law (and for important analyses of earlier spells of military
rule), see various issues of the excellent Karachi magazine, *Defense Journal*; the charges
against Bhutto are summarized in several White Papers issued by the Government of Pakistan in 1978 and 1979.

the problems of the diversity of Pakistani society and the slow growth of what the military would regard as a community of responsible politicians make it difficult for it to relinquish power. Once in power, the officer corps is tempted to tinker with the political system and "adjust" it, and again one can trace this back to the British. One subtradition of British India was a paternalistic but activist Punjab school of administration.[25] Pakistani officers sound very much like their British predecessors when they discuss the various civil works they have constructed, the hospitals and medical services they provide for ex-servicemen and others, and the businesses and factories they run.[26] They are eager to prove that they are not a drain on the resources of the state and actively contribute to its modernization. Yet they are reluctant to assume complete responsibility for these larger tasks: again and again they repeat that they will do so only within their proper sphere—in this case welfare for ex-servicemen—and tasks (such as the construction of the Karakoram Highway) that civilian authorities cannot handle.

The army's involvement in water projects and roads would be of only passing interest if the military were not guided by essentially the same limited-reformist approach when it deals with Pakistan's politicians. Raymond A. Moore concluded that although the army's contribution was "absolutely indispensable" in external-defense and internal-security matters, "it was peripheral rather than central in the areas of social and economic development. The country would have scarcely ceased to grow without the army's peaceful uses of military forces, but that it grew faster and more efficiently because of them is clear."[27]

Moore is skeptical of the Pakistan Army's political involvement, and urges it "to strengthen the civilian sector (and) avoid the pitfalls of prolonged assumption of political power," along the lines of the Indian model. Yet, these two roles of the Pakistan Army, its so-called nation-building activities and its political involvement, cannot be easily sepa-

25. Shahid Javed Burki, *Pakistan Under Bhutto, 1971–77* (New York: St. Martins, 1980), pp. 13–15.

26. One of the main activities is the Fauji Foundation. When India and Pakistan were partitioned they shared in the welfare contributions donated by other ranks during World War II; India distributed these to individual ex-soldiers, but Pakistan used the money to capitalize the Fauji Foundation, which in turn used it to develop a chain of hospitals, light (and heavy) industries, and various service facilities, largely but not entirely for ex-servicemen. The foundation is headed by a retired general, and employs a number of retired officers. A detailed account of the foundation's activities is contained in its annual calendar and several reports. It was rumored in 1982 that the foundation was one channel for the clandestine import of equipment used in the nuclear-weapons program.

27. Raymond A. Moore, *Nation Building and the Pakistan Army, 1947–1969* (Lahore: Aziz Publishers, 1979), p. 332.

rated from each other and from the army's role in national defense. Many officers recognize this, and are aware that their integrity will be strained beyond limits if they attempt to perform economic and political as well as military tasks at a high level of efficiency and quality. This cannot be done without the lavish expenditure of resources together with the development of a doctrine of total military intervention in any "weak" sector, a doctrine that does not exist in Pakistan. My analysis of this problem in 1964 seems to be still essentially valid today:

The difficulty in defining and establishing a suitable civil military relationship is intimately connected with the military's problem of re-shaping and re-establishing Pakistani politics. If civilian and military have their own spheres, there is as little justification in the military intervening in politics as the politicians in military matters ... The justification for the breaking of this rule in Pakistan is that the politicians first broke the 'rules of the game' by meddling foolishly in military matters. Significantly, the official position today is that the military is no longer in politics: the army is above politics and parties. The justification for [Ayub's] coup is that the army restored the balance between the military and the civil spheres by rebuilding the political structure (as one would rebuild an army after defeat or partition). But, of course, political problems are not the same as military problems.[28]

The difference that fifteen years has made is that the present military leadership is aware that the efforts of Ayub, Yahya, and even Bhutto to reform Pakistani politics and create a stable balance between the military sphere and the political one have all failed, and are therefore to some degree discredited—hence their interest in religion and "Islamization" as a new strategy. After 1978 they pursued the rebuilding of Pakistan along "Islamic" lines with little enthusiasm; what is striking is the generals' loss of confidence in their ability to find a working solution to the problem of balancing military and civilian interests as well as to carry it out.

CIVILIAN CONTROL AND DECISION-MAKING

The present situation is doubly serious because there is widespread belief within the military's upper ranks that a stable, orderly civil-military relationship is vital to the future security of Pakistan itself. After he became Prime Minister, Bhutto received full military cooperation in a careful study of civil-military relations and decision-making. The study was carried out largely by retired and serving officers, and they concluded that

28. Stephen P. Cohen, "Arms and Politics in Pakistan," *India Quarterly* (October–December 1964): 413–14.

the 1971 war with India disclosed serious flaws in the military's performance and organization.[29] Even though Bhutto was interested in discredit-
ing his military predecessors and downgrading the reputation of serving
officers, his steps to reform the decision-making structure were strongly
supported by the military, and they have been partially implemented under Zia. Bhutto's *White Paper on Defense Organization* was part of a
concerted effort to ensure civilian control over Pakistan's defense process.
The 1973 Constitution provided harsh punishment for challenging civilian rule, and the *White Paper* set forth the intellectual justification for
such punishment.[30] At times, the *White Paper* reads more like a lecture to
the troops than a government document (criticizing earlier regimes for
incompetence and mismanagement), but it makes the case for civilian
control in practical terms:

It is only a representative Government and the exertion by the Government of
supreme authority over the country's Defense Establishment that ends the separa-
tion of the Armed Forces from the people and eliminates the element of caprice
from decisions of war or peace. An unrepresentative regime, lacking a perception
of the national interest as distinguished from the interest of a class or group, draws
guidance from subjective appreciation ... and may have no correspondence to
realities. National defense policy is no longer a military affair alone ... the evolution of national defense policy and its administration requires (a) effective political control at the top ... and (b) a number of institutions and agencies at the base,
to produce the necessary data and appreciations on which political decisions can
be based.[31]

29. A number of studies appeared after 1972, some of them clearly inspired by Bhutto.
The most comprehensive was written by Fazal Muqeem Khan, a respected retired lieutenant-general. See *Pakistan's Crisis in Leadership* (Islamabad: National Book Foundation,
1973); also, the texts of a *White Paper on Defense Organization* and a Staff study can be
found in *Defense Journal* (July–August 1976) 2:7–8; this publication regularly included
analyses of Pakistan's higher defense organization throughout the 1970s. In the course of his
analysis, Fazal Muqeem summarized his conclusions (pp. 106, 261):

In Pakistan, at the military level, there has never been any joint planning in the true sense of the word. At
best, unilaterally produced service plans have been coordinated through bilateral discussions between the
services. The army, the senior service, was usually the sponsor ... and the other two services formed an
appendage to this plan. The air support which the navy wanted was never catered for ... The PAF plan
was exclusively its own and did not take into consideration its impact on the operations of the other two
services. It never occurred to them [army or navy] to ask for the PAF plan, including the siting of planes,
deploying of radar and activation of airfields. They just accepted what the C-in-C, Air, promised them
vaguely. Consequently, owing to the lack of joint planning and inter-service coordination, there were
dangerous flaws in the plans of each service.

30. The 1973 Constitution provides that any attempt to abrogate it by force or threat of
force is treasonous (sec. 6), the principle of civilian control is firmly laid down (sec. 243–5),
and an oath is specified for members of the Armed Forces, which states in part that "I will
not engage myself in any political activities whatsoever" (third schedule).

31. *White Paper on Defense Organization*, Sec. 3.

According to one general who helped write the *White Paper,* Bhutto and the military were in agreement on the principle of civilian control. The military saw this "civilian" as restricted to the political leadership:

The first important consideration was that we must accept the principle in Pakistan—as is done in all democratic countries—that the civil supremacy must be maintained; and we still wish to and we still follow that policy that in Pakistan the overall supremacy is that of the civilian government—that is, the chief executive along with the cabinet. But it does not mean that is the rule of the civilian servants in any way, the CSP (Civil Service of Pakistan), in other words. The CSP should not boss around the service chiefs as such. We distinguish between civilian supremacy and the dominance of the civil-service officers over the service chiefs.[32]

This is a critical and revealing point. It shows the limits to which the Pakistan military was willing to go in submitting to "civilian" control even when it was demoralized and discredited. Specifically, several generals referred both to periods of their own history during which the civil service became especially powerful (under Ayub), and the example of the Indian defense-policy process, where civil servants play a critical role in controlling and directing the military. One senior general recalls a conversation with his Indian counterpart, who complained bitterly that his report of their meeting (to discuss cease-fire demarcation) would be gone over and edited by a "babu" second-class clerk. Such conversations may be apocryphal, but the Pakistan Army does know enough about the Indian system to be reluctant to accept it as a complete package, although the army certainly has been willing to accept components of it (such as control by a political defense minister and a political prime minister).

The structure that emerged after several years of analysis and planning is quite similar to that found in many democratic countries.[33] It is now entirely in place, but because there is no effective civilian leadership it has not really been tested.

At its upper levels the system is now marked by anomalies, because the man who is Chief of the Army Staff (and therefore subordinate to the Defense Minister and the Prime Minister) is also President. Serving soldiers are not technically members of the Defense Committee of the Cabinet, the DCC (which is responsible for determining the size, role, and shape of the armed forces) yet a military man presides over it and appoints all of its members (who should be elected civilian officials, but are not,

---

32. This is a common theme among serving officers; part of the legacy of the Ayub era is a belief that he was led astray and used by civilians; Bhutto also had little love for the CSP.

33. The most comprehensive study of current Pakistani defense decision making is in Shirin Tahir-Kheli, "Defense Planning in Pakistan," *Defense Planning in Less Industrialized States,* Stephanie Neuman, ed. (D. C. Heath, forthcoming).

because of the absence of elections). Below the DCC is the Defense Council. Military men are members of this council, which is supposed to advise the DCC on military matters; it includes the External Affairs Minister, the Finance Minister, and other cabinet members with a special interest in defense policy. In turn, it receives recommendations from a Joint Chiefs of Staff Committee, patterned after both the American and British systems. The JCSC gave Pakistan—for the first time—a thoroughly integrated interservice mechanism for the higher direction of war, and it does function now, although for some time it lacked a chairman (the chairman was a senior army general who resigned when Zia became President). Under the JCSC are a Director-General, a Joint Staff, and a complex bureaucracy made up of officers drawn from all three services (but still dominated by the army). At the lower levels the system seems to be functioning, but it is impossible for an outsider to speculate as to its effectiveness—indeed, several officers who are not part of this new system of decision making expressed their puzzlement as to how it actually works.

What is true is that for the first time in the history of Pakistan an administrative structure exists above and beyond the army's own chain of command. In military terms, this is vital for several reasons. First, in 1965 and 1971 the three services of Pakistan went to different wars. No overall strategic plan existed, and tactical cooperation was limited. Pakistan's new security-policy-making process will (if it is ever implemented) ensure that there will at least be a framework for decision making. Secondly, it enables the military and the state to allocate resources better for weapons acquisition and the development of Pakistan's own defense-production infrastructure. For the first time, there is central direction of the growing defense-production system and a way to process and evaluate individual service requests for weapons. However, having a service chief as head of state distorts the entire process. Because officers at the level of the JCSC and the planning staff can be retired or transferred by a decision of their superiors (and at the highest level that means Zia himself), they cannot perform their military duties without calculating political and personal consequences. Unless they seek early retirement, or unless Zia himself is willing to encourage dissent, debate, and discussion between himself and his immediate subordinates, it is likely that the "decision-making process" will be in the hands of a series of yes-men, and beneath them, the "nodders," smiling their way up to higher rank.[34] This may help to keep the peace within the military (which is one condition of Zia's continua-

34. The term "nodder" was coined by P. G. Wodehouse and has found its way into the Pakistan Army.

tion in power), but it hardly resembles the tough-minded and systematic decision-making process envisaged in the *White Paper*.

THE ZIA SYSTEM

In 1983 President Mohammed Zia ul-Haq completed his fifth year as President of Pakistan, his sixth year as Chief Martial Law Administrator, and his eighth year as Chief of the Army Staff.[35] He thus holds positions of authority within the military, the martial-law system that prevails in Pakistan, and the government itself.

This is an astonishing accomplishment for a man who was universally regarded outside the army as a temporary "front man" for the group of generals who deposed Zulfiqar Ali Bhutto. Except for a few officers who had linked their careers to his, Zia was not even well known within the army itself, having been a very junior lieutenant-general when Bhutto reached down and promoted him to Chief of the Army Staff in 1976. His military career was marked by competent service and his personal demeanor inspires neither awe nor fear.[36]

Although Zia's rule is not based upon wide popular support, and may be ended abruptly, it is important to note both how he has functioned since 1977 and what steps he has taken to build a political structure to replace the one he destroyed. Our term for Zia's method of operation and the structure he is erecting is "the Zia system."

Immediately after the arrest of Bhutto in 1977, Zia received a congratulatory message from one of Pakistan's oldest and most respected generals, a former associate of Ayub. This general drew the analogy between 1977 and his own involvement in Ayub's coup of 1958; "the time came when we felt the army had to be protected, they were forming groups in the army." The Pakistan Army, he explained in 1980, was and is highly professional.

There is no political ambition, but the army gets infected by its environment, by the politics, by the chaos, by the instability. All these politicians who make state-

35. For a survey of Zia's rule, almost five years after he came to power, see Stephen P. Cohen and Marvin G. Weinbaum, "Pakistan in 1981: Staying On," *Asian Survey* 22:2 (February 1982): 36–146, and Marvin G. Weinbaum and Stephen P. Cohen, "Pakistan in 1982: Holding On," *Asian Survey* 23:2 (February 1983).

36. Zia's early anonymity was both an advantage and a disadvantage. It worked to his benefit in that his opponents in and out of the military grossly underestimated both his ability and his tenacity; in this he resembles Indira Gandhi after she became Prime Minister in 1965, or her predecessor, Lal Bahadur Shastri. All three quietly undercut their political opponents, or set them against each other, while consolidating power. By 1983 Zia was no more charismatic than he was in 1977, but he was much more assured and confident; indeed, a sign of his success is that he is beginning to be taken for granted.

ments, they are third-rate, useless. Bhutto's mission was to destroy Pakistan, Asghar Khan came to carry on with the same mission; I was so moved when Zia took over I sent him a telegram, "Well done!" I was so delighted, I called him up and told him, "you have saved the country—well done, and you've saved the army!"[37]

This is an extreme view, even for those who support Zia. More representative of officers of the British generation (who are now almost all retired from public life) was the judgment of another of Ayub's associates. He was unsure as to whether the military could involve itself in national politics and still retain its professional outlook:

As you know, it depends on the involvement. In Ayub's time the army's involvement was never very deep, the army had only professional duties, the initial period of the martial law when the army assumed direct responsibility was very short-lived. And Ayub realized that the army must go back to its old duties. Afterwards, however, the service structure was upset, because all the senior officers were involved in it [martial law] and naturally, new officers have to be appointed. So you do tend to destabilize the rank structure to that extent. But personally, I believed that professional soldiers are professional soldiers, and no matter how good a head you may have, you can't wear two caps all the time, you can for a short time. Ayub was the one who kept the army out of politics and would always tell us, never interfere in politics, 'till such time as he took over, and even then he took the army back to barracks. And I feel the army should do its own job, and the sooner we establish [political] institutions, the better, because eventually the army gets hurt—we are all human beings, and we come to the same temptations.

This cautious advice was widely regarded as prudent in 1977–78, and even as late as 1980. It was not followed, according to Zia's supporters, because of the failure of civilian politicians to come forward and accept the responsibility of governing Pakistan; the politicians, of course, contend that to do so would have been political suicide, for it would have associated them with an unpopular military government. For supporters of the executed Bhutto there were other matters to settle. Finally, it was not clear until 1981 that Zia was in a position to transfer power: some generals regarded him as a lightweight (and did not hesitate to tell visitors this with witnesses present), and there were indications that several younger officers had organized a small conspiracy to assassinate him.[38]

37. Interview with General Mohammed Musa (retd.), Lahore, 1980.
38. Various reports indicate that a number of young officers (with some hope of associating various senior officers in their activities) planned to assassinate Zia. At least one retired officer with a grievance against Zia was also involved; a few generals who were told about the plan reported it to military-intelligence authorities, and some of those who did not were subsequently retired. Although he often ventures out into public—distributing blankets in cold weather, cycling to his office, and appearing at public meetings—Zia is unusually well guarded and wears a bulletproof vest.

Zia and his close advisors moved first in April 1980 to retire, transfer, or reduce the responsibilities of a dozen senior officers, some of whom were suspected of disloyalty.[39] This also created new opportunities for younger men whose promotion had been blocked. Sometime in this period Zia and his closest associates also came to the conclusion that their own futures were better served by remaining in power than by a quick devolution of power to the civilians, or by Zia's resignation and retirement. A number of factors contributed to this decision: their concern for their own careers, the reluctance of responsible politicians to come forward, fear of a Pakistan People's Party revival and the belief that a change in the senior leadership would further eat away at the integrity of a demoralized army. They concluded that Pakistan could not be effectively governed under these circumstances without a drastic change in the 1973 Constitution, and they have moved to create an entirely new, "Islamic" system of political life.

As was described earlier, the Pakistan Army officer corps is increasingly drawn from middle-class, more orthodox and religious families. Zia himself is quite representative of this class of officers. Zia and his close advisors have launched Pakistan on a new political course, combining both their religion and their military subtradition of order, discipline, and building organizational structures from below, piece by piece. There are strong similarities between their efforts to create a system of Islamic advisory councils at the provincial and national level (the Majlis-i-Shura) and Ayub Khan's earlier efforts at building "basic democracies." Where they differ from Ayub is in their use of Islam and their systematic attempt to control, intimidate, or uproot all traces of independent centers of political power (including the press, the judiciary, and Pakistan's already enfeebled intellectual class).[40]

Although a number of practical considerations account for this effort to "Islamize" Pakistan by the military (few officers are willing to challenge Zia and his colleagues so long as stability is maintained and the army does not have to deal too extensively with civilian opposition), these steps do have a theoretical justification. In Chapter 4, we cited the views of one senior advisor to Zia who argued that not only were the leaders of

39. Lt.-Gen. F. A. Chishti, who was Corps Commander and Martial Law Administrator of Islamabad-Rawalpindi area, Cabinet Minister, and reportedly one of the prime movers against Bhutto, was the most prominent general who was retired.

40. These efforts are most fully documented by Amnesty International in a major report, *Pakistan: Human Rights Violations and the Decline of the Rule of Law* (London: Amnesty International Publications, 1982). The Pakistan government has vehemently contested both the particulars of the report and its general conclusions.

Pakistan progressive and enlightened individuals by any standard—Western or Islamic—but that the Pakistani people had yet to reach such a level of development.[41] Hence, the tough punishments ordained by some Islamic codes were appropriate to Pakistan at its present stage of development—more appropriate than the permissive and unacceptable laws passed in some Western democracies.

These views of Islam and its relationship to Pakistani society clash directly with those of many educated Pakistanis. During a series of protest marches by Pakistani women, held in February 1983, the two views confronted each other in the press and on the streets of Karachi, Lahore, and Rawalpindi. The women were objecting to the proposed adoption of an "Islamic" law, which weighs the testimony of a female witness as half that of a male; not only were the women prohibited from completing their march but several in Lahore were severely beaten. However, for most senior military leaders of Pakistan these marches were evidence of both the ignorance and bad intentions of those who opposed Zia's Islamic reforms. They argued that the women were not "true" Pakistanis, and asserted that some were Hindus, or married to Hindus and that they did not understand that the requirement of two female witnesses applied only to special cases. Some Islamic scholars deny this, and point out that there are important Shia-Sunni differences in these matters, and that the government of Pakistan has merely selected those facets of Islamic doctrine that are convenient for its purposes.

Those Pakistani leaders who hold hard-line views of their role in society are not likely to yield power quickly or to regard domestic opposition as anything but further proof of its degeneracy. They share a widely held view that the West is in moral decline, and criticism from that direction is only further evidence that they have chosen the correct, albeit difficult, path. Not all of those who hold power in Pakistan would subscribe to these views, and there is some evidence to indicate that Zia is more flexi-

41. Another senior retired general, Fazal Muqeem Khan (who has served in civilian administrative positions under both Bhutto and Zia), wrote that the people of Pakistan have "an innate lack of political maturity" and are "besotted by wishful thinking" (*Pakistan's Crisis in Leadership,* p. 249). This view is widely shared by Bangladeshi generals (most of whom served earlier in the Pakistan Army), who also complain of civilian political immaturity. Lt.-Gen. H. M. Ershad contended that the military role had to be institutionalized in the constitution "for all time to come," because Bangladesh was not like India, where the leadership was "very mature." Bangladeshi officers, moving faster in this direction than their Pakistani counterparts, argue that an Indonesian-like system in which army officers could hold civilian jobs without loss of seniority would be desirable. For these remarks see report by Salamat Ali, *Far Eastern Economic Review,* Nov. 27, 1981; for a broader survey of the Bangladesh military, linking it to its Pakistan Army traditions, see Lawrence Lifshultz, *Bangladesh: The Unfinished Revolution* (London: Zed Press, 1979).

ble on these issues than he has been made out to be. He has freely added and dropped advisors, he has yielded to public opposition on several occasions (most notably after the protest of Shias over the imposition of *Zakat*, a religious tax), and he has shown great flexibility and creativity in strategic decisions. He many yet come to resemble a latter-day Ayub, so aptly described by Herbert Feldman:

Notwithstanding the impressive exterior and the choice of blunt soldierly language, it had already been demonstrated that his was no stern and unrelenting character, firm in its decisions and in the determination to pursue to the end clearly defined objectives. On the contrary, he had shown himself to be, in essence, a conciliator, a man ready to compromise and come to terms with any movement, organization or individual, even within the country itself, wherever there was a genuine point of view and the courage to pursue it.[42]

It remains to be seen whether Zia and his advisors have a vision beyond that of merely holding on to power, distracting the citizens of Pakistan with Islamic doctrine, and maintaining a revolving political-prisoner population of unknown but apparently substantial size. Their alternatives are not, however, attractive. The military certainly would not be willing to yield power to any group that sought to raise the issue of Bhutto's death; given the wording of the Pakistan Constitution this might be fatal for Zia himself. Nor does most of the army have a clear vision of a radically different way of organizing Pakistani life.

They have been professional soldiers throughout their careers, and although most generals have learned how to "play politics" both within the military and in dealing with politicians and bureaucrats, they are often lacking in speculative or conceptual skills, let alone the ability to articulate their ideas in such a way that a mass public would find them intelligible. What is great cause for concern is that this generation of generals (and, one might add, their civilian counterparts in the bureaucracy, as well as the entire intellectual class of Pakistan) are barren of imaginative plans for the future. The optimism of the Ayub era was replaced by the opportunism of Yahya and the hyperbole of Bhutto; they have all failed and perhaps Zia's major contribution to Pakistan will be to lower popular expectations and merely to survive until a trustworthy civilian leadership or a more ambitious group of generals emerges. I very much doubt the latter, unless the army itself is adversely affected by the continuation of its chief as President and by the perpetuation of martial law.

42. Feldman, *From Crisis to Crisis*, p. 5.

CONCLUSION

In his brilliant study of the military and society, Stanislav Andreski distinguishes between four kinds of "militarism."[43] There is idolization of the military, rule by the military, the peacetime militarization of society (even under civilian leadership), and the gearing up of a society for war. Pakistan has seen only the first two, and even those on a sporadic basis. Military rule in Pakistan has been fitful, carried out with some embarrassment and apology. The present regime is no exception. Zia's rule could deteriorate into violent and corrupt palace politics, ruining the military and destroying the state, but it could be the first step back toward legitimate and effective (and civilian) rule.

As for the future political role of the military in Pakistan, it is futile to debate whether the military has been pulled into politics (because of the incompetence of civilian leaders) or pushed its way in (to ensure that civilians did not pursue policies anathematic to military interests). Due weight must be given to political explanations, cultural explanations, and considerations derived from the historical and doctrinal ethos of the Pakistan Army itself. Not only does the army believe that it defends society from external enemies, but a number of officers will argue that the military has an important role in ensuring that Pakistan society itself modernizes and yet remains pure and truly Islamic. Not only should the military defend Pakistan (they claim), but Pakistani society must remain worthy of the military; there is still a belief that it is the only institution in Pakistan that can hold the country together. A friendly critic would point out that there is more than a small trace of self-fulfilling prophecy in this argument, inasmuch as the military has intervened on several occasions when it was dissatisfied with the power or performance of the bureaucracy or the political parties: it will not permit the latter to become effective national institutions.

Consequently, if Pakistan is to recover from its intellectual and political exhaustion and if it is to break the cycle of intervention, reform, demoralization, and breakdown, many groups will have to be involved. Pakistani civilians of all regions must appreciate the military's sensitivity to domestic disorder, a disorder that may threaten the integrity of the military itself; they must also be capable of demonstrating their own competence and authority to run Pakistan. The soldiers are not blameless, and

43. Stanislav Andreski, *Military Organization and Society*, 2d ed. (Berkeley: University of California Press, 1968), pp. 184–86.

will have to accept a decline in their relative status and influence as a price that must be paid to reduce the necessity of intervention. A series of agreements, compromises, pacts, or understandings—possibly complete with timetables and election schedules—could still be worked out between civil and military for the sake of national survival, if not national unity.

This is clearly the central agenda item of Pakistani politics. The military is reluctant to withdraw from power because of doubts whether any of the current civilian leaders are capable of running the state to its satisfaction. Unsurprisingly, in view of Bhutto's fate, civilians are reluctant to come forward. There is also no assurance that the military will not try to play a covert political role even if formal power should pass to a civilian government. But the notion of partial military rule is not accepted by most Pakistanis, even in the military, whose perspective has been strongly shaped by the British tradition of parliamentary democracy and civilian control. The divergencies between civilian and military opinion on these basic questions are enormous.

The generals will not satisfy the politicians unless they allow free elections and restore a reasonable range of civil liberties. Those parties with grievances against the military will probably have to pledge that they will not seek retribution. The military may have to be given a constitutional voice in the making of policies that most greatly concern it (such as defense and foreign policy). A staged (in both senses of the word) withdrawal from politics would reassure both the military and civilian politicians that both sides were keeping their promises. From a realistic standpoint, it is unlikely that this will occur. With Bhutto's death it is not clear whether any single party or individual can effectively run Pakistan even if the military should remain neutral; nor are there any political figures that seem willing to serve as a front for the military; nor as of 1982, has the military offered a coherent, attractive alternative to some form of civilian democratic government.

In addition to military and civilian groups, however, Pakistan's friends and the states that surround it do contribute to the role that its army plays in politics.

In the case of India, so long as Indians (incorrectly, I believe) associate military rule in Pakistan with a belligerent Pakistan, they make it difficult for the military to either withdraw from power or pursue a negotiated settlement of bilateral disputes.[44] There is very little sympathy within India for

44. Many informed Indian journalists and scholars have begun to rethink their views of Pakistan as a result of increased visits to that country. For a selection of their opinions see Pran Chopra, ed., *Contemporary Pakistan: New Aims and Images* (Delhi: Vikas, 1983).

helping Pakistan find both stability and security. India is burdened with its own problems and the generals are hardly candidates for sympathy. Yet, as we shall discuss in the next chapter, the Indian desire to see Pakistan as a weak buffer is being reexamined in the light of the 1978 Afghanistan coup and the subsequent invasion of that country by Soviet forces.

In the case of Pakistan's friends, only the United States has both the leverage and the interest to hasten the restoration of representative government. The renewed American relationship with Pakistan has been harshly criticized by liberal Americans, who probably exaggerate the degree of influence that one state can have over another when it provides some economic aid and sells (at commercial terms) military equipment. Yet the Reagan administration and its advisors have erred in the other direction: they assume both that Pakistan is inherently a military-run state and that such a state will in the future be sympathetic to American interests. Our analysis in this and preceding chapters indicates that neither assumption is true: unlike Iran, Pakistanis share (with India) a heritage of liberal democracy; moreover, there are no illusions among the generals about America's "friendship."

American and Indian encouragement of a return to a more open political system, even in phased steps, is an important but insufficient condition. Pakistan's political future will ultimately be determined by the degree of trust between Pakistanis. Despite all of the bravado of the military and the potent symbolism of Pakistani nationalism, the absence of such a fellow-feeling may yet tear the state apart; the military, more than any other group, must come to understand its role in creating this state of affairs. Its suspicion of Pakistani (especially Baluchi and Sindhi) politicians, "poets," and professors is beginning to lead some of the latter to speculate whether their future might not be brighter within a shattered Pakistan or even a larger India. This warning would be rhetorical in the case of virtually any country other than Pakistan, whose own blood-stained past provides the strongest precedent.

CHAPTER SIX

The Army, Strategy, and Survival

Pakistan has to fight a three-front war. First, there are the Indians, who cannot accept our existence. Then, there are the Russians, who also want to see us out of the way. Finally, there is the third front: at home, against those who would destroy us from within.

Retired Lieutenant-General, Pakistan Army (1980)

Two great uncertainties characterize today's international system. The first is whether the domination of two superpowers will continue or whether the major regional states will emerge and form a new multipolar international system of three, four, five, or even six powers. The second is whether an international order based largely on nuclear deterrence will survive the proliferation of nuclear weapons. The two uncertainties are linked at every turn. Both are of direct importance to a Pakistan so deeply enmeshed in the web of superpower and regional-great-power politics that its survival, growth, or decay will provide some important clues as to the future of the international system itself.

To paraphrase Freud, territory is destiny. Pakistan, with more than 80 million people, a martial tradition, and a large and well-trained military establishment, would ordinarily be counted as a major power. Such a country would dominate its neighbors were it situated in Africa, Latin America, or Southeast Asia. But compare it with the world's three largest states and one quickly observes the importance of relative power.

This is Pakistan's central strategic dilemma, a dilemma shared by those states whose interests depend upon a viable Pakistan. Although over thirty years old, it still struggles for identity and security in the reflected brilliance of three megastates, Russia, China, and India. Its chief (but inconstant) ally is thirteen thousand miles away, its borders are permeable, and its population spills over into unstable Afghanistan and Iran, as well as India. Some regard Pakistan as a latter-day Prussia, strategically placed to the south of the Soviet Union (and a ready-made surrogate for American strategic plans), but others speak of Pakistan in terms of eighteenth-century Poland—to be swallowed up piece by piece by its neighbors—or expect it to be crushed in a vise whose jaws consist of the Soviet Union to the north and India to the south. At best, Pakistan might be an Asian Finland, required to subordinate its security policy to the will of its powerful neighbors.

There can be no immediate answer to the question of Pakistan's future—whether it will be a nuclear-armed Prussia, a Poland, or a Finland. The country's fate depends upon the evolution of its unsettled domestic political system, the ambitions of its neighbors, and the actions of its allies. Its survival is therefore likely to be in part the result of superpower and great-power rivalry, a state of dependency uncomfortable for any state, but particularly so for one that has viewed itself as a rugged, tough, and independent power.

This description of Pakistan's strategic dilemma embraces only the visible half of the problem. The invisible half is to be found within the minds of those responsible for Pakistan's foreign policy. Not only do Pakistanis disagree in their identification of reasonable foreign-policy goals and the strategies that can best be deployed to achieve such goals, but there are fundamental organizational and structural problems associated with the foreign-policy process. These parallel many of the issues discussed in the preceding chapter and stem from the same cause: the Pakistan military—by tradition, structure, and temperament—is part of a whole that does not fully exist. By force of will and threat of gun the generals have controlled the politics of Pakistan, but they do so without full training, experience, or legitimacy.

As we shall examine below, the service schools encourage the Pakistani officer corps to expect and prepare for the worst (especially from India), just as Indian officers are taught to expect the worst from Pakistanis or Chinese. In India, Britain, and other democracies, however, effective civilian institutions check and balance the military perspective; the military are encouraged to plan for the worst, but others make the final decisions on matters of war and peace. In contrast, because the military holds political power in Pakistan, these partial perspectives on foreign affairs have been injected directly into the Pakistani foreign-policy-making process. When the folklore of the officers' mess becomes state policy, disaster is not far away.

As we have argued in chapter 5, it is not inevitable that Pakistani generals will be hawkish, and many civilian advisers have urged war when the generals have urged caution. Nevertheless, Pakistan's neighbors cannot be blamed for concern. That India has at times exhibited the same mentality (although civilian hawks, not soldiers were chiefly responsible) further complicates the situation.

After a brief survey of Pakistan's shifting international position, this chapter will focus on several security and foreign-policy issues of particular concern to the military itself. These include the permeability of Pakistan's frontiers, the ranking of security threats, the various strategies that have been developed to protect Pakistan, and the looming threat of regional nuclear proliferation.

ALIGNMENT STRATEGIES

THE FIRST PHASE: NONALIGNMENT

Pakistan's early years were dominated by active conflict with India over the terms of partition, the disposition of Kashmir and other disputed territories, and access to vital river and water resources. From 1947 to 1953, Pakistan pursued a policy of nonalignment, and early established close relations with the new People's Republic of China, the major superpowers, and the Muslim world. The latter effort was particularly important, although it has been retrospectively judged as "overoptimistic and amateurish" by a leading Pakistani diplomat.[1] It retains its significance because it is a path to which Pakistan has recently returned.[2]

In those years Pakistan proclaimed itself to be the fifth largest nation in the world and the largest Muslim state. It actively pressed Muslim causes in the United Nations and shaped its foreign policy so as to support liberation movements in Islamic states. For example, Pakistan opposed Dutch military action in Indonesia in 1948, banned KLM from its air space, and declared a public holiday on the occasion of Indonesian independence. Yet this policy (along with similar support for the Egyptian revolutionaries) brought few dividends. Pakistan discovered to its dismay that both

---

1. By S. M. Burke. An Indian analysis of Pakistan's early search for alliances and friends is given by Aswini K. Ray, *Domestic Compulsions and Foreign Policy* (New Delhi: Manas, 1975).

2. For a comprehensive history of Pakistani foreign policy from the viewpoint of a retired government officer, see S. M. Burke, *Pakistan's Foreign Policy: An Historical Analysis* (London: Oxford University Press, 1973). An American view is in William J. Barnds, *India, Pakistan, and the Great Powers* (New York: Praeger, 1972).

Indonesia and Egypt regarded Indian support as more effective and important. The Indian leadership was established and well known, and Pakistan found it difficult to compete with India for the attention of third-world states—even those that were entirely Muslim in population. The exceptions were Iran and Turkey. Iran was the source of much of Pakistan's Islamic culture, and Turkey was also a modernizing state dominated by the military; both were to join with Pakistan in CENTO.

Finally, Pakistan's alignment strategy was shaped by a lively dispute on its border with Afghanistan. Pakistan inherited a militarized and disputed border with Afghanistan, complicated by the presence of unruly tribal groups that straddle the border.[3] Moreover, just as Pakistan was encountering a competitive Indian presence in countries that it thought were its "natural" friends, it saw the emergence of an Afghan-Indian linkage. A sense of foreboding grew, as Pakistanis came to believe that Indian hostility had taken a new and ominous form. The turning point came in 1950–51, when the two countries were on the verge of war, and Pakistan saw that its military and political position vis-à-vis India was precarious. By 1951, therefore, Pakistan had begun actively to seek outside support. India had effectively blocked such support from the Commonwealth and the Muslim countries, and though Pakistan's relations with China were good, it had little to offer in the way of military hardware. This left the United States, and the apparent coincidence of interests ultimately led to a military association that was to last for fifteen years.

ALIGNMENT: 1953–65

Although the early negotiations with the United States took place while Harry Truman was President, the two countries did not formally enter into an alliance relationship until 1954. First came the Turco-Pakistan pact of February 19, 1954, in which Pakistan and Turkey declared their intention to study collaborative measures in a wide range of fields, including security policy. A few days later, Pakistan disclosed that it intended to seek American military assistance under the Mutual Security Act, and Eisenhower then publicly announced a favorable American response. A mutual-defense-assistance agreement was signed on May 19, 1954, although both governments declared that it did not establish a mili-

3. A partial survey of the border issue is provided by Sir Olaf Caroe, *The Pathans* (London: Macmillan, 1958; reprint ed., Union Book Stall, Karachi, 1973) and sources cited below in note 11.

tary "alliance" and would not provide for any military bases in Pakistan for the United States.

Later that year Pakistan became a member of the Southeast Asia Treaty Organization (SEATO) and the Baghdad Pact (later, CENTO). It joined CENTO with considerably more enthusiasm than it felt for SEATO because the former represented a special tie with some Islamic countries to the west. Furthermore, Pakistanis were far more concerned with Soviet than Chinese aggression. In both cases, there was no assurance that Pakistan would receive assistance in case of an attack from India. Although the American interest was in containing communism, and it regarded the Pakistanis as anti-Soviet, United States political relations with India continued to be good—and, indeed, India became the largest recipient of American economic assistance.

Faced with this ambivalent American policy, Pakistan pressed for further commitments. It received a clarification in the form of a U.S.-Pakistan cooperation agreement dated March 5, 1959. The United States committed itself to the "preservation of the independence and integrity of Pakistan," and agreed to take "appropriate action, including the use of armed force" in support of that goal. There was no public mention of India, but private assurances led Pakistan to believe that the United States would indeed support it in the event of an Indian attack. American officials now admit that such pledges were made but contend that they were not binding.

What were the consequences of these agreements? Externally, Pakistan lost ground in the nonaligned world and gradually came to boast that it was the "most allied" of American allies. Internally, the alliance relationship was greeted with mixed although generally positive feelings. Pakistan's military situation was desperate, and this was thought to be the only way in which it could be quickly rectified. There are grounds to believe that these ties with the United States enhanced the relative power of the military vis-a-vis an enfeebled civilian political elite; the military in fact negotiated some of the early agreements virtually on its own. Finally, the American tie had a profound effect on the military situation in South Asia. Between 1954 and 1965, Pakistan received over $630 million in direct American grant assistance and over $670 million in concessional sales and defense-support assistance.[4] This allowed it to build a small but fairly modern army of 300,000 to 400,000 troops, and a medium-sized air force (about 250 combat aircraft), thus precipitating an arms race with

4. See Stephen P. Cohen, "U.S. Weapons and South Asia: A Policy Analysis," *Pacific Affairs* 49, 1 (spring 1976): 49–69.

India and raising new fears in Afghanistan, which became entirely dependent upon the Soviet Union for military equipment by the 1960s.

RECONSIDERATIONS, 1963–71

When India and China fought a war in 1962, there were those in Pakistan who urged military action against India and the seizure of Kashmir. Ayub Khan demurred, hoping that the Indians would return to the bargaining table.[5] To his dismay they did not, and he then saw American, British, and Soviet equipment flow into India. Two of Pakistan's principal alliance partners were actively supporting its greatest enemy. A major reconsideration of these alliances took place as the credibility of the Western alliance partners came under severe attack.[6] Pakistan initiated the 1965 war with India—fearful that if it waited any longer, India would reach a position of commanding dominance—but the United States reacted by terminating its military programs to both India and Pakistan. A new American arms-transfer policy was considerably more restrictive, and in any case the United States had lost interest in the region as its involvement in Vietnam grew. The 1971 conflict with India was the turning point for most Pakistanis, for despite public support from Nixon and Kissinger (who were primarily concerned about the evolving United States relationship with China), there was virtually no material support as Pakistan was dismembered.

By 1972, Pakistan became a de facto nonaligned state. Most of its American military equipment was wearing out and it set about diversifying its arms sources. By the mid-1970s, Pakistan was receiving equipment from North Korea, China, Italy, West Germany, and even the Soviet Union. After a brief flirtation with the United States (including an offer by Zulfiqar Ali Bhutto of a full-scale alliance), Pakistan plunged ahead into the nonaligned movement.

The final break came in the late seventies when Pakistan was officially admitted to the Nonaligned movement after it left SEATO and CENTO. In addition, it has become one of the leaders of the pan-Islamic

5. Ayub's supporters defend his "honorable" inaction. Such a move would have had unpredictable military and political repercussions, and would have forever earned Pakistanis the label of "jackals," to be blamed for a "stab in the back" which "was not in our character," according to a former head of the Pakistan Artillery. See Maj.-Gen. Shaukat Riza (retd.), *Izzat-O-Iqbal: History of Pakistan Artillery, 1947–1971* (Nowshera: School of Artillery, 1980), p. 133.

6. Bhutto's own writings convey this reconsideration most effectively. See his *The Myth of Independence* (London: Oxford University Press, 1969).

movement. Pakistan has thus returned to something approaching its original foreign policy—nonalignment, with an Islamic orientation. It has yet to return to the Commonwealth (which Bhutto left in anger in 1972), because India has blocked reentry, but it does maintain good-to-cordial relations with a number of states. Pakistan receives economic assistance from Saudi Arabia and the Soviet Union and military equipment from China and the United States.

From being the most allied of allies, Pakistan prided itself from 1972 to 1980 on being the most nonaligned of the nonaligned. Yet its underlying strategic problems remain unchanged, and nonalignment is widely perceived as only marginally more effective than the old alignment policy. Pakistan elites are realistic enough to know that no major outside power will offer them the kind of commitment that would guarantee absolute security in an insecure world; indeed, they see nonalignment as permitting multiple relationships that enhance security; in President Zia's words, "We hope that we now have a trilateral strength from our association with China, our new relationship with the United States and our traditional relationship with other Islamic countries, headed by Saudi Arabia."[7]

To ensure that its nonaligned credentials remain intact, and to avoid putting too much weight upon any leg of the triad of support from China, the United States, and Saudi Arabia, Pakistan has so far been careful to avoid any public statement that implies the existence of a major external commitment in case of war. Even in the case of an assault on Pakistan by the Soviet Union, Pakistanis have acknowledged that they do not place much faith in the 1959 mutual-security treaty with the United States. They realistically assume that such an assault will be part of a broader conflict, or that the United States will be tied down elsewhere; therefore, one would have to be living "in a fool's paradise," to quote Zia, to believe that the United States "will come and fight our battle in the thick of affairs." Pakistanis insist that they will meet such a threat out of their own resources. Zia has also argued that involving the Americans in a land battle over Pakistan might get out of hand, and it might even be better for Pakistan to absorb such a Soviet attack, "to get a bit of a beating on the knuckles . . . rather than being an instigator of a third world war."[8] Such statements are designed to reassure Zia's domestic critics (who are concerned about dependence upon the United States), the Soviets (Pakistanis have publicly stated that understandings do exist between Pakistan and

7. Interview with President Zia ul-Haq, *Far Eastern Economic Review*, Oct. 16, 1981, p. 46.
8. Ibid.

the Soviet Union which rule out the prospect of a major attack on Pakistan), and the Americans, for one concern in the United States has been a too-close identification with Zia and a fear of being dragged into an unimportant regional conflict.

STRATEGIC ANALYSIS

Pakistan has one of the most complex security environments of any state in the world. To the east is India, a state with vastly superior industrial resources and a much larger population base;[9] to the west lies Afghanistan—never a friendly power but now occupied for the indefinite future by the Soviet Union. At home—the third front—there are important grievances that include dislike of military rule. Moreover, two of Pakistan's provinces have important populations with strong ethnic and tribal ties across the border in Afghanistan; even on the Indian frontier an unresolved dispute exists over the status of Jammu and Kashmir.[10] Domestic Pakistani politics remain intimately linked to political relations with Pakistan's neighbors; any analysis of threats to Pakistan's security must emphasize this overlap between internal and external problems. Additionally, many in the military raise questions about the loyalty of the country's intellectuals, poets, and professors to both Islam and the state of Pakistan. A fear held by some generals is that such ideologically "impure" groups may constitute a massive fifth column.

On the ground, specific conventional military threats have been identified. Whereas civilian strategists tend to treat states as abstract statistical entities, army staffs are taught to look first to geography and terrain. One senior general, closely associated with strategic planning, saw Pakistan's geo-military situation in these terms:

Ideally, a country is safe when it has a very large area but a very small frontier to defend; on the other hand, a country that has a small area but must defend its entire frontier is very precariously placed. And Pakistan happens to be in that difficult position [although not quite so severely as Israel, another officer interjects]. Although we have a large surface area we must defend our entire border, eleven hundred miles on the east and now [January 1980] an equal number of miles on the west, with Afghanistan and also an unstable Iran. And we have a

9. See Stephen P. Cohen and Richard L. Park, *India: Emergent Power?* (New York: Crane, Russak, 1978) and John W. Mellor, ed., *India: A Rising Middle Power* (Boulder: Westview, 1979).

10. The best study of the complex Kashmir issue remains that of Sisir Gupta, whose *Kashmir: A Study in India-Pakistan Relations* (Bombay: Asia Publishing House, 1966) is a humane and perceptive analysis.

coastline of almost five hundred miles to defend—then in the north we have a not very friendly neighbor [the U.S.S.R.]. So therefore, Pakistan finds itself in [such] a position that its geography forces it to defend almost every inch of its territory.

Moreover, the particular topography of Pakistan and the distribution of its population and lines of communication severely complicate the defense problem:

Pakistan is narrow, that is from north to south our lines of communication, our industrial centers, our towns, our major cities lie fairly close to a country [India] that is not very friendly with us, and with which we have a border that has no geographical impediments: no major river divides us, no high range of mountains separates us from our potential enemy. It is an area where tanks can roll easily, whether it be desert or the plains of Punjab. Our other borders are not quite so vulnerable, but they can be penetrated; even our seacoast is open.

Two major wars were fought over the Punjab-Sind-Rajasthan frontier; at its northern end is a cease-fire line that is suited to guerilla activity. Parts of the cease-fire line are observed rather ineffectively by a token United Nations presence that serves no real peacekeeping function. Pakistan's only port, Karachi, is close to the Indian frontier and can be attacked by land or air and be blockaded by any state with a moderate naval capability. To the west is the Durand Line, the historic frontier between British India and Afghanistan, which until recently was publicly challenged by the Afghan government.[11]

When military assistance to Pakistan was being publicly discussed in the United States in early 1980, it was often asserted that such assistance was useless because Pakistan was helpless in the face of the Soviet threat. In fact, this is not the view of the Pakistan military itself. It analyzes the threat from Afghan/Russian forces in the following way: (1) If for some reason the Soviet Union wanted to undertake a massive invasion of the North-West Frontier Province, there is little incentive for the Soviets to undertake an invasion that would lead them away from the strategic prize of the Persian Gulf. (2) A massive Soviet push through Baluchistan, toward either the Arabian Sea or Iran, would make somewhat more strategic sense but might precipitate American intervention whether or not there was a Pakistan-United States agreement; Pakistan itself could do little that would prevent the Soviets from attaining such an objective, but as in the case of point 1, above, it could (at considerable risk to itself)

---

11. The Durand Line is discussed in the context of Afghan history in Louis Dupree, *Afghanistan*, rev. ed. (Princeton: Princeton University Press, 1980). A detailed Pakistani study of legal aspects of the border is in Mujtaba Razvi, *The Frontiers of Pakistan* (Karachi-Dacca: National Publishing House, 1971).

resist with ground and air forces. (3) Far more containable would be direct Soviet or (Soviet-supported) Afghan attacks on refugee camps in Pakistan, some of which are within artillery range of Afghanistan and most of which could be struck by air or ground raids. Pakistan could not prevent such attacks, but it might do some damage to the attackers and retaliate upon support facilities in Afghanistan. It could also increase the flow of weapons to the Afghans, offer training to them, and allow Pakistani "volunteers" to join them, as the Indian Government allowed Indian Army personnel to join the Mukti Bahini. There is no evidence that Pakistan has done any of these things, but they could form part of a response to Soviet-Afghan pressure on Pakistan's highly permeable border. (4) Finally, there remains the possibility of long-range Soviet support for Baluchi and other tribal groups in their continuing struggle against the government of Pakistan.[12] Such a struggle could probably be contained by the present Pakistani government; if not, it might corrode the integrity of the state, its economic base, and the loyalty of most of its citizens.

Even before the rise of the Soviet threat, Pakistan planners had to assume that a conflict with India could develop very quickly, so quickly that there would not be time to raise new forces. Furthermore, because of the length and topography of the border, a small, even fast-moving mobile force would not be able to defend it. Unlike Israel in a confrontation with several Arab armies, it is improbable that Pakistan could strike in one place, defeat an Indian force, and then rapidly redeploy and strike elsewhere. It no longer has air superiority, it cannot raise new forces during the course of a short war, and its present army—though a strain on Pakistan's resources—is less than half the size of the Indian Army. Moreover, it would be impossible to move large numbers of troops from north to south during a war without considerable improvement in road and rail transport and the assurance of freedom of movement. The problem is insurmountable when one considers the possibility of simultaneous pressure on the Afghan frontier. Even the British never expected the Indian Army to hold out against a hypothetical Russian or German invasion of Baluchistan or the N.W.F.P., and imperial strategy assumed that the Indian Army would only delay the enemy until British forces arrived.[13]

12. See Caroe, *The Pathans*, for a short discussion of the Baluchis; several of the papers in Ainslie T. Embree, *Pakistan's Western Borderlands* (New Delhi: Vikas, 1977) include a brief discussion of the Baluchis; the most comprehensive account is by Selig S. Harrison, *In Afghanistan's Shadow: Baluch Nationalism and Soviet Temptations* (New York: Carnegie Endowment, 1981), which has been highly praised by Baluchi leaders themselves.

13. For the texts of various contingency plans see Historical Section (India and Pakistan), Official History of the Indian Armed Forces in the Second World War, *Defense of*

When this defense problem is considered from the perspective of a military staff, it is clear that something must give way. A number of responses have recently been discussed publicly and privately: (1) Pakistan has tried to acquire new conventional weapons, especially high-performance aircraft and armor, and is trying to manufacture some of these itself, with limited success on both counts. (2) The idea of a militia, or lightly armed defense force, to defend large amounts of territory at low cost has been revived. (3) Privately, some generals will seriously discuss the possibility of rapprochement with one or more of Pakistan's more dangerous neighbors, even the Soviet Union, in order to reduce the threat of a two-front war. (4) Nuclear weapons are often talked about as a possible substitute for conventional defense forces.

STRATEGIC STYLE

The preparation of strategic doctrine in Pakistan closely resembles an attempt to hit numerous moving targets from a moving vehicle. But the capacity of the state itself to respond to such threats has drastically changed within a short time. For example, in 1965, the decision not to defend East Pakistan was reaffirmed and only token forces were stationed there; this neglect of East Bengal contributed to growing separatism in that province, but the units necessary to control that separatism could not be released from West Pakistan because the Indian military continued to pose a threat there. Another example: Pakistan is faced with the prospect of incursions along the Durand Line but cannot risk a massive transfer of forces to its western frontier for fear of leaving its border with India open to attack. Yet it must not run the risk of allowing incursions to occur just now because of the relatively weak political position of the military in the country; one major military defeat might mean the end for those responsible for strategic planning. In both of these cases Pakistan did not (or does not) have the resources to enable it to fight a two-front war, yet there were (and are) compelling political reasons to prevent it from redefining the strategic threat so that it would not have to fight such a war; one of these was and is the hope that outside powers will provide substantial military assistance to Pakistan (or, in the case of China, create a two-front problem for India), but even this outside support is unreliable and unpredicta-

---

India: Policy and Plans (n.p.: Combined Inter-Services Historical Section, distributed by Orient Longmans, 1963).

ble. Despite Pakistan's essential strategic dilemma—it is a big enough state to play the game, but not big enough to win—it has evolved a strategic style. The main components of that style, which has remained remarkably consistent over the years, are outlined below.

Given Pakistan's size, location, and the terrain along its eastern border with India, its strategists have always been attracted to the doctrine of the "offensive defense." That is, in time of heightening crisis Pakistan has not hesitated to be the first to employ the heavy use of force in order to gain an initial advantage. This was clearly the pattern in 1965 and possibly in 1971; in both cases it was thought that a short, sharp war would achieve Pakistan's military as well as political objectives. However, in view of India's larger territory and population, this strategy has always assumed the availability of high-performance armor and aircraft and superior generalship. Looking at a map, it is easy to see why Pakistanis have always been reluctant to adopt a strategy of trading space for time.

Secondly, Pakistan has usually regarded war as an opportunity to bring longstanding conflicts to the attention of the international community and to mobilize its friends in the Islamic world and fellow alliance members (and more recently, the People's Republic of China). Over the years, however, the world has grown tired of Indians and Pakistanis shooting at each other. Pakistan cannot count on anyone caring much about a new war with India, and at the same time its ability to avoid defeat at the hands of the Indians has been sharply reduced. War for political purposes now represents an enormous risk to the survival of the state.

A third component of Pakistani strategic doctrine has been deterrence of an Indian attack. In recent years this has become the dominant theme of Pakistani defense planners, for they realize that the risk of initiating war becomes greater. In the words of one major-general responsible for defense planning, "The posture that we have decided to adopt is a policy of 'strategic defense.' You can call it a policy of deterrence or whatever, but it is our policy to maintain adequate armed forces to insure that our territorial integrity and independence is assured." And a brigadier interjected,

We think that we have a threat from India—we may be wrong but that is what we think. To meet that, what we must have is a minimum force which would be a deterrent. Now to maintain that, we have a problem of financing it, it affects our economic needs. But we want to be in a position where no adventurist feels that he is attracted to our side.

To put it bluntly, some Pakistanis hope to kill as many Indian soldiers as they can, raising the cost of an Indian attack to unacceptable levels.

In view of the Soviet occupation of Afghanistan, Pakistani strategists have now begun to develop a strategic doctrine to deal with various kinds and levels of threats from the west. As we indicated above, present force levels are adequate to deal with insurgency and limited probes by conventional Afghan forces across the border. No forces would be adequate, however, to deal with a major Soviet thrust backed by the threat of nuclear attack on troop concentrations or urban areas. Pakistan is forced to play a very dangerous game, that of maintaining enough of a military presence to deal with (and thus deter) limited probes, but not so large a force that the Soviets would fear Pakistani intervention on behalf of the Mujahiddin or that units facing India would be depleted.

Two different kinds of strategic responses have been widely debated in Pakistan and must be noted here. One, the nuclear option, will be examined below. The other grows out of three military traditions, all of them familiar to the Pakistan Army.[14] This may be termed a "people's guerilla war." It argues that instead of relying for deterrence and defense upon very expensive and very high-technology weapons, nuclear or conventional, Pakistan should train and arm its population so that any invader would be unable to occupy the country. The cost of victory would be so great that such an invader would have to retreat or would be deterred from attacking at the beginning. A variation on this people's guerilla war involves a more activist strategy: train and arm friendly populations in the territory of your enemy, tying him down in a hundred places.[15]

Pakistanis are taught at Quetta that only certain kinds of states can have an effective "people's" army. "The effectiveness of such forces," in tne view of Staff College lecturers, "is directly related to an ideological orientation and social solidarity such as only China and North Vietnam can boast of in modern times, and India cannot." India is too diverse, its population too divided, to sustain such a force effectively; Pakistan is socially diverse, but its population does have a common bond in Islam, and Pakistanis therefore believe that their territorial forces will stand a good chance of being effective, at least as a second line of resistance or as a local guard force.

However, all-out people's guerilla war is unlikely to be favored by the current military leadership of Pakistan.[16] It had been tried earlier in Kash-

14. These include American Special Forces training given to many Pakistanis, recent Chinese doctrine on people's war, and the two-thousand-year-old tradition of tribal guerilla war that exists in Pakistan's North West Frontier Province and Baluchistan.
15. The boldest statement of this strategy is in Akbar Khan, *Raiders in Kashmir*, 2d ed. (Islamabad: National Book Foundation, 1975).
16. Although Zia has been reported as having considered "a massive increase in the size of the country's armed forces to create a people's army on the Chinese model," others have

mir and was not successful. Whether this was due to the unwarlike character of the Kashmiris or to poor planning is not clear. What is certain is that the military of Pakistan favors regular, conventional formations, except for light patrol and police work in the tribal areas. Further, it is highly unlikely that a relatively unpopular regime will risk the widespread distribution of small arms and explosives to its own population. Finally, Pakistanis have the terrible example of Afghanistan before their eyes. The Afghans have a proud and ancient martial tradition, but this has merely slowed down the Soviet military machine; the price of their resistance is fearful. Would a Pakistani accommodation—even with the Indians—be preferable to invasion?

The strategic choices open to Pakistan never were extremely attractive and are now increasingly risky and limited in number. It would be suicidal for the Pakistan Army to provoke a confrontation with the Indian forces today; even managing limited incursions from the Indian or Afghan frontier runs great risks of escalation; above all, there remains the possibility of active Indian-Soviet cooperation, based on the 1971 treaty of friendship, which would place Pakistan in a hopeless strategic position. As one distinguished retired general phrases it: "I have eaten many chicken sandwiches, but this is the first time I have ever realized what it is like to be the chicken." However, an assessment of Pakistan's strategic problem is not complete without taking into account two additional factors: the weapons and manpower that Pakistan is able to devote to its defense.

FORCE LEVELS AND DISPOSITION

A brief examination of Pakistan's defense effort further clarifies the strategic dilemma of that state. The numbers and quality of weapons held by the Pakistan military are determined by factors largely beyond its control: the attitudes of weapons suppliers and of financial supporters and the slow growth rate of the Pakistani arms industry. The actual disposition of forces was severely limited by geography even before the 1980 Soviet invasion of Afghanistan; that event has complicated even the simplest defense task. We shall consider the geo-military problem and take note of Pakistan's arms-production capabilities in the context of a discussion of allies and arms suppliers.

---

expressed doubt as to whether such a mass army might not be too expensive. See Reuters dispatch from Islamabad, reprinted in *India Abroad*, Aug. 29, 1980, for Zia's ambivalent remarks, and the 1981 speech by Agha Shahi (then Foreign Minister) before a Pakistani audience, explaining that a mass army would cost too much.

When the British ruled South Asia, the old Indian army had four major tasks. One was internal security: large numbers of troops were stationed in cantonments situated outside major population centers. Another task was to patrol the long (and sometimes undefined) frontier of India. Thirdly, the military was used intermittently as an expeditionary force. The battleflags of Indian and Pakistani Army units even today bear the names of such places as Cassino, Peking, Lhasa, Basra, El Alamein, Burma, Saigon, and Japan. And fourthly, the Indian Army maintained a series of forts and posts in the northwest, and engaged in a number of campaigns, the purpose of which was to check an advancing Russian Empire.

With some modifications, the Pakistan military today still carries out internal security, border patrol, and expeditionary tasks. The last now takes the shape of service by thousands of officers and men as pilots, gunners, advisors, and training cadres in a number of foreign military establishments, especially in the Middle East. But the military has, in effect, given up the task of checking Russian/Soviet advances in exchange for a new role, that of preparing for conventional ground war against India. Most of the Pakistan Army's four hundred thousand soldiers and approximately 900 tanks are dedicated to the long border with India. Conflict clearly exists between the self-image of the Pakistan military as the legatee of the British side in the "Great Game" of Central Asian politics, balancing out the Russians, and the reality of Pakistani troop dispositions. There is also a substantive reason for that conflict, in that Pakistan, in 1947–48, could not afford to maintain a far-flung and costly series of forts (much less challenge the Soviets in Afghanistan or elsewhere) without the complete backing of a major power, and at the same time defend itself against India.

Consequently, Pakistan's main-line forces, organized into approximately twenty divisions, grouped into six corps, largely face east, not west. One corps, based in Peshawar, probably has two infantry divisions; another, in Quetta, is in the process of formation; but four major corps (containing most of Pakistan's armor) face the Indian Army in the east.

The troops that actually patrol the border, especially along the Afghan frontier and in Kashmir, are usually not regular army units but belong to one of several special formations. Units such as the Mohmand Scouts, the Pishin Scouts, and the Khyber Rifles are raised from local tribes but are officered by regular Pakistan Army officers on deputation. They are quite small in numbers, but effectively combine Kiplingesque romanticism, light weapons, and mobility of foot. Because of their local ties, their actual use is a serious political as well as military question—they may be fighting their own kinsmen. Yet when they are used it is often seen as a "local" matter; their presence is considerably more acceptable than that of regular Pakistan Army units that may be drawn from distant provinces. These scouts thus stand somewhere between the regular army and local-police units, with some of the firepower of the former and the local contacts and mobility of the latter.

As we have noted, there are special topographical problems associated with the defense of Pakistan. Lahore and the main north-south railway, canal, and road systems are very close to India and must be protected at all costs with static formations. Pakistan's only port, Karachi, is 800 miles from Islamabad, and far from the likely scene of major combat in Kashmir and the Punjab. The two most rebellious provinces, Baluchistan and the N.W.F.P., do not have well-developed road or rail systems (except for the Khyber-Peshawar area). Quetta (the capital of Baluchistan) is screened by a number of small mountain ranges, although it does have rail connections. But the rest of Baluchistan is both inaccessible and inhospitable. The army cannot count on quickly moving units around Pakistan during a major crisis. New threats—such as that from the Afghan border—require new units, and Pakistan would probably like to form several new divisions dedicated to the Durand Line.

Before 1980 the Pakistan Air Force was entirely oriented toward the Indian border.[17] The situation is now transformed. Most of Pakistan's major military airfields were placed well back from the Indian border; this now means that they are very close to the Afghan frontier and major Afghan military airports. Published reports indicate that the Soviet Union has introduced a large number of aircraft and missiles into Afghanistan, supplementing aircraft already supplied to the Afghan Air Force. Some of these aircraft are less than a minute's flying time from Pakistan, and the Pakistan Air Force (PAF) finds itself vulnerable to a surprise attack from the west. It must assume that if there were to be major Soviet or Afghan incursions into Pakistan—in hot pursuit of Afghan tribesmen or for purposes of harassment—PAF airfields would be under attack. This led the PAF to generate a minimal requirement for improved advance-warning and SAM systems and substantial numbers of new high-performance aircraft to enable it to meet and counter regular intrusions by Soviet or Afghan MiG 21s and other aircraft. Much of the American arms-sales program developed in 1981 by the Reagan administration is geared to meet this request.

17. The most complete description of PAF history and operations is in John Fricker, *Battle for Pakistan: The Air War of 1965* (London: Ian Allen, 1979), which was written with the cooperation of senior PAF officers.

WEAPONS ACQUISITION

This discussion of the possible expansion of the army and air force brings us to one of the central constraints on the Pakistan military—its dependence upon outside sources for weapons.

Pakistan is a very large country and possesses a substantial pool of educated, trained manpower, but it cannot manufacture a crankshaft.[18] Pakistan became completely dependent upon the United States in the 1950s for all major and most minor kinds of equipment, and it was not until 1965, when American arms transfers were practically terminated, that Pakistanis began to think seriously about building up an indigenous arms industry. Since 1965 there has been considerable progress in that direction, largely with Chinese and French help, but Pakistan is still dependent for new tanks, armored personnel carriers (APCs), aircraft of all kinds, soft-skinned vehicles, artillery, electronics, radar, fire-control systems, and many other items. Pakistan does produce virtually all of its light-infantry weapons (the excellent G-3 rifle and a machine gun, both built under West German license), and most ammunition, shells, explosives, and mortars, and it has recently acquired the capacity to completely rebuild and reconstruct its 700 Chinese-supplied T-59 tanks and French Mirage III aircraft. It will soon be able to rebuild the Chinese F-6 (MiG 19) aircraft and it can perform major repairs of most of its heavy armored vehicles.[19]

Inasmuch as a number of these projects are geared to an international market (the Mirage rebuild facility expects to handle aircraft from all over the Middle East and Asia), it can be said that Pakistan belongs to the category of "intermediate" arms supplier. It must acquire the most advanced equipment from others, yet it is capable of supplying simpler arms. Some of these projects having been bankrolled by Saudi Arabia and other Arab states, there is some truth in the claim that Pakistan hopes to become the arsenal of the Islamic world. This, however, is a long-term project, fraught with difficulties and risks, and Pakistan cannot wait until it develops an indigenous capacity to manufacture high-performance weapons. For these it must turn to the commercial international arms market or its friends.

18. According to Lt.-Gen. Abdul Hamid Khan (retd.), "Organization for Defense," Na-wai-Waqt, Lahore, Apr. 10–11, 1979. However, Pakistan has been able to manufacture a number of military items for several years, including the excellent 106 mm. recoilless rifle, an American design.

19. The F-6 and tank-rebuild facilities are being provided by the PRC; the Mirage rebuild facility is French-supplied but is paid for by Pakistan; the repair facilities of the Pakistan Army have been built up over the years, with a major American contribution in the 1950s.

Both have proven to be uncertain sources. The Chinese are regarded in Pakistan as reliable, tactful, and steadfast, although there has been concern about both the quality of equipment they can supply and its future level. China is itself seeking assistance in defense technology from a number of Western states, and Pakistan does not want to wait for this to "trickle down." The French have sold Mirage aircraft and other technology to Pakistan, but have insisted on cash payments; more recently, there has been a shift in French interests in South Asia, and in 1982 they concluded a major sale of advanced fighters to India.[20] That country may insist that the French limit sales to Pakistan as one condition for its own purchases. The Soviet Union once provided a hundred T-55 tanks to Pakistan, but demanded a settlement of the Kashmir issue as the price of further assistance. The United States, of course, has twice cut off Pakistan from arms purchases (in 1965 and 1979), and it maintained a restrictive sales policy from 1967 onward; only the invasion of Afghanistan brought about a change in American policy. The Carter administration sold Pakistan some ships and other equipment, but it was not until the Reagan administration took office that a major program was developed.

The military component of the Reagan package had two parts. One provided for the sale of $1.55 billion worth of armor and support equipment.[21] There was little public objection to this part of the package, even from the Indian government. The latter concentrated its opposition on the separate sale of forty F-16 Hornet aircraft and their spare parts and repair facilities. American Congressional and academic critics objected that the F-16 was unnecessarily provocative, because it has an excellent long-range ground-attack capability as well as an air-defense capability.[22] They reasoned that a detuned F-16 or the Northrop F-5G would provide adequate air defense without enabling Pakistan to attack Bombay, Delhi,

20. The Indian and French governments have initialed an agreement for the purchase and eventual manufacture of France's latest fighter-bomber aircraft, the Mirage 2000.

21. In addition to the forty F16s, the United States has promised the following items: one hundred M48 A5 tanks, thirty-five M88A1 recovery vehicles, twenty M109A2 self-propelled howitzers, forty M110A2 8″ self-propelled howitzers, seventy-five M198 towed howitzers, and ten AH-1S attack helicopters. Pakistan did not seek the more modern M-60 tank because of its weight and because it already had a number of M48 tanks in its inventory. In addition, it has received at least four destroyers, optimized for antisubmarine operations. A separate economic agreement provided credits and loans at concessional interest rates for a five-year period; the military component of the package provides some credit, but at commercial levels (about 14 percent), hardly a bargain. Both programs must receive annual congressional approval; their future is in doubt if Pakistan should detonate a nuclear device, as restrictive clauses have been written into the legislation.

22. James L. Buckley, then Under Secretary of State for Security Assistance, presented the outline of the agreement in testimony before the House Committee on Foreign Affairs on Sept. 16, 1981; critical and supportive witnesses appeared on Sept. 22 and 23, 1981.

or other major Indian cities. Moreover, the F-16 has a capability for the delivery of nuclear weapons.

Although the technical qualities of the F-16 are important, the larger problem is political. In the Indian view, such a weapon symbolizes a broader American commitment to support Pakistan, and in turn postpones the day when Pakistan will accept its status of relative inferiority. Furthermore, it may induce Pakistan to reopen the Kashmir issue. From the Pakistani standpoint, the F-16 and other items of American equipment barely restore their military credibility. They insist that genuine peace cannot exist between Pakistan and India unless Pakistan has the ability to defend itself against the much larger Indian military machine; because Pakistan now has a live frontier with Afghanistan, its overall military position has suffered, whatever new equipment it may receive.

These positions are not irreconcilable, but it is evident that because of the impending nuclearization of the South Asian region the stakes are much higher now than they were in 1954, and America's store of goodwill in both India and Pakistan is nearly exhausted. It is an open question whether the new mutual dependencies that will be created between the United States and Pakistan as a result of this major program will in the long run enhance or weaken Pakistan's security.[23]

THE NUCLEAR OPTION[24]

The military in Pakistan does not like nuclear weapons—no soldier really likes them. A few active and retired generals have spoken and written in opposition to a Pakistani nuclear program; most have come to accept with varying degrees of enthusiasm the idea of a nuclear weapon. Pakistan did not embark upon a nuclear-weapons program without some consideration of the relevance of such weapons to the security environment of the state. Zulfiqar Ali Bhutto had long been an advocate of a Pakistani nuclear option (that is, a civilian program which could be con-

23. See Stephen P. Cohen, "Pakistan and America: The Security Dimension," *Defense Journal* 7, 8 (Karachi, 1981): 7–11.

24. I have dealt with this issue at greater length in *Perception, Influence and Weapons Proliferation in South Asia* (Washington: U.S. State Department, Bureau of Intelligence and Research, Contract No. 1722-920184), August 1979. A number of perceptive articles on nuclear strategy and theory are to be found in various Pakistani military journals. For an indignant Indian view, see Maj.-Gen. D.K. Palit (retd.) and P.K.S. Namboodiri, *Pakistan's Islamic Bomb* (New Delhi: Vikas, 1979). A more balanced approach is made in Zalmay Khalilzad, "Pakistan and the Bomb," *Survival*, November/December, 1979, pp. 244–50, and a detailed British analysis is contained in the BBC program, "The birth of the Islamic bomb" (transcript distributed by the New York Times Syndication Sales Corporation, 1980).

verted to military ends), but it was not until 1974 that the military seriously addressed itself to the strategic implications of an Indian—and then a Pakistani—nuclear weapon. It was then asked by Bhutto to explore the military implications of nuclear proliferation in 1974, although evidence exists that plans for a nuclear program began before that date. The army's analysis includes the following major points.

First, it assumes Indian possession of several nuclear weapons, or at least the capacity to "go nuclear" quickly (no published Western report has verified this). Secondly, Pakistanis believe that such Indian weapons are directed primarily against them, not China. They ridicule the idea of India catching up with the Chinese or that there are any serious grounds for an India-China conflict. Thirdly, if Pakistan is the target, then the Indian bomb must have a military as well as a political rationale. They generally see it as enabling Indian conventional forces to seize the rest of Kashmir from Pakistan or even to dismember all of Pakistan; nuclear weapons held in reserve as a threat against Lahore, Karachi, Islamabad, and other vital targets would effectively paralyze Pakistan and make it unable to resist. Fourthly, such strategists conclude, a modest, "limited" Pakistani weapons program is essential to deter India's nuclear forces. Taking their lead from Indian writers on the subject, the Pakistanis have observed that the only time nuclear weapons have been actually used was when the enemy did not have them. Fifth, possession of nuclear weapons not only deterred a nuclear attack, but (referring to the NATO example) was an effective deterrent against conventional attack.

Some Pakistani and many Indian strategists argue that such a Pakistani bomb, besides neutralizing an assumed Indian nuclear force, would provide the umbrella under which Pakistan could reopen the Kashmir issue. A Pakistani nuclear capability would paralyze not only the Indian nuclear decision, but also Indian conventional forces, and a bold Pakistani strike to liberate Kashmir might go unchallenged if Indian leadership was indecisive. To a lesser extent, such a nuclear force might enhance Pakistan's deterrent along the Durand Line. A major incursion into Pakistan could trigger a Pakistani nuclear response, directed against "purely military" targets in Afghanistan or the Soviet Union. The weight of these arguments has led Pakistan to pursue the acquisition of fissile material through both the reprocessing and enrichment routes, and perhaps other channels.

Those Pakistanis who have thought about nuclear proliferation generally believe that although the rapid spread of nuclear weapons is not necessarily in Pakistan's interests, it does not threaten those interests, because the states most likely to confront Pakistan already either have nuclear weapons or are capable of acquiring them. Nor did the behavior of Pakistan's allies do much to challenge the obvious implications of this analysis: China had long refused to transfer nuclear technology and subscribed to a doctrine of self-reliance in nuclear matters; the American government at first seemed to ignore the Indian explosion but then turned its fury upon both India and Pakistan for failing to sign the Non-Proliferation Treaty (NPT). It was in any case unwilling to provide conventional weapons to Pakistan in sufficient numbers to balance an Indian nuclear capacity (there is some question whether any quantity of arms can—in the view of most Pakistani officers—balance a nuclear weapon in Indian hands).

The Pakistanis apparently reached the same conclusion that most other states would reach when faced with a growing conventional military imbalance, domestic disorder, and shaky allies. A small nuclear program would enable them to do in nuclear terms what their armored divisions and air force do in conventional terms: punish an Indian attack so severely that it would be deterred at the start. And the bonus is that such deterrence would work against a massive conventional attack as well. One does not have to be an Indian strategist to calculate also that a Pakistani bomb might enable Pakistan to reopen the Kashmir issue by the threat of force: if nuclear weapons deter each other they may also inhibit direct military conflict between states that possess them; a Pakistani leadership that was bold enough could attack and seize Kashmir at a time when India was in disarray. Pakistani analysts make the opposite case: an Indian government could do the same to a weak Pakistan.[25]

Possession of the bomb will entangle both India and Pakistan in an endless series of calculations of "if I do this, he will do that, and I shall have to respond, so why don't I move first?" But in the present state of bilateral nuclear options, the same calculations are necessarily carried out, and this has served to increase the pressure within the two governments to go ahead with military nuclear programs as insurance against the other side. India's situation is complicated by the existence of a Chinese nuclear force, part of which could be targeted on India itself. The fact that a Pakistani nuclear weapon would probably lead to an Indian one is not in itself a sufficient barrier for Pakistani officers; they have not fully

---

25. Pakistani and Indian strategists are also aware of Western arguments that nuclear weapons have, indeed, prevented a general war from breaking out between the United States and the Soviet Union, and that they have probably kept the Russians from invading Western Europe. Those strategists ask why—if Bernard Brodie, McGeorge Bundy, and others can justify American possession of nuclear weapons in these terms—a state in a far more vulnerable position cannot acquire "just a few" nuclear weapons.

thought through the strategic balance of forces that would result from unlimited proliferation in South Asia, but they do not think that it would be more disadvantageous than the present situation (in which they assume that India already has a covert nuclear capacity). If Indians find this conclusión to be in error, they must privately reassure the Pakistan government in whatever way that will be convincing.

To sum up, there are extremely persuasive strategic reasons for Pakistan to go ahead with a military nuclear program, even if the political, diplomatic, and economic cost is substantial. Assuming that Pakistan is going to acquire a nuclear weapon, can we speculate on its strategic role? There has been some interesting discussion of this question in Pakistan recently, and a few remarks can be offered.

As in the case of India, Pakistani nuclear planners will have the choice of utilizing their nuclear force for tactical or strategic ends. That is, nuclear devices can be used against massed troop concentrations or can be dropped on urban populations as sheer terror weapons. Given the nature of both economies, there are also various targets that are of an ambivalent character. These would include major power-production centers, dams, and irrigation projects; none of these would directly cause much loss of life—according to preliminary studies—and would thus not be "provocative" in the way that destruction of urban areas would be; but such attacks might in the long run cause more loss of life.[26]

Such writing as does exist on the subject seems to indicate that Pakistani strategists favor the most dramatic (but realistically the most conservative) use of nuclear weapons. We have discussed this at length earlier in the context of a discussion of Islam and strategic doctrine. Nuclear weapons are "terror" weapons *par excellence*. There is no need to use them; mere possession is enough to ward off the threat; the Quran and modern deterrence theory neatly dovetail. Such a strategy would also simplify the command and control problem of Pakistan and would require the minimum number of weapons. Accuracy and timing not being crucial, it would also simplify targeting and delivery requirements. If proliferation does come to the subcontinent, it is possible that both India and Pakistan would adopt such deterrence-cum-terror strategies at first, and later, when a stockpile of fissionable material is developed, consider diverting some of this stockpile to produce a few "tactical" nuclear weapons. This could well happen if Pakistan felt that it was falling farther behind in its conventional arms imbalance with India, and that its stockpile of "strategic" weapons was not adequate to deter a conventional war.

26. This is the conclusion of one informal study at the University of Illinois.

All of this is grim, but Pakistanis are not necessarily irresponsible for engaging in such calculations. It is the melancholy duty of the professional soldier to think of such things. Nor is there much substance in the charge that Pakistan is somehow a candidate for "crazy" status—that it would irresponsibly detonate nuclear weapons or that it would transfer them to areas of the world where they would probably be used. The military of Pakistan have done self-destructive things in the past, and it cannot be assumed that they will not do them in the future. But I believe that the Pakistan Army has done much to rebuild its professional character; it is not likely that it will make such decisions in the future any more irresponsibly than any other state confronted with the same perplexing set of security constraints.

If a Pakistani bomb has some relevance to the threat of India, how relevant is it to Pakistan's new hot frontier with Afghanistan or to the turmoil of domestic politics? The same reasoning that applies to a hypothetical Indian attack upon Pakistan may be relevant to a hypothetical Soviet-Afghan attack. Pakistan would be no match for an all-out attack, nor would nuclear weapons be of much practical use, but they might contribute something to the deterrent force at work, and they could also serve as a plausible substitute for several new divisions. Pakistan would not be threatening the Soviet Union itself, but only a neighbor acting with clear hostile intent. Given the vulnerability of Pakistan, such a threat might be as credible as an Israeli "Masada" bomb. But there is a rub.

If Pakistan were in such dire straits that it actually contemplated the use of a nuclear weapon against an attacking enemy, it might have already lost the military edge that would allow it to deliver such a weapon upon enemy targets. If confronted with the Soviet Air Force (or even the Indian Air Force), not to speak of a combination of the two, could a handful of PAF nuclear-capable aircraft survive an initial attack or penetrate fully alerted and hostile air-defense screens?[27] Pakistan might well find its nuclear force both provocative and ineffective.

A Pakistani nuclear weapon would be greeted with widespread support at home (it is practically the only issue that Pakistanis do agree on), but there is some doubt that it will help any regime that does build, test, and deploy it. This is the "life-insurance" facet of nuclear weapons; as the

27. This point is raised by Jeffrey Kemp in the context of a hypothetical Israeli last-ditch nuclear retaliation, in "A Nuclear Middle East," in John Kerry King, *International Political Effects of the Spread of Nuclear Weapons.* Some Western analysts who have studied the problem conclude that if a Pakistani nuclear force survived a conventional air attack it would be unstoppable, especially if it flew north or west through mountainous territory.

Indians discovered a number of years ago—and as all other nuclear powers found out earlier—nonpossession creates some unease and public anxiety, but possession barely returns the needle to normal.

Our analysis of Pakistan's nuclear program indicates that it is actuated by many motives. The most important of these are survival of regime and state, but other factors include considerations of national prestige, nuclear weapons as "bargaining chips" with friend and enemy alike, and the near-unanimous support for the nuclear program among Pakistanis of all political persuasions. If any outside state wishes to influence the Pakistani decision eventually to "go nuclear," it must understand that proliferation in South Asia is a complex affair. It is not an event as much as a process; the process does not end with a test detonation, let alone the acquisition of special nuclear material. Nor is more necessarily less; at certain force levels—should the region become nuclearized—relations between South Asian states and between the region and external powers may become more rather than less stable. And this proliferation process is not casual. States seek nuclear weapons (and other weapons as well) because of the pressures of technology, the presence of an action-reaction syndrome (an arms race), their relevance to a search for status and symbolic gratification, and their utility as instruments of policy and strategic discourse.

To deal effectively with the proliferation process of South Asia, and to enable the states of South Asia to deal with more basic threats to their security, such as slow rates of economic development, the unequal distribution of wealth, and political disorder, more is required than quick fixes. The best strategy for dealing with nuclear proliferation may not be the best possible strategy if it triggers a conventional war.

The irony is that the "best strategy" devised by nonregional states (especially the United States) to deal with the proliferation problem may also have increased rather than decreased the rate of proliferation. An effective antiproliferation strategy for South Asia would have to identify the minimum-security requirements of both India and Pakistan; it would also have to treat the nuclear issue as part of the security calculation of regional states, and not try to eradicate it.

The most effective approach would be one that assists regional states in isolating South Asia (or what remains of it, after the Soviet Union has finished its task in Afghanistan) from superpower conflict and simultaneously settles major regional disputes. If these can be dealt with at the negotiating table rather than on the battlefield, much of the concern about the "threat" of Pakistan to India, of India to Pakistan, and of China to India will be dissipated. The states involved can move toward their own version of a regional peace agreement and devote their resources to their only permanent enemy: domestic disorder, poverty, and low growth rates. Pakistani arms can be left at a level sufficient to deter the unlikely straight-on Soviet or Indian attack but not so large that it would enable Pakistan to carry out a successful attack on India. There is an upper limit of arms which Pakistan need not cross, for to do so would be threatening to India; but there is an important lower limit. Below this mix of numbers, quality, and tactical disposition Pakistan cannot fall; India and Pakistan must jointly determine these upper and lower limits. The role of outsiders in such an effort might be to help fill in those gaps and deficiencies so as to strengthen the security of both states. Pakistanis may have to reconcile themselves to second-rank regional status, but India cannot expect Pakistan to effectively disarm and assume the status of a Sri Lanka or a Bangladesh.

A regional settlement leading to a balanced imbalance of conventional arms must necessarily deal with the nuclear problem. It may be that the states most directly involved are willing to live with neighbors that can quickly cross the nuclear threshold; if this did not imply proliferation to other regions there is no reason for the United States and other powers not to endorse such an agreement and strengthen it with material inducements, including jointly controlled energy-generating facilities.[28]

CONCLUSION

Pakistan is the only former colonial state that has been divided by war. The successors to the military regime that governed at the time are aware that neither the international nor the domestic environment has improved since 1971. Pakistan is now flanked by the Soviet Union and India; three million Afghan refugees have crossed the Durand Line, and more are on the way; and Pakistan's international friends do not match their verbal encouragement with material support. In terms of equipment the military was in relatively poorer shape in 1980 than it was in 1971; politically, it is even more unpopular, and there appears to be no civilian leadership capable of assuming power. Moreover, ethnic, regional, religious, economic, professional, and class groups periodically express their unhappiness

28. This was suggested by David E. Lilienthal just before his death in 1981. An attempt to project four strategic futures for South Asia and to suggest a way to pursue the most desirable course is in Stephen P. Cohen, "India, South Asia, and the Superpowers: War and Society," in Paul Wallace, ed., *Region and Nation in India* (forthcoming) and Stephen P. Cohen, "Prospects in South Asia: How to Promote Cooperation," *Times of India*, December 12, 1982.

with continued military rule. It is widely perceived as incompetent, and some in the military feel that it may be damaging to the army itself. A few Pakistanis and foreigners do not believe that Pakistan will survive in its present form beyond this decade. Pakistan faces the unenviable prospect of becoming a latter-day Poland, partitioned out of existence.

Without underestimating the possibility that civil war, revolution, external invasion, or some other calamity may lead to another dismemberment of Pakistan, certain factors may enable Pakistan to surmount its present crisis. First, though it is not popular, the military leadership is not irrational and is aware of the predicament that it is in. Zia and other generals have encouraged debate, discussion, and criticism within the military, although they have not always allowed civilians to speak their minds. They are painfully aware of the technical shortcomings of the military, of the regional dominance of India, of the ruthlessness of the Russians, and of the unreliability of their American ex-allies. Nor do they think that the Islamic world, not to mention the nonaligned movement, will do very much to help them. They hold the stark but realistic view that they must rely upon their own resources and keep on their own path at a moment of great peril. But this path is not immediately apparent to anyone, Pakistani or non-Pakistani.

If, as seems most likely, the military continues in power in Pakistan or retains a veto over security-related decisions, there is not likely to be a major change in the present strategic style. That style represents a consensus within the military hierarchy itself, and it is improbable that there will be a change in Pakistan's attempts to maintain a conventional retaliatory capacity (in the form of armor, air support, and mobile infantry) to crush an invader or make his attack more costly. Yet Pakistan finds it difficult to create and maintain expensive armor units, it cannot produce its own high-performance aircraft, and it must commit large forces to the static defense of major urban areas and lines of communication. Increasingly, the strategy of deterrence is stretched thinner and thinner, and it may lose credibility altogether. One "solution" for Pakistan may be the acquisition of nuclear weapons. They serve the purpose of forcing the enemy out of massed concentrations on the ground and may be used in a punishment strategy. However, nuclear weapons are hardly attractive to the professional Pakistani officer, and pressure for their acquisition probably first came from civilians. Pakistan will acquire nuclear weapons if it can, but it is not likely that they will be used as a substitute for conventional ground and air force so long as the military remains in power or retains a veto over security policy.

However, should the Pakistan Army be persuaded to withdraw from power and its dominant role in defense-policy making, it is conceivable (though unlikely) that a future civilian government would reshape both structural and strategic components of security policy. They would be following in Bhutto's footsteps, and might envisage an expanded role for nuclear weapons or attempt to create a people's army. It is improbable that the Pakistan Army as it is now constituted would yield power to those who would dismantle it. Pakistan itself would have to be on the verge of civil war and anarchy for such a radical departure to be even contemplated.

More conceivable would be a civilian attempt to limit the size, role, and mission of the military without altering its characteristic structure. A number of thoughtful officers have argued that Pakistan could survive with a much smaller and more efficient and effective military establishment, even without nuclear weapons, and that even Indian regional dominance does not necessarily mean the destruction of an independent Pakistan. Some have gone so far as to argue for a "deal" with the Soviet Union. The dangers here lie not in the present but in the future. Would a Pakistan subservient to either India or the Soviet Union be required to alter its Islamic character? Would strategic dependence lead to political and cultural penetration, undoing the partition of 1947? Then, too, there is the small but (in view of 1971) not incredible possibility that one of Pakistan's neighbors will seize upon its disorder and end the "Pakistan problem" once and for all. If the Pakistan Army were defeated and disarmed, Pakistan would disintegrate into separate, independent states, each virtually disarmed and under the protective influence of India or the Soviet Union. It is inconceivable that India would want to reabsorb much of the present Pakistan, but it might conclude that an unstable, fragile, nuclear-armed, and hostile Pakistan held greater risks than an immediate war.

Pakistan must thus search for a *via media* between concessions that would undo the state itself and a hard-line strategy that threatens total war as a form of defense—and might lead its neighbors to conclude that it is unredeemably irresponsible. This is especially true in the case of India. Pakistan has little choice except to learn to live with its newly powerful neighbor and to accept its own *de facto* strategic inferiority. Such acceptance, however, is in turn dependent on Indian statesmanship. If India insists that Pakistan has no legitimate defense needs, then Pakistan is in an impossible position. If India recognizes, on the other hand, that it has an interest in the continuing existence of a Pakistan that is capable of defending itself—even against India—because that capability is one condition for the integrity of the state, but not the only one, there may be an opportunity for a general regional-security agreement.[29] However, given the unstable domestic politics of some of the states involved, their impending nuclearization, and the unpredictable policies of both superpowers toward South Asia, there may not be much time.

29. Senior members of the Pakistani leadership were aware of this in 1980, and they stunned India by offering it a no-war pact on Sept. 15, 1981. (India itself had made such an offer as early as 1949, and Pakistan had in turn routinely countered with a "joint defense" proposal.) After two months' exchange of press releases and innuendos, India formally responded positively to the offer on November 25, 1981; however, negotiations were broken off by India in March 1982 (when Pakistan raised the Kashmir question in a UNESCO committee meeting) but soon resumed. They have led to the establishment of several sub-commissions, regular exchanges of journalists, and even discussions between the two countries over the exchange or sale of electric power, natural gas, and—according to the highest Pakistani sources, Pakistani purchase of weapons manufactured in India.

Epilogue to the 1998 Edition

The years 1984-97 saw a full measure of drama and trauma in Pakistan. Four years after this book was first published in the United States, President Zia, many of his senior generals and the distinguished American ambassador, Arnold Raphel, died in a still-mysterious air crash. This event paved the way for a transition, first to a quasi-democratic regime (in which the military were key players), and then, in early 1997, to the apparent restoration of full constitutional democracy—albeit one in which the army seems to play an important role. These years also saw the end of the Cold War, the continuation of the conflict in Afghanistan, two major crises with India (1987 and 1990), and the *de facto*, if unacknowledged, spread of nuclear capabilities to India and Pakistan.

This Epilogue will survey some of these developments, particularly the gradual withdrawal of the military from politics, the internal structure and ideology of the army, and Pakistan's altered strategic environment.

The Army and Politics

THE TALE OF THE TROIKA

The term "troika" has been rather loosely applied to describe Pakistan's governing system after 1988.[1] However, even before the

1. For example, the IISS' Strategic Comments, December, 1996 refers to an informal power sharing arrangement between the three, and that "competition for power among the three has been

major constitutional changes of 1997 (which decisively tilted the balance of power between the President and the Prime Minister in favor of the latter—"troika" never quite captured the shifting balance of influence between the army, the Prime Minister, and the President. While the army may still be Pakistan's most important potential political force—and has long been referred to as the most important Pakistani political "party"—its role has been in continuous recession over the past six years, a trend that could continue for at least the duration of Nawaz Sharif's tenure as Prime Minister. Indeed, the stage may be set for a dramatic transformation of relations between the military and the political community.

Shortly after Zia's death—he had served as army Chief from 1976 and President from 1984, and in the latter capacity had dismissed Mohammed Khan Junejo in May 1988—the term "troika" was coined to describe the three-party arrangement between the Prime Minister, the President, and the army.[2]

Junejo had become Prime Minister after the (party-less) election in 1985: the year also saw the re-creation of the Muslim League, the passing of the Eighth Amendment (which strengthened the hand of the President), and the lifting of martial law. Junejo had tried to expand the powers of the Prime Minister, and may have differed with Zia on important nuclear and foreign policy issues (he was bypassed during the Brasstacks crisis of 1986-87, when Zia and Gen. Mohammed Arif were in tight control over Pakistani decision-making).

Zia died in August 1988, replaced by Mirza Aslam Beg as COAS, and by Ghulam Ishaq Khan (then Chairman of the Senate, and thus constitutionally next in line) as President. In November 1988, Beg presided over Pakistan's freest election since 1970. Benazir Bhutto was elected Prime Minister and Ghulam Ishaq Khan was elected President after the federal and provincial polls. Ishaq had been an important civilian advisor of Zia, his election was not a surprise, but he was in no way Benazir's favorite, having been in the inner circle of advisors that decided on the death of her father. The first, and most

responsible for much of the instability since Zia's death," citing Benazir's "second sacking," i.e. 1996, as having "the full support of the army leadership." This conclusion appears to be based on the generally shared, and inaccurate view of the military's role in politics *circa* 1996. International Institute of Strategic Studies (London), *Strategic Comments*, Vol. 2, No. 10, December 1996, "Political Turmoil in Pakistan," p. 1.

2. For a remarkable and forthright overview of the Zia years by one of his closest army associates, see Lieutenant-General Khalid Mohammed Arif, *Working With Zia: Pakistan's Power Politics—1977-1988*. (Karachi: Oxford University Press, 1995).

important "troika" in Pakistani politics was in place: Benazir, Aslam Beg, Ghulam Ishaq Khan.

Benazir's Pakistan People's Party won the election with a small majority but she was immediately thrown into domestic and foreign policy crises in which both the President and the army chief saw themselves as key policymakers. Beg and Ghulam Ishaq probably determined nuclear policy, although Benazir claims, unpersuasively, that she was not fully informed of the existence of a military nuclear program. Her role in the January-May 1990 confrontation with India over Kashmir is not clear.

A sustained domestic crisis began in late 1990, highlighted by bloodshed in Karachi and Hyderabad. There was speculation that Aslam Beg, as a Muhajir, was supporting the MQM. Both the President and Beg tried to undercut Benazir, regarding her as too weak, and too conciliatory towards "extremist" Sindhi groups, and remnants of her brother's Al-Zulfikar organization.

Benazir was subsequently dismissed by Ghulam Ishaq who charged her with tolerating corruption, an inability to pass bills, and the deterioration of the law and order situation in Karachi and Hyderabad. The October 1990 election saw heavy army/ISI rigging, recently acknowledged by Aslam Beg and others. Nawaz Sharif was elected Prime Minister with a massive majority; Beg briefly remained COAS, Ghulam Ishaq continued on as President. The second "troika" was short-lived, since Beg retired immediately after the Gulf War.

Beg's successor, Asif Nawaz Janjua made Sindh his first order of (domestic) business. Janjua apparently developed his own plan to deal with the MQM in an operation reminiscent of the army's crackdown against East Bengal in 1970. Janjua's contribution to "troika" lore was brief but impressive: he managed to outflank both the President and the Prime Minister, pursuing army rather than political interests.

Janjua died suddenly in January 1993, and was replaced by the least visible of the serving corps commanders, Lt.-Gen. Abdul Waheed. The selection of Waheed created a conflict between Ghulam Ishaq and Nawaz, one then inherent in the division of powers between the President and the Prime Minister. The "new" troika was very short-lived, however, because Nawaz was dismissed in April, 1993 by GIK on the same grounds he had dismissed Benazir: corruption, and the breakdown of law and order. At this critical point, with the army's command integrity at stake, the hitherto politically invisible Waheed stepped forth and asked both Nawaz and Ghulam Ishaq Khan to resign.

The elections of October 1993 produced a new lineup: Benazir, Farooq Leghari, and Waheed. Leghari demonstrated his independence by appointing Lieutenant-General Jehangir Karamat as the new COAS in January 1996, without consulting Benazir (she had apparently wanted another officer for the position).

Karamat's role in this period seems to have been very restrained. Virtually the entire conflict between Benazir and Leghari was bilateral in nature, although Leghari may have been confident of Karamat's support. During this period there was some public discussion of the need to *strengthen* the President, and perhaps restructure the constitution to produce a truly presidential system. If he had wanted to, Karamat could have managed the dismissal of President Leghari or forced a change in the constitution to strengthen the presidency.[3] There were also reports that the army was irritated at "political" budget decisions and weapons purchases, partly because of rumors of kickbacks in a Mirage deal and submarine purchases for the navy. To the degree that a "troika" was in operation, the army third played a minor role during this critical period.

It is still not clear what role the army played in December 1997, when President Leghari resigned. There had been a major public demonstration of Nawaz Sharif's "street power" (a mob attacked the Supreme Court building) and the army refused to intervene as local forces stood by and watched. It would have been surprising if the army had intervened against a popularly elected Prime Minister, but popularity is one thing that cannot be assumed forever in politics. The November-December 1997 crisis (when the military was reported to have cautioned President Farooq Leghari about confronting the recently-elected Nawaz Sharif) will not be Pakistan's last political crisis. It may, however, have brought the next civilian-military crisis closer if Nawaz Sharif ever attempts to pack the upper reaches of the army with his followers as he attempted to pack the Supreme Court with sympathetic judges. His salvation, and that of any political alternative, will be in good policies, not manipulative politics.

3. This was also the position of Moeen Qureshi, who had been caretaker Prime Minister during the interregnum after Nawaz's dismissal. Qureshi's view was that a wide range of issues were not being successfully addressed by a weak prime ministerial system. See interview with Qureshi, *Newsline*, January 1997.

THE ARMY'S PERSPECTIVE

If the army has been less inclined to play an active role in politics it may be because the social ties between the military and the political community have grown closer. The army comes from the same "class" that now produces most of Pakistan's politicians, as well as from the region that dominates the entire country politically—urban and central Punjab. The army is still drawn from the middle classes, typically the sons of Junior Commissioned Officers. This makes them middle class, upward mobile, and with a strong belief in a system that is, more or less, based on merit recruitment and promotion, although "sifaarish" does not hurt, either.[4]

The army faces the same problems as other Pakistani professions (the Press, the judiciary, and academia) that have tried to preserve their integrity. Ironically, these groups dislike and distrust the army and the military-bureaucratic "establishment" that play such an important role in Pakistan. These institutions survived because they were attentive to international norms of how journalists, lawyers, judges, professors, and soldiers behaved. Of course, the critical profession—politicians—did not survive long after independence; since then, the military have been searching for politicians that could build a Pakistan worthy of its army.

The army views Pakistan's current political crisis with a mixture of dismay and embarrassment. Most officers are aware that while the politicians may be corrupt and incompetent, it is now recognized that the military interregnum of 1977-88 did nothing to strengthen the political infrastructure of the state. Indeed, it hurt the military in the eyes of those Pakistanis who, in their commitment to a modern, progressive state, most resemble the army itself.

Thus, the army has joined other Pakistanis in deep reflection over what has gone wrong. The Zia years are now regarded with a degree of embarrassment, although particular policies of that era are praised. This is quite different from Zia's own perspective. He and his colleagues were aware of, but not embarrassed by, the mistakes committed during the military rule of Ayub and Yahya. Zia was determined to avoid those mistakes, especially the personal corruption

---

4. See the discussion of *sifaarish* (undue favour) and *rishwat* (bribery) by one of Pakistan's most distinguished generals, the late Lt.-Gen. M. Attiqur Rahman in *Back to the Pavilion*, (Karachi: Ardeshir Cowasjee, 1990), 276 ff.

and venality of Yahya—which was largely screened from the Pakistani public by an overpowering public relations machine.[5] They stressed the importance of reform and purification, encouraging Islamic-style changes in Pakistani society—although less so in the army itself. These are now seen as excessive and detrimental to the professionalism of the army. They failed to transform Pakistan, they brought the army into disrepute, and they encouraged the tiny minority of proactive Islamists in the army—a subset of "the bearded ones"—to press for the introduction of Islamic principles and practices into the army itself—a trend culminating in the abortive *coup* of 1995.

The army's own mistakes (as seen by the officer corps itself), while serious, pale in comparison with those of the politicians, especially Benazir Bhutto. The politicians are seen as responsible for a host of domestic and foreign policy failures. A summary list would include: the continuing inability to develop a coherent national strategy, let alone a national ideology that would serve as a unifying force for all Pakistanis, the no-win stalemate in Kashmir, the worsening of relations with Iran, the loss of American support, an uncertain situation in Afghanistan (and little progress towards achieving the grandiose goal of projecting Pakistani power into Central Asia), an economic disaster at home, the specter of widespread political corruption undermining Pakistani democracy, tainting the military (possibly weakening national security). Only the much vaunted nuclear program, under army control, seems to have produced positive results, as Pakistani generals believe it deterred an Indian attack in 1990.[6] But a nuclear weapon cannot balance Pakistan's budget, it cannot bring in foreign investment, it cannot initiate a dialogue between embittered social and ethnic groups, and it will not ensure Pakistan's security, which is now threatened from within more than from across its borders.

---

5. The sad history of the manipulation of public opinion by the army's own public relations apparatus is well-documented by Brig. A.R. Siddiqui (ret.) who is also the founder-editor of the unique and very useful *Defence Journal*. See Siddiqui, *The Military in Pakistan: Image and Reality* (Lahore: Vanguard Books, 1996).

6. Their conclusion is not shared by others who have examined the crisis closely, and Indians are themselves divided over the impact of Pakistan's weapons, and possible threats, on the outcome of the crisis.

GENERATIONAL CHANGES

The first edition of this book developed a "generational" analysis of the officer corps. This became part of the discourse about Pakistani politics and its army.[7] The concept of generation was a shorthand way to explain how significant events shape the world-view of a group of officers, independent of their regional or social origin. I noted the emergence of a possible "Zia generation" of officers: individuals who were socially more conservative, perhaps more "Islamic" in orientation, and not overly worried about the army's role in Pakistani politics. Further, this generation's chief foreign policy experience was, in 1982, the 1971 humiliation at the hands of India. Many officers spoke and wrote at that time of the need to revenge that defeat.

Yet, the long tenure of Ziaul Haq as army chief itself had its own impact on the officer corps. While there may now be a "Zia generation" of officers who conform to the above description, many of them, fifteen years later, have undergone further and more significant experiences. They seem to have modified their view of the army, of Pakistan, and of the army's role in the state. Zia's long tenure as Chief and President shaped a generation of officers (and influenced the whole officer corps) in seemingly contradictory ways.

First, Zia's stress on Islam, in an already conservative society, encouraged the Islamic zealots in the army. In the words of one recently retired major-general, "Zia did great damage to all of Pakistan, and the military by his Islamization policy: he wasn't sincere about it, but in a conservative society it makes people more bigoted, intolerant, and fanatic—we want to rid ourselves of this legacy."

But for some officers the secret war in Afghanistan became the prototype of a new Pakistani strategy—war by proxy against domestic and foreign foes. These officers made no secret of their views, publishing them widely in official outlets. One of the leaders of the aborted September, 1995 *coup*, Major-General Zahir ul Islam Abbasi, had served as attaché in India and upon his return was promoted and spoke publicly about the need to "Islamize" both Pakistan and its army. He wrote in the Staff College's professional journal of the importance of "Islamization" and resisting the domination of an

---

7. See, for example, Captain (ret.) Ayaz Amir, "Soldiering On," *The Herald*, November 1995.

aggressive, sinister India and other foreign, anti-Muslim states.[8] That Abbasi was part of a larger *coup* effort comes as no surprise. The *coup* was fully reported, in alarming terms, by the leading publication devoted to security and military affairs, *Defence Journal*, which contains extracts of the speech that Abbasi was to deliver as well as extracts from doctrinaire Islamic articles that appeared in the army's own weekly, *Hilal*, and a speech by Benazir Bhutto.[9] This speech, to PMA graduates, encouraged the new officers to "make themselves ready for jihad." Benazir was here following a strategy developed by her father of being more "Islamic" than the mullahs.

The idea of a *coup* followed by the Islamic transformation of Pakistan was *not* one that Zia subscribed to, nor were his close associates cut from this cloth. He was more concerned about holding on to power, influencing Pakistani politics and society on the margins, and developing the professionalism and competence of the army. Even the officers who pushed Zia into his own *coup* were not "Islamic" types— in that sense, Zia, his colleagues, and the Zia experience did not promote a "Zia generation" in the officer corps.

However, two aspects of the Zia years did produce a "generation" of sorts, and these seem to differ remarkably in their implications. On the one hand, as a senior officer once said, "who would have joined the army during the Zia years?" Certainly not the best and the brightest, but more likely the time server, the politically conservative, the socially disengaged. This officer had entered the military in the Bhutto years, full of hope and idealism for the remaking of a then-shattered Pakistan.

On the other hand, the Zia experience, viewed in retrospect by most of the military, is seen as a period of excess, an embarrassment to the military, especially the army. Conservative officers who had no compunctions about joining the army in the 1977-88 years, now look back on that period with regret. Many officers note that one or another aspect of the Zia period was good for the army, and good for the country, but on balance they would not like to see the experience repeated. Thus, while the Zia period was important in shaping the outlook and mentality of a generation of officers, it affected the entire army in a negative fashion, and the "lesson" of the period—driven

---

8. For a sample, which reads very much like his never-given *coup* speech, see the article Abbasi wrote for the Staff College's professional journal: "The Quranic Concept of Leadership: Its Adoption and Application in the Pakistan Army," *Citadel*, No. 1, 1992, pp. 35-51. For a good overview of the *coup* see Zafar Abbas, "The Coup that Wasn't," *Herald*, November 1995.

9. *Defence Journal*, Vol. 21, April-May 1996.

home by one after-effect, the "Islamic *coup*" of 1995—has been to reinforce the senior commanders' concern with professional development. Speculation about the dangers of a "Zia generation" of officers moving up over the years needs to be tempered by an understanding of the overall experience of the period. From many officers' perspective it was negative.

There has been public discussion in Pakistan of an increasing "Islamization" of the officer corps, as well as speculation about its professional deterioration.[10] These, however, are two different trends. There is no necessary correlation between a decline in the quality of officers and officer-candidates and an increase in Islamist or Islamic extremist views.

As for ideological motivation, there is some evidence that the Tablighi Jamaat has grown in influence in the officer corps (as it has expanded its activities in Pakistan and among Indian Muslims). The Tablighi are not Islamist, but a devout, pious, loosely organized proselytizing group, themselves opposed to the doctrinaire Wahabis of Saudi Arabia. There is no evidence of organized Jamaat i Islami infiltration in the Pakistan army. One of Zia's goals appears to have been to ensure that they, and other Islamist groups, were kept out of the army. Zia certainly held the view that a devoted Muslim might be a better officer than one less committed, but he never formally introduced Islamic criteria for promotion or recruitment. However, some officers have publicly argued for the introduction of Islam when considering promotions. This perspective flourished under Aslam Beg; it was detected and challenged after Asif Nawaz Janjua became COAS.

While Islamist, or Islamic fundamentalist trends could be important in the future, especially if they were linked to one of Pakistan's Islamist parties, the central army-society issue in Pakistan is not, for the moment, Islam, but whether the army should redefine and restructure itself in such a way as to reduce itself in size, maintain its professionalism, and make the army attractive to smart, ambitious Pakistanis. Here, the Pakistan army is responding to the same social, economic and technical challenges facing many armies created on a pre-nuclear, low-technology, infantry intensive model. Educated Pakistani youth need to see the army as leading to a useful career later

10. Ayaz Amir, "Soldiering On."

in life: whether in technology, or management, not just the development of martial skills that cannot be marketed in later years.

Finally, some mention should be made of the newest, post-Zia generation of officers. Some senior and retired generals claim that younger officers are not so much "Islamic" as they are materialistic, nationalistic, and politicized. They entered the army in the 1970s, during a period of great agitation in the universities and schools of Pakistan. They are accused of lacking the spirit of self-sacrifice and modest living that (presumably) characterized their predecessors. It is hard to judge the accuracy of this view, but if it is true then there are several explanations. First, in Pakistan as in India (where the same phenomenon is observable), society itself is becoming more materialistic—such changes may reflect the broader society itself, and the greater appeal of business and commerce. Second, the Pakistan army is increasingly seen as just another profession or occupation, having lost its special panache as a higher calling. The ablest young Pakistanis (and across the border, their Indian counterparts) head for other institutions, although a small core of very fine officers remains.

This "newest" generation is probably not yet a politically important phenomenon. As in the past, promotion up the ladder is determined by merit and by the subtle criteria established by senior officers who tend to look for younger candidates just like themselves. The Pakistan army has found a way to promote certain types to higher ranks: the "fighting" officer, the "thinking" officer, and so forth. For the most part extremists have been weeded out or sidetracked. The biggest question here is whether the next generation of officers will imbibe the notion of the army as a corporate entity, an army that must stay united. If the sense of corporateness should weaken, then it will be easier, with concomitant risks, for civilians to attempt to divide the army along ideological, class, or personal lines. It will also increase the risk of sharp ideological divisions within the officer corps.

THE FOREIGN POLICY OF AN ARMY

The higher command of the officer corps is not a monolith. While there are different strategic schools, such differences are to be expected in a country which borders on Central Asia, West Asia, and South Asia and which once saw itself as a major global player. However, like most professional institutions, there is a common core of strategic assumptions—an "operational code" that most officers subscribe to (or are taught). The current (1998) version seems to be:

- Avoid a war with India, without yielding to Indian pressure on vital issues;
- Support Kashmiri separatists, but not to the point where it leads to confrontation with India;
- Try to maintain good relations with all of the major Islamic states, both to broaden the base of economic and potential military support, and to avoid the appearance of tilting towards one or the other, thereby triggering sectarian conflicts within Pakistan itself;
- Maintain and expand the nuclear program, but without risking Pakistan's residual relationship with the United States and other anti-proliferation states;
- Avoid a too dependent relationship with the US, the state that has "let Pakistan down" many times in the past, but remain close enough to make Pakistan's case in Washington, and to balance Indian influence;
- Do whatever is possible to hold together Pakistan's most important proto-alliance—that with China—recognizing that Chinese interests in Pakistan have diminished.

More recently, the army's attention has been diverted by internal security issues. In the past this has been seen as a "civilian" problem, which might require military intervention from time to time to sort out Sindhis, or Muhajirs, but several recent developments have intensified the domestic security role of the army and brought back unpleasant memories of the failure to cope with the Bengali separatist movement.[11] Senior officers raise the issue with visitors as a "new" and urgent security task facing the army, and the army's own professional literature devotes an increasing amount of space to the subject.

First, the Afghan war made Pakistan a center for terrorism, narcotics, and adventurers; while some of these groups were supported and directed by ISI, the regular army tends to view them with concern when they meddle in Pakistan itself. Second, a number of "friendly"

---

11. Since the first edition of *The Pakistan Army* a number of excellent studies of this event have been published; for an overview see Richard Sisson and Leo E. Rose, *War and Secession: Pakistan, India, and the Creation of Bangladesh* (Berkeley: University of California Press, 1990 [Pakistan reprint edition, Oxford University Press, 1992]).

Islamic states have made Pakistan a base for proselytism; the interior conflicts of Islam have, in this way, been carried to the streets of Karachi and Multan. The most acute of these conflicts, between Iran and the Gulf Arab states, threatens Pakistan's own sectarian balance, and has led to the formation of extremist Shi'a and Sunni groups, possibly funded from abroad.[12] Finally, it is widely assumed by the military that India's hand is at work in Pakistan, although this is seen as an extension of the larger India-Pakistan conflict.

Pakistan's recurrent nightmare is that its "three legged stool" of outside support from China, America, and the Islamic world, has collapsed. Beijing, Washington, and Tehran all openly advocate a dialogue on Kashmir, and have offered their services as facilitators. The Pakistani "establishment," including the military, has probably not formulated a coherent response. On this issue policy in the past few years has been reactive.

At the strategic level Pakistanis have (privately) argued with China and the US that their apparent move to India presents dangers to them, not just to Pakistan. This view resonates among hard-line Chinese, and within the PLA, which all remain very suspicious of a "rising" or emerging India. China is likely to continue just enough support to Pakistan to ensure that they retain the ability to pressure an India which could emerge as a rival; they also want Pakistan to help the Peoples' Republic contain the spread of Islamist and Islamic-powered nationalism to China itself (as they fear expanded Indian support for Tibetans).

PERCEPTIONS OF NEW DELHI

The army's major foreign policy interest remains India, closely followed by the need to have good relations with potential arms suppliers. In order of importance these are China, the United States, the Gulf states (for financial support), and European states. Most in the army still regard China as Pakistan's greatest friend, and see China as a partner in containing India, and as a provider of nuclear technology and some weapons.

12. For one of the best overviews of the sectarian problem—by one of Pakistan's most distinguished journalists—see Khaled Ahmed, "The Shia-Sunni Conflict in Pakistan," *The Friday Times,* Jan. 30-Feb. 5, 1997, p. 9.

On the whole, the army's judgment of India has become slightly more realistic in the past dozen years. Some of the cruder stereotypes of India have disappeared from army writings. One Commandant of the Staff College spoke (in 1990) of the palpably false image of India contained in Staff College texts and lecture notes. He regarded them as detrimental to sound professional thinking and commissioned an important, comprehensive study of India, which has been adopted in the Staff College and is now distributed by the army's own Press.[13] While a considerable improvement over earlier studies of India, *India: A Study in Profile* is still deeply problematic, although extremely well researched.

With a strong civilian leader as Prime Minister in Pakistan and with recent attempts by new Delhi to normalize its relations with its other neighbors, the Pakistan army may have to face the question as to whether normalization with India is possible. Should it be conducted on the basis of strict reciprocity, or should Pakistan move on some issues regardless of what India does—or even change its policies regardless of Indian positions? Should the army continue its hardline opposition to dialogue, or should it allow—or even encourage—the civilian leadership to gradually move towards normalization and even an accommodation on Kashmir?

While senior officers are not in principle averse to unilateral steps it is generally their position that important policies need to have at least the appearance of reciprocity, with assurances that India will not back out at the last moment, humiliating Pakistan and throwing its weight around. Pakistan's generals cite India's failure to conclude a Siachin withdrawal agreement. With their overwhelming self-image of Pakistan as the smaller and weaker state, they are worried about predominant Indian power being used to pressure Pakistan. They tend to be less sophisticated when it comes to the nuances of international negotiations, and leave these to the diplomats. The establishment of an arms control cell in GHQ (with one officer detached to the MFA), is an indication that the army is aware of the need both to participate in such decisions and inform them with military expertise. This is a welcome development: if the army can be persuaded that negotiations or even unilateral actions do not weaken Pakistan's immediate position in terms of hard security considerations, there may be fresh thinking.

13. Brig. Javed Hussain, *India: A Study in Profile* (Rawalpindi: Army Press, 1990). Hussain was a colonel when he wrote the study.

Senior officers are interested in the way in which agreements between adversaries have been monitored in recent years, and are curious to learn about verification mechanisms which would lessen the risks of both surprise and embarrassment should the Indians fail to stick to the terms of a security agreement.

THE ARMY AND REGIONAL NORMALIZATION

While they seem to be unlikely advocates of arms control, the Pakistan army has a realistic sense of what could be gained by a series of verifiable agreements with India. Senior officers express their concern at the dangers of an arms race with a richer, more powerful India; Pakistan's nuclear program would be irrelevant, as India builds up its regional capabilities, and its power-projection role. Even if there was no direct India-Pakistan confrontation, the perception of Pakistan as a declining state would make Pakistan a less attractive regional partner to China, the United States, Iran, and others.

However, all of these arguments for negotiation and compromise are more than balanced by their profound distrust of India. Pakistani officers have a grudging respect for New Delhi, and most believe that Indian strategy is driven by deeper, chauvinist motives, and that in the long run it will be hard to get the Indians to abide by *any* agreement—whether it is mutual withdrawal from Siachin, the demarcation of the Sir Creek boundary, improved notification of major troop movements, or discussions about the regional intake of next-generation weapons. Army officials are aware of the success of the Indus Waters Treaty, but they retain a professional soldiers' skepticism of the difficulty of verifying and enforcing any arms control agreements with New Delhi.

There are indicators that this resistance to regional dialogue could change. The senior levels of the army are aware now that arms control can be an extension of security policy, and that there might be advantages to be gained from slowing down or constraining Indian weapons acquisitions, and the army has established an arms control cell. The published army literature on the subject, while replete with warnings about Indian duplicity, has begun to discuss the issue objectively.[14]

14. For example, 'South Asia—Prospects of Mutual Disarmament,' the report of a Group Study in the 1995 Class at the Staff College, has the usual stereotyped view of India, but also includes a balanced set of recommendations. *The Citadel*, No. 1, 1996, pp. 26-35. See also

THE NUCLEAR ISSUE

When this book was first published, the idea of a nuclear Pakistan was still a concept. Now, with the apparent development of at least a "non-weaponized" capacity, nuclear strategy is freely discussed within the army, and hints of an emerging consensus are evident in the few published articles on the subject that have appeared.

The consensus army view seems to be that the present situation of non-declaration of nuclear possession serves Pakistan's strategic interests better than nuclear renunciation *or* the public declaration of a nuclear capability. Pakistan's nuclear choices are not seen as between no rungs on the ladder (renunciation) and one rung on the ladder (an all out nuclear response to any Indian provocation).[15] Nuclear renunciation is strategically risky since Pakistan would be threatened by India's latent nuclear capability. It is also politically impossible because of the popularity of nuclear weapons. Overt nuclear weapons status also has its risks: declaring Pakistan to be a nuclear power would bring down severe foreign economic and political sanctions, and would not materially improve Pakistan's security situation.

However, the army has developed what they call an option-enhancing policy that will not require such choices:

- The first rung of an "escalation ladder" might be private, then public, warnings to India not to move its forces in a threatening fashion (again, following the 1990 precedent).
- The second rung would be a demonstration explosion of a small nuclear weapon on Pakistan's own soil—a warning shot during a mounting political crisis. This fits in well with recent Pakistani responses to Indian missile development and preparations for renewed nuclear testing. Should this not deter a conventional Indian attack, Pakistan could threaten to move further.
- The third rung could be the use of a few nuclear weapons on Pakistan's own soil, against Indian attacking forces.[16] The potential

Lt. Col. Babur Idris, 'Arms Race—The Case of India and Pakistan,' *The Citadel*, No. 2, 1995, which argues that India's pursuit of conventional advantage in South Asia is now irrelevant that nuclear weapons have stabilized the relationship between it and Pakistan (and China).

15. Lieutenant-Colonel Syed Anwar Mehdi, 'Nuclear Ambivalence Versus a Well Defined Policy Involving Minimum Political Fallout,' The Citadel, No. 2/1994, p. 59.

16. Unlike Europe, a decision to use nuclear weapons on Pakistani soil to resist an Indian attack would not be encumbered by allied pressures, and could help balance India's larger conventional forces.

battle areas could be identified as "Nuclear Test Sites," (in one scenario, desert terrain that might be traversed by invading Indian armor units—á la Brasstacks) and prepared for a nuclear detonation.[17] Areas which were not covered by "NTS" (urban and populated areas) could be covered by flexible delivery systems; either missiles or aircraft, and defended by Pakistan's conventional forces;

- A fourth rung would be use against critical but purely military targets in India across the border from Pakistan, thinly populated areas which are "desert or semi-desert" with little infrastructure, this would have little collateral damage. Both uses would, in the eyes of some Pakistan officers, lessen the risk of Indian retaliation against Pakistani cities, since Pakistan's response would be confined to military targets;

- Finally, some of Pakistan's nuclear weapons could be held in reserve for the counter-value role. Here there is little to fear from an Indian pre-emptive attack, since an airborne nuclear system and nuclear tipped missiles could be moved around the country. They would be impossible for the Indians to locate, attack, and destroy, without a high risk of failure.

The search for a strategy somewhere between renunciation and immediate, all-out response to Indian provocation is well underway. It matches up well with Pakistan's current public posture of nuclear ambiguity: not declaring that it has a nuclear weapon (which helps Pakistan in its relationship with the United States, among other things).

However, there are risks associated with a strategy of graduated escalation, or many "rungs," especially in an environment where public discussion of this strategy is discouraged.

One hazard is the malfunctioning of an unreliable command and control system. When I asked Zia about this just before his death, he would only mutter, "Hmm, that could be a problem." A second risk is even less well-understood: the mis-perception of Indian intentions and capabilities. Since the army has so few objective sources of information about India, and the internal military culture hardly encourages balanced thinking, one rarely encounters a Pakistani officer who might suggest that his own system regularly misinterprets India.[18]

17. Mehdi, p. 65.

18. Indeed, privately and in journal articles, Pakistanis are irritated at the suggestion that they, or even the Indians, are irrational. One colonel has examined the question at length and concludes that in the three India-Pakistan wars there was "overall caution, restraint, and even gentlemanliness in their military behaviour." Idris, p. 75.

For example, a recent Staff College group study of the prospects of arms control and disarmament between India and Pakistan begins with page after page of simplistic text that grossly distorts Indian policy and history (and Pakistan's for that matter).[19] However, the study ends with a set of quite pragmatic and realistic recommendations. This disconnect remains troublesome. In a crisis, which set of attitudes would prevail: the "official" stereotypical view, or the actual, more pragmatic interpretation of India? The answer, of courses, is that it depends on the context of the crisis and the individual officers making the decision. Further, there are few civilians who are capable of pointing out past Pakistani misjudgments of India. One of the greatest risks in the region stems from this combination of an undeveloped command and control system and the chronic misjudgment of India that characterizes the thinking of the entire Pakistan military, regardless of service, rank, or experience.

A SUCCESS SCENARIO

It is easy to develop "failure" scenarios for Pakistan: its own history and partition provides one, the Soviet Union suggests another, and the Yugoslavia/Bosnia case still a third. Yet one must remain impressed with the resilience of Pakistan, or at least that very small core of Pakistanis who remain dedicated to a modern, relatively secular (albeit formally Islamic) state. Although much disparaged by their liberal civilian critics at home and abroad (sometimes with good reason), many officers believe they represent, and defend, this vision of Pakistan.

For that reason, I remain cautiously optimistic about the fate of Pakistan, and would suggest that in addition to the many scenarios leading to failure, that we contemplate strategies that will incrementally, but conclusively, ensure the security and success of this kind of Pakistan.

Such a strategy must include the incremental normalization of relations with India. Without this, Pakistan will continue to bear a crushing defense burden, its politics and society will remain excessively militarized, and India will remain at risk from a hostile and potentially unstable, but nuclear-armed Pakistan. The worst-case scenarios of a

19. Group Research Study, "South Asia—Prospects of Mutual Disarmament," *The Citadel*, 1/96.

nuclear war over Kashmir have been overdrawn, especially by Americans, but there is still some risk of a nuclear holocaust.

Going back to basics, the core strategic dilemmas India-Pakistan relations over the past fifty years has been that neither believes it can negotiate a reduction in threat unless it is "strong"—both states have been dominated by the slippery slope school of statecraft—one can only negotiate from a position of strength. Of course, when one side feels strong enough to be confident in its ability to negotiate, the other side may not be prepared. Rarely do both countries find themselves equally interested in negotiating issues which are threat-generating. We are now in a period where there may be an opportunity for both sides to peacefully resolve security-related threats. The next few years could see some remarkable breakthroughs. If this is true, what are the chances of the Pakistan army intervening to prevent a peace process from achieving significant agreement between the two states?

In the past it has been widely assumed that the army blocked serious negotiations with Delhi to protect its own institutional interests, and to pursue what it regarded as Pakistan's legitimate stake in Kashmir. I would speculate that a large minority of officers hold these views: perhaps 20-40% of the officer corps; a smaller minority of true fanatics would be opposed to any dealings with India and seek to "bleed" India. An equally small minority (which included Zia in the past) believe that if Pakistan's vital interests are protected, then serious negotiations with India are not only possible, but desirable, given Pakistan's economic, political, and other foreign policy problems. If the present dialogue between India and Pakistan is to move forward, the politicians and the foreign ministry will have to persuade the moderates in the army that Pakistan's security will be enhanced by such a process; in turn, the moderates in the army will have to persuade their colleagues that this is the best that they can hope for, and that no vital Pakistani interest will be at risk.

Bibliographic Note

Ten years ago there was only a handful of books and articles dealing with the Pakistan military or with that country's security policy. There is now a substantial literature and two new journals dealing with Pakistani strategic affairs. Most of these books and articles have been written by Pakistanis; a number of them deal with the experiences of 1971, others reach back to 1965, and a few attempt a comprehensive critical reexamination of the very ethos of the Pakistan Army.

This bibliographic note will discuss only those books that I believe to be essential for an understanding of Pakistan's military and security policy. There are many excellent studies on Pakistani history, politics, economics, and culture, but only a few will be noted below.

It should be stressed that some of the most valuable books and articles concerned with Pakistan's military and security policy are not polished or objective studies. They are useful precisely because their authors are trying to persuade or conceal. Even some of the public-relations material is valuable when read carefully. The same comment can be made about many of the articles in such military journals as *Pakistan Army Journal* (Rawalpindi), published by the Inspector General, Training and Evaluation Branch, GHQ, now on a monthly basis. Some of these are staff or exercise papers repackaged for a broader audience, others appear to be wildly irrelevant to modern warfare (for example, the studies of early Islamic battles), but all are valuable when one considers the context in which they appear and the audience to which they are addressed. Such material should be taken as seriously, in its own way, as the major full-length books written by distinguished retired generals.

Two new civilian journals have appeared in Pakistan in recent years and must be carefully followed by anyone interested in regional security affairs. One is a quarterly, *Strategic Studies* (Islamabad), the journal of the recently founded Institute of Strategic Studies. This journal publishes comprehensive studies of regional security and military affairs. The Institute may eventually become the most important "Islamic" strategic-studies center. It also publishes the *Islamabad Papers* on an irregular basis. A move to larger quarters and a new director have given *Strategic Studies* new weight. The second journal seeks a more popular audience and is addressed largely to Pakistanis themselves. *Defense Journal* is edited by a retired army officer once associated with military public relations; it has been in existence for several years and appears every other month, with occasional special issues. It serves as a forum in which Pakistanis can debate a number of highly sensitive issues: the military in politics, the 1965 and 1971 wars, strategy, and defense organization. It survived Bhutto's downfall and continues to be both provocative and thoughtful.

THE MILITARY

A by-product of the 1971 conflict was a burst of writing about the Pakistan military. One author in particular stands out for his lucid, perceptive analyses—Lt.-Gen. M. Attiqur Rahman (retd.). Two of his books are certainly required reading for anyone dealing with the military: *Leadership: Senior Commanders* (Lahore: Ferozsons, 1973) is a sequel to his first book, *Leadership: Junior Commanders,* which is a widely used text on military principles. Attiq's third book, *Our Defense Cause* (London: White Lion Publishers, 1976), is even more comprehensive and also deals with strategic issues. Although published in Britain, it is available as a paperback in Pakistan. *Senior Commanders* and *Our Defense Cause* are indispensable, but it should be remembered that no single author is fully representative of the range of thinking in the army.

An able Pakistani scholar, Hasan Askari Rizvi, is the author of the most comprehensive history of the involvement of the army in politics, *The Military and Politics in Pakistan,* 2d ed. (Lahore: Progressive Publishers, 1976). Almost four hundred pages long, it contains a number of useful appendices listing key personnel and giving the texts of several important documents pertaining to the role of the military in politics. See also the recent and thoughtful study of a former air marshal turned politician, Mohammed Asghar Khan, and written while under house arrest, *Generals in Politics* (Delhi: Vikas, 1983).

The closest to a history of the Pakistan Army is (the then) Maj.-Gen. Fazal Muqeem Khan's *The Story of the Pakistan Army* (Karachi: Oxford University Press, 1963). It contains much useful information but is not the comprehensive objective history that the Pakistan Army deserves. For a critical review of this book, see Stephen P. Cohen, "Arms and Politics in Pakistan," *India Quarterly,* October–December 1964. Fazal Muqeem's second book, *Pakistan's Crisis in Leadership* (Islamabad: National Book Foundation, 1973), deals entirely with the 1971 crisis and provides a great deal of useful information about the inner politics of Pakistan and the actual fighting in East Pakistan.

On the subject of the predecessor of the Pakistan Army, three books take different approaches. My own *The Indian Army* (Berkeley: University of California Press, 1971) focuses on civil-military relations, recruitment, and the indigenization of the officer corps in the preindependence period, and deals briefly with the postpartition Pakistan Army. A superbly written "account" of the Indian Army, concerned more with specific personalities and military battles, is in Philip Mason, *A Matter of Honour* (New York: Holt Rinehart and Winston, 1974). T. A. Heathcote's *The Indian Army,* (London: David and Charles, 1974) deals with the pre-1922 army and attempts to capture some of the exotica of the imperial period. Pakistan has now begun to produce it's own regimental histories. Two very good ones are Maj. M. I. Qureshi, *History of the First Punjab Regiment, 1759–1956* (Aldershot: Gale and Polden, 1958) and Lt.-Gen. M. Attiqur Rahman (retd.), *The Wardens of the Marches: A History of the Piffers, 1947–1971* (Lahore: Wajidalis, 1980).

A first-hand account of the 1971 war, written by a senior public-relations officer who was eventually captured in Bengal, is the excellent *Witness to Surrender,* by Siddiq Salik (Karachi: Oxford University Press, 1977). He presents an eye-witness account of the deterioration of moral, political, and military authority in East Pakistan. There are a number of other books written by Pakistanis on events in East Pakistan, but none as good.

Several books have been published about the 1965 conflict with India, some of them quite recently. Brig. Gulzar Ahmed (retd.) wrote *Pakistan Meets Indian Challenge* (Rawalpindi: Al Mukhtar, n.d.) shortly after the war itself, and although the book contains much useful information (especially extracts from a captured Indian general's personal diary), it is not an objective work. Perhaps the best account is by an American journalist, Russell Brines, in *The Indo-Pakistan Conflict* (London: Pall Mall Press, 1968). Also dating from about 1968 is the account of M. Asghar Khan,

The First Round, Indo-Pakistan War, 1965 (New Delhi: Vikas, 1979).
This edition contains an important recent foreword by Altaf Gauhar, who
was a key civilian advisor to Ayub Khan in 1965. Bhutto leaked substantial information about the 1965 war in the *White Paper on the Jammu and
Kashmir Dispute* (Islamabad: January 1977), some of it distorted, and
several issues of *Defense Journal* (for example, September 1979) have
been devoted to a survey of the literature on that war. Many Pakistani
authors have concluded that the 1965 war was a turning point for Pakistan, and there is justifiable interest in discovering how and why Pakistan
went to war and the way it was fought. The only detailed account of the air
war is John Fricker, *Battle for Pakistan* (London: Ian Allan, 1979), which
is by a professional military writer who was given access to PAF documents. No Indian equivalent exists, but a useful work is Air Marshal M. S.
Chaturvedi, *History of the Indian Air Force* (Delhi: Vikas, 1978). The
Indian military literature has been dominated by studies of the 1962 conflict with China (which generated some fine books), but a few Indians
have written about the wars with Pakistan. D. R. Mankekar is a journalist
but was given official assistance to write *Twenty-Two Fateful Days: Pakistan Cut to Size* (Bombay: Manaktalas, 1966). Lt.-Gen. B. M. Kaul, who
achieved notoriety for his part in the 1962 fiasco, did write a long and
confused book about India's wars with Pakistan, *Confrontation with
Pakistan* (Delhi: Vikas, 1971). The 1971 war has been the subject of several Indian books, among the first being D. K. Palit, *The Lightning Cam-
paign* (New Delhi: Thompson, 1972), which many Pakistani generals
criticize strongly; and M. Ayoob and K. Subrahmanyam, *The Liberation
War* (Delhi: S. Chand, 1972). This is an important book, as much for
what it tells us about Indian attitudes as for the actual political framework
and battles of the war itself.

Two books written by Pakistani soldiers attempt to examine the relationship of Islam and strategy. "Rangrut" [Maj.-Gen. M. A. Khan, retd.],
The Islamic Pattern of War, vol. 1, *Theory* (Karachi: Islamic Military Sci-
ence Assn., 1968), is comprehensive but obscure; more recently Brig. S. K.
Malik published *The Quranic Concept of War* (Lahore: Wajidalis, 1979), a
very important study, not least because General Zia provides the foreword
and A. K. Brohi, one of Pakistan's eminent legal minds, the preface. One of
Pakistan's most disinguished and influential soldier-scholars, Lt.-Gen. A. I.
Akram (retd.), not only directs the newly-formed Institute for Regional
Studies in Islamabad but is the author of several well-researched and per-
ceptive histories of Islam at war. A recent study is *The Muslim Conquest of
Spain* (Rawalpindi: Army Education Press, n.d. [probably 1982]).

Not much literature on the internal organization of the military is publicly available. Raymond A. Moore, Jr., provides a comprehensive account
of the army's involvement in civil works, disaster relief, education, reha-
bilitation, sports, industry, and related activities, but not its military activities, in *Nation Building and the Pakistan Army, 1947–1969* (Lahore:
Aziz, 1979). One chapter is devoted to the armed forces of Pakistan in
Richard F. Nyrop, et al., *Area Handbook for Pakistan* (Washington: Government Printing Office, 1975), which has some useful information and a
certain amount of misinformation (for example, it states that "all service
Headquarters are at Islamabad" which is not true—the Army is in Rawalpindi, twelve miles away, and the Air Force was in Peshawar as recently as
February, 1983).

Finally, two books by army officers deserve special mention. One is a
brief study by "ex-Major-General" Akbar Khan, *Raiders in Kashmir*, 2d
ed. (Islamabad: National Book Foundation, 1975), which not only discusses the Kashmir problem but illustrates the revolutionary and unortho-
dox streak found within at least part of the officer corps; the other study,
still worth reading, is Ayub Khan's autobiography, *Friends Not Masters*
(London: Oxford University Press, 1967). Written with the assistance of
several advisors, it still remains a remarkable book both as a history of
Ayub's involvement with the military and as a statement of Pakistan's goals
and ideals. The chapters on foreign policy are especially useful.

FOREIGN POLICY

Although no comprehensive study of Pakistan's defense policy exists,
there are a number of excellent books that deal with foreign policy and
discuss military and security dimensions of foreign policy at length. The
authoritative official versions are by a retired Pakistani diplomat, S. M.
Burke, *Pakistan's Foreign Policy* (London: Oxford University Press, 1973)
and *Mainsprings of Indian and Pakistani Foreign Policies* (Minneapolis:
University of Minnesota Press, 1974). A scholarly and detailed analysis of
Pakistan's borders (which includes East Pakistan/Bangladesh) is Mujtaba
Razvi, *The Frontiers of Pakistan* (Karachi-Dacca: National Publishing
House, 1971); a somewhat older but still important study of foreign-pol-
icy choices open to Pakistan is Aslam Siddiqi, *A Path for Pakistan* (Karachi: Pakistan Publishing House, 1964). Quite recently a group of Pakistani
and foreign scholars contributed to Masuma Hasan, ed., *Pakistan in a
Changing World* (Karachi: Pakistan Institute of International Affairs,
1978), an outstanding memorial to K. Sarwar Hasan, a distinguished

Pakistani scholar. The best study of India-Pakistan relations remains that of the late Sisir Gupta, *Kashmir: A Study in India-Pakistan Relations* (Bombay: Asia, 1966). Pakistanis might find much to object to in this book, yet few other studies on this issue match it for comprehensiveness and sensitivity.

A large literature exists that examines Pakistan's relations with the superpowers. Among the best are William J. Barnds, *India, Pakistan and the Great Powers* (New York: Praeger, 1972), G. W. Choudhury, *India, Pakistan, Bangladesh, and the Major Powers* (New York: The Free Press, 1975), and Norman D. Palmer, *South Asia and U.S. Policy* (Boston: Houghton Mifflin, 1966). Aswini K. Ray's *Domestic Compulsions and Foreign Policy: Pakistan in Indo-Soviet Relations* (Delhi: Manas, 1975) is highly specialized but quite informative. Another able Indian scholar is no less critical of the American tie to Pakistan: Jayanta Kumar Ray, *Public Policy and Global Reality* (Delhi: Radiant, 1977). A Pakistani scholar, Sattar Babar, examines the American presence in Pakistan in *U.S. Aid to Pakistan* (Karachi: Pakistan Institute of International Affairs, 1974); more recently, an American scholar of Pakistani origin (who joined the Reagan administration in 1982) is the author of the most comprehensive and balanced study of U.S.-Pakistan relations. See Shirin Tahir-Kheli, *The United States and Pakistan: The Evolution of an Influence Relationship* (New York: Praeger, 1982). Dr. Tahir-Kheli is the author of an earlier study of Soviet policy in Central and West Asia, *Soviet Moves in Asia* (Lahore: Ferozsons, n.d.). Perhaps the most interesting source for Soviet views of the region is in the March 1974 issue of *Asian Survey*, which contains nine articles by leading Soviet scholars on various problems of the subcontinent; this has been reprinted in Pakistan as Yuri V. Gankovsky, ed., *Soviet Scholars View South Asia* (Lahore: People's Publishing House, 1975).

PAKISTANI POLITICS

A vast literature is available on this subject, and only a few books can be noted. In rough chronological order, the early days of Pakistan are skillfully analyzed in Wayne Ayres Wilcox, *Pakistan: The Consolidation of a Nation* (New York: Columbia University Press, 1963); Keith Callard's *Pakistan: A Political Study* (London: George Allen and Unwin, 1957) remains a classic, and Khalid B. Sayeed, *The Political System of Pakistan,* (Boston: Houghton Mifflin, 1967), is still useful. Three books

by Herbert Feldman cover the Ayub and Yahya periods with great perception and balance: *Revolution in Pakistan: A Study of the Martial Law
Administration* (London: Oxford University Press, 1967), *From Crisis to
Crisis: Pakistan, 1962–69* (London: Oxford University Press, 1972), and
The End and the Beginning: Pakistan, 1969–71 (London: Oxford University Press, 1975). The breakdown of Pakistan and the Bangladesh movement is recorded by a Bangladeshi scholar, Rounaq Jahan, in *Pakistan:
Failure in National Integration* (New York: Columbia University Press,
1972). The Bhutto years have been comprehensively treated in two books,
one by a distinguished Pakistani scholar and the other by an Indian academic who analyzed Pakistani affairs for the Government of India. The
former is Shahid Javed Burki, *Pakistan Under Bhutto, 1971–77* (New
York: St. Martins, 1980); the latter is Satish Kumar, *The New Pakistan*
(Delhi: Vikas, 1978). A liberal Muslim interpretation of the transformation of the ideology of Pakistan over the years, by one of Pakistan's most
distinguished jurists, is in Chief Justice Muhammad Munir (retd.), *From
Jinnah to Zia* (Lahore: Vanguard Books, 1980). This informed criticism
of the Zia regime was freely available in Pakistan after its publication.

Zulfiqar Ali Bhutto's own writings are required reading for the serious
student of Pakistan but all are not publicly available in Zia's Pakistan.
Bhutto often wrote and spoke for dramatic effect, but his speeches and
writings are still vital. Two books are most readily available, *The Myth of
Independence* (London: Oxford University Press, 1979), and his death-
cell testament, *"If I Am Assassinated . . ."* (Delhi: Vikas, 1979). A perceptive short biography is Dilip Mukerjee, *Zulfiqar Ali Bhutto* (Delhi: Vikas,
1972), and a more definitive one is Salmaan Taseer, *Bhutto: A Political
Biography* (London: Ithaca Press, 1979). Four anthologies contain a number of extremely useful articles and bibliographies covering several facets
of domestic politics, foreign policy, and economic development and social
change: Ainslie T. Embree, ed., *Pakistan's Western Borderlands* (Delhi:
Vikas, 1977); W. Eric Gustafson, ed., *Pakistan and Bangladesh: Bibliographic Essays in Social Science* (Islamabad: University of Islamabad and
Columbia University, 1975), and Lawrence Ziring et al., eds., *Pakistan:
The Long View* (Durham: Duke University Press, 1977).

To conclude, the single most comprehensive and useful source of information about the entire subcontinent must be noted. *An Historical Atlas
of South Asia* (Chicago: University of Chicago Press, 1978), edited by
Joseph B. Schwartzberg, not only conveys the sweep of history through an
unparalleled series of maps, but contains extensive bibliographies, pho-
tos, and a full descriptive text.

Index

Index